ETHICS AND CONSULTANCY:
EUROPEAN PERSPECTIVES

Issues in Business Ethics

VOLUME 7

The titles published in this series are listed at the end of this volume.

Ethics and Consultancy: European Perspectives

edited by

HEIDI VON WELTZIEN HOIVIK
Norwegian School of Management

and

ANDREAS FØLLESDAL
Researcher, ARENA Research Program,
Research Council of Norway,
Oslo, Norway

KLUWER ACADEMIC PUBLISHERS
DORDRECHT / BOSTON / LONDON

A C.I.P. Catalogue record for this book is available from the Library of Congress.

ISBN 0-7923-3377-2

Published by Kluwer Academic Publishers,
P.O. Box 17, 3300 AA Dordrecht, The Netherlands.

Kluwer Academic Publishers incorporates
the publishing programmes of
D. Reidel, Martinus Nijhoff, Dr W. Junk and MTP Press.

Sold and distributed in the U.S.A. and Canada
by Kluwer Academic Publishers,
101 Philip Drive, Norwell, MA 02061, U.S.A.

In all other countries, sold and distributed
by Kluwer Academic Publishers Group,
P.O. Box 322, 3300 AH Dordrecht, The Netherlands.

Printed on acid-free paper

Contents

About the Contributors

Rupert Ahrens is managing partner, Ahrens & Behrent Agentur für Kommuni-kation GmbH, Frankfurt, Germany, a consultancy firm specializing in dialogical approaches to corporate communications. He has lectured at different universities and published various articles and books on dialogical communications campaigns.

Antonio Argandoña is Professor and Secretary General of IESE, International Graduate School of Management, University of Navarra, Barcelona, Spain. He is Treasurer and member of the Executive Committee of the European Business Ethics Network (EBEN) and co-founder and Secretary General of "Etica, Economía y Dirección (EBEN - Spain).

Paul Batchelor is responsible to the European Board of Coopers & Lybrand for the development of the firm's management consulting services across Europe. He is also Chairman of Coopers & Lybrand's International Management Consulting Ser-vices Executive.

Øystein Blymke is Director at the Norwegian Directorate of Civil Defense and Emergency Planning. He has previously worked with Statoil Norway on an exchange program for management development between public administration and industry.

Stanley Crossick is Chairman of Belmont European Community Office and Bel-mont European Policy Center in Brussels, Belgium. The Belmont firms specialize in public policy, strategic and political advice, in particular issues of European integra-tion and EU-US relations.

Collean Evans-de Souza is the founder of the Office for International Policy Services. This company provides effective policy development, strategic planning and project management to organizations working in transitional economies. The company has a significant reputation for their work in Central and Eastern Europe and the states of the former Soviet Union.

László Fekete is Associate Professor in Philosophy at the Budapest University of Economic Sciences.

Andreas Føllesdal is the Director of the Norwegian National Committee on Research Ethics in the Social Sciences and Humanities. He is also associated with the Research Council of Norway on the project, Advanced Research on the Euro-peanisation of the Nation-State (ARENA).

Wessel Granzevoort is Chairman of KPMG Klynveld Management Consultants in The Netherlands, Vice Chairman of KPMG Management Consulting Europe, member of KPMG International Management Consulting and Chairman of KPMG Quality Assurance Steering Group. He is also a member of the board of the Dutch Management Consultancies Council (ROA).

José Mª Ortiz Ibarz is Dean of the School of Philosophy and Professor of Business Ethics at Universidad de Navarra in Pamplona, Spain. He is also vice president of the Permanent Seminar, Enterprise and Humanism.

Knut Johannessen Ims is Associate Professor at the Norwegian School of Economics and Business Administration in Bergen, Norway, where he teaches business ethics.

Haavard Koppang is an Assistant Professor at the Norwegian School of Marketing, part of the Norwegian School of Management. He has previously been employed at the Directorate of Public Management.

Bente Løwendahl is Associate Professor of Strategy at the Norwegian School of Management. Her main area of research focusses on strategic management of knowledge-intensive firms, including but not limited to consulting companies.

Josep H. Lozano teaches Social Philosophy and Business Ethics at ESADE (Barcelona). He is currently pursuing a doctorate, researching the correlation between concepts of ethics and management. He is the vice president of Ética, Economía y Dirección (EBEN - Spain).

Patrick Maclagan is a Senior Lecturer in organizational behavior and managerial ethics at the School of Management, University of Hull, UK. He has published widely in the fields of management development and business ethics.

Domènec Melé is a senior professor of Business Ethics and Chairman of the Department at IESE, the International Graduate School of Management, University of Navarre in Barcelona.

Lidmila Nemcová currently is employed by the Czech Department of Small Business, where she specializes in business ethics, non-profit organizations and cooperatives in the free market economy and marketing.

Adrian Payne is Professor of Services Marketing and Director of the Center for Services Management at the Cranfield School of Management in Great Britain.

Joseph A. Petrick is a founding partner, with John Quinn, of Organizational Ethics Associates. The company works with companies, industries and governments on assessing and developing ethical work cultures that increase ethical effectiveness, congruence and integrity.

Fleming Poulfelt is Professor of Management at the Copenhagen Business School in Denmark. He serves as the school's representative in the Inter-faculty group on business strategy in the organization Community of European Management Schools (CEMS).

John Quinn is Senior Partner in the US firm Organizational Ethics Associates. He is also an Associate Professor in the Departments of Philosophy and Management and the School of Law at the University of Dayton, Ohio, US.

Barto Roig is Professor Emeritus of Business Policy at IESE. He is former president of the Academy of International Business in the European International Business Association, and a consultant and counselor for several companies. He is author of more than 250 cases and documents on Business Policy.

Francis Sejersted is Professor of Economic and Social History at the University of Oslo. He is also Chairman of the Norwegian Nobel Committee as well as the Director for the Centre for Technology and Culture.

Alejo José G. Sison has been a Professor in the Faculty of Philosophy and Letters (Pamplona, Spain) and in the International Graduate School of Management, IESE, Barcelona. He is currently at the Center for Research and Communication in Manila, Philippines. He is a senior researcher of the Permanent Seminar "Empresa y Humanismo".

Horst Steinmann is Professor at the University of Erlangen-Nürnberg, Germany and holds the Chair for General Business Administration and Management. He is Executive President of EBEN Germany and served on the Executive Committee of EBEN Europe until 1994.

Mitja Tavcar is Professor of Corporate Policy and International Management, Faculty of Economics and Business Administration, at the University of Maribor in Slovenia. He is also Program Director of the Core Curriculum for the MBA Program, a member of the Expert Committee for ITEO Consulting Ljubljana, a member of Expert Listing for the Slovenian Management Institute and an expert of the Association of Slovenian Economists.

Jan van de Poel is a member of the executive board of Royal Sphinx, Maastricht, The Netherlands. He is also president of the board of directors of the Maastricht Accounting and Auditing Research Center (MARC) and a part-time professor at Limburg University.

Heidi von Weltzien Høivik is Associate Professor at the Norwegian School of Management, where she also served as provost and dean of faculty from 1989 to 1993. In 1994 she was associated with the Centre of Technology and Human Values as a visiting researcher. She is Vice Chairman of the Executive Board of the European Institute of Business Ethics, Nijenrode, Netherlands.

Ansgar Zerfaß is a Research Assistant with Professor Horst Steinmann at the Institute for Business Administration, University of Erlangen-Nürnberg, Germany, working in the area of public relations and business ethics.

Introduction

The present volume in a series of books produced from European Business Ethics Network (EBEN) conferences in Europe, is a compilation of plenary speeches and papers presented at the 1993 EBEN conference in Oslo, Norway. The theme of this year's conference was "The Use of Consultancy: Ethical Demands and Requirements" and there was a special focus on Eastern Europe. Of over 40 papers presented at the conference from 165 participants representing 23 countries, we present here 20 selected by the editors as providing an overview of the latest thinking from both academicians and practitioners on the subject of ethics in consulting. Due to strict constraints on space in this volume, several valuable papers presented at the conference must be published elsewhere. We have also tried to maintain the unique flavor of the papers by authors whose mother tongue is not English.

The consulting profession is booming in Europe, both in the West and in the former Communist Bloc countries. However, it has not previously been subjected to rigorous scrutiny from the ethical point of view. The conference planning committee thus sought to put the spotlight on the spreading phenomenon of buying and selling consultancy services within the European Union, within Europe and with the new Eastern Europe. The conference addressed several ethical challenges facing either the buyers or providers of consultancy services in both the private and public sectors.

The roles of consultants are often vague, allowing for consultancy services that require ethical reflection: What, precisely, may a manager properly ask of consultants? and, What may consultants properly offer? A manager can avoid blame by shifting the responsibility for controversial decisions onto a consulting company. Outside consultants, on the other hand, may too easily recommend policies because they need not take responsibility for the effects of their suggestions. As you will see from the articles here, in a profession where money is made by analyzing situations and making recommendations on which decisions are based, doing what is best for the client, staying honest, and making money often conflicts with each other.

We have divided the book into five sections; Ethics and Consulting, General Issues in Consulting, Special Areas of Consulting, Consultancy and Ethics in Eastern Europe, and Concluding Issues. The first section, Ethics and Consulting, begins with a paper from the Oslo Conference's keynote address by Francis Sejersted, chairman of the Nobel Peace Prize Committee and Director of the Center for Technology and Culture, University in Oslo. Sejersted looks at different theories of management in his discussion of managers and consultants as manipulators, where business peoples'

1

H. von Weltzien Hoivik and A. Føllesdal (eds.), Ethics and Consultancy: European Perspectives, 1-4.
© 1995 *Kluwer Academic Publishers. Printed in the Netherlands.*

norms in their functional roles within the organization and in their roles as managers of people are brought into focus. This means reconciling the need to make money on the one hand with the moral obligation to treat people 'right' on the other.

Paul Batchelor's article on the use of consultancy focuses on issues concerning the ethics of the consulting process and looks at the role of consultants from his point of view as a practitioner. Jan van de Poel, both an academician and practitioner, looks at the moral issues in consulting and asks if it is possible to take a systems approach to the subject. Van de Poel concludes, that the ideal consultant is a friend, someone who is both committed to you and yet independent. We are next introduced to consultancy in the EU arena by Stanley Crossick. He offers a few tips to consultants, who abound in the EU organizations, on how to get around in the multicultural environment of the EU where it is often difficult to establish the idea of ethics. J. Wessel Ganzevoort then goes through the business process of a consulting firm to find some ethical dilemmas that consultants encounter. He believes that both consultant and client must be aware of each other's ethical obligations.

In the second section on general issues, our first article by Flemming Poulfelt and Adrian Payne is an examination of the Danish management consulting industry from the perspective of the consulting firm's managing partner and the client organization's CEO. The results of the survey confirm several beliefs regarding the value of using consultants, but question some of the consultants' capabilities and ethical behavior. Patrick Maclagan and Collean Evans look at two European cases in their article on the purchase of organizational consultancy services. They are primarily concerned with the client managers' motives when it comes to nepotism, self-interest and ethics in purchasing services that can lead to abuse of their authority to spend moneys and obtain resources.

The ethics of occasional consultancy – those informal, unpaid requests for advice – is taken up by Antonio Argandoña. His position is that this advice is hardly trivial and should therefore meet certain conditions for all concerned; the seeker, the giver, their organizations, etc. Argandoña analyses this sensitive area and makes some recommendations for both the advice seeker and the advice giver. Haavard Koppang and Bente Løwendahl look at "hidden" factors that could lead to unethical outcomes in the consultancy process. They describe these factors as "hidden agendas" where consultants may, in some situations, end up taking on the role of the scapegoat for their client. The authors call for an expanded research agenda in business ethics to include process-related issues such as unconscious agendas, dyadic and group interaction and the dynamic evolution of relations over time.

Our third group of papers deals with special areas of ethics in consulting beginning with an article by Øystein Blymke on government and consultancy. Blymke looks at the basic clash between the structure of government bureaucracy and consultants from the business world. He admits that both groups have a lot to learn from each other but that the differences in their worlds can lead to possible ethical conflict. Domènec Melé and Barto Roig look at ethical issues in executive search consultancy, or headhunters. After identifying relevant issues in the executive search industry, they suggest some ethical criteria for these consulting firms from the basic moral values of justice, veracity, and trustworthiness.

Managerial ethics consulting is discussed by Joseph A. Petrick and John F. Quinn in their article on the ethical culture in the health care environment of Children's Medical Center in Dayton, Ohio, US. The authors feel that the models and methods of managerial ethics consulting adopted by the Ohio medical center show the value added to client health care by professionally addressing stages in the consulting process. These benefits can be translated to any health care organization worldwide. Horst Steinmann, Ansgar Zerfaß, and Rupert Ahrens tackle the ethics of consultants' roles and responsibilities in public relations consultancy. They approach the subject by looking at the corporate ethics, dialogical communications as opposed to traditional one-way communications, and the ethical demands this new approach puts on public relations consultants.

The subject of consultancy and ethics in Eastern Europe is explored through three articles by Lidmila Nemcová, László Fekete and Mitja Tavcar, representatives from the Czech Republic, Hungary, and Slovenia. All the authors agree that the changes occurring in their countries have been phenomenal with the opportunities for a great deal of abuse in the consultancy arena. The articles provide enlightening examples of situations from consulting projects after market reforms have taken place. The authors also agree that it is hard for non-East-European consultants to fully appreciate the shifting ethical environment of the ex-Communist Bloc countries. It is difficult for these countries to change overnight and there are many people taking advantage of what they perceive to be the naivete of the local citizens. What is needed for consulting to succeed in these culturally different environments, according to Tavcar, is an enlightened use of situational ethics, however disturbing this may sound.

Finally, we conclude this volume with four articles addressing the discipline of business ethics. The first article deals with the dilemmas of teaching business ethics, by José Mª Ortiz and Alejo José G. Sison. They begin their article by asking the question: Is business ethics an oxymoron? That is, is it self-contradictory to put these two words together? The article looks at the inclusion of ethics in undergraduate and master-level programs in economics and business administration followed by a discussion of the "a-rationality" of the doctrines forced on the students. The authors offer concrete recommendations for the reformation of business ethics courses, with an emphasis on rational commitment, as opposed to "value neutral" presentations.

The seeming contradiction of business ethics and ethics in business is also taken up by Josep M. Lozano. In his article, Lozano looks at several studies on morals and ethics and concludes that any contradiction in business ethics and ethics in business might be seen as a means of clarifying and complementing a process of personal and organizational development. He admonishes teachers and consultants not to limit themselves to teaching skills, techniques and abilities. His article very much supports the lament from the Eastern European countries of Western consultants placing their black and white moral codes on peoples who cannot understand them.

Andreas Føllesdal looks at the philosophers as consultants. Føllesdal says that the unique contribution of philosophers as consultants is in a role of educator or coach, clarifying and improving the moral reasoning of groups, committees, etc. They are trained in arguing on ethical dilemmas and can help clients arrive at reasoned agreement on common ground.

Lastly, Knut Ims addresses the importance of the quality of the consultant-client relationship. It is not just a question of substance, but the process of what is going on in the relationship – the dyadic relationship. The concept of self is central to Ims' discussion as he tries to get us to understand that knowing oneself is perhaps a condition of quality performance, whether one is the client or the consultant.

We are grateful to the sponsors of the conference, KPMG Management Consulting Europe; College of Business Administration, University of Notre Dame; Skandia Fonds A/S, Miljø-Invest, Bergen, Norway; National Westminster Bank; and Norwegian Telecom. Particular thanks is given to the Norwegian School of Management for their hospitality, graciousness and support in hosting the conference.

The other members of the review committee have provided invaluable service. These include Professors Antonio Argandoña of IESE, Arnold Schilder of Coopers & Lybrand, and Hans De Geer of the FA Institute, Stockholm.

Brit Giertsen, and later Mari Wolstad, managed the conference with aplomb, providing the opportunities for discussion and reflection on the papers presented at the conference. Svanhild Blakstad was instrumental in the preparation of the manuscript in its final form. Peggy Simcic Brønn has provided indispensable editorial assistance, managing the complex process efficiently, and with a smile, illustrating the invaluable role that consultants can play.

Heidi von Weltzien Høivik
Andreas Føllesdal
Oslo, August 1994

PART ONE

Ethics and Consulting

1

Reflections on the Suspension of Ethics: Managers and Consultants as Manipulators

Francis Sejersted

The Problem: The Manipulated Efficiency

Business people act, qua business people, in two institutional contexts which in principle are completely distinct, and normally entail two different ways of relating to other people. On the one hand they are actors in the market, and on the other they are their employees' managers. We shall assume that different sets of norms govern how to relate to trading partners in the market and how to relate to subordinates in the company. The moral problems which arise in the two different institutions for conducting human relations consequently also differ. The main problem relating to market operations originates in the fact that one achieves the most desirable consequences when the objective as such is difficult to justify on moral grounds.[1] Profit is the target, if necessary at the expense of the person one is dealing with. In this context – i.e. in the market – altruistic considerations, or acting out of consideration for the other party, can produce socially undesirable results. The problems confronting the business person as manager are of a different nature. We shall not be considering all aspects of management or consultancy ethics, only what we regard as in principle the fundamental problem, one which in fact applies to all management in modern society.

Two observations will serve to indicate the problem. Although beginnings were made here and there, modern western social sciences never really won a foothold in the totalitarian communist regimes. Analysis of individual actors in markets, the principal aim of economics, was never an issue in command economies, nor was sociology's programmatically detached analysis of social conditions suitable in highly ideological regimes. There was nevertheless one type of research in which those regimes did take a special interest, even setting up institutes for it, and that was "management research." One should pause a moment over the question of what totalitarian regimes thought they could learn from precisely that field of research. How did they think they stood to gain?

The second observation derives from close reading of Peters and Waterman's best

7

H. von Weltzien Hoivik and A. Føllesdal (eds.), Ethics and Consultancy: European Perspectives, 7-26.
© 1995 *Kluwer Academic Publishers. Printed in the Netherlands.*

seller *In Search of Excellence*, in which the authors in effect recommend one both to brainwash one's employees and to treat them as individuals.[2] Any potential conflict between two such strategies is not discussed. The moral problem highlighted by these two observations relates to what I would describe as basically manipulative attitudes to inter-personal relations, a tendency to treat man as an object or a means of achieving goals beyond man himself. In so far as there is such a tendency, it is contrary to a fundamental principle of our ethical tradition. It was clearly formulated by Kant, and states that man must not be treated as a means but as an end in himself.

The prominent contemporary moral philosopher, Alasdair MacIntyre, sees this manipulative tendency as a core problem of modern society as a whole, by no means limited to commercial life, but he uses business management as a main example; the choice is natural, since the business enterprise is a core institution in our society. The point of departure for MacIntyre's thinking is that in modern society, moral judgements are based on chance preferences, attitudes or emotions. Society is merely a meeting-place for such individual preferences. In a society of this kind, the distinction between manipulative and non-manipulative social relations is bound to disappear. The absence of any shared impersonal criteria to refer to makes it hard to discuss moral problems. Rational argument has to give way to more subtle modes of exercising influence. This disqualifies the modern manager, in the capacity of manager, from even participating in moral debate.[3]

Modern managers will normally be seeking efficiency, which requires control of certain aspects of social reality. They are not accustomed to regarding efficiency as a moral concept. But that, according to MacIntyre, is precisely what it is. Control of important aspects of social reality implies the manipulation of people to adapt them to particular patterns of behavior or life-styles. In reality, the life-style called for by efficiency competes with alternative ways of living. Since in our society any common frames of reference have more or less been dissolved, such control can only be exercised by manipulation; in other words, it requires subtle ways of influencing people. It is by virtue of his effectiveness in this function that managers can legitimize their management.[4]

Another prominent contemporary moral philosopher, Charles Taylor, does not go as far as MacIntyre. He does, however, see some symptoms of disease in modern society, primarily an individualism which has declined into narcissism and loss of a sense of meaning in existence. That individualism is intimately related to an instrumental rationality, the rationality "we draw on when we calculate the most economical application of means to a given end. Maximum efficiency, the best cost-output ratio, is its measure of success."[5] When individuals become detached from the significance which their place in a larger world order gave them, they are "open to be treated as raw materials or instruments for our projects." In contrast to MacIntyre, however, Taylor believes that a joint frame of reference does exist, but that it is hidden. What we need is reflection on the original moral inspiration that lay behind modern society.

The fact that we have lost sight of the moral wellsprings of modern society is due among other things to a conspiracy between on the one hand the technology pessimists or critics of civilization, who see us enslaved by modern technology, and on the other the technology optimists or industrialists, with their uncritical instrumentalism. What those two prototypes of modern society are conspiring about is not to discuss the essential issue, which is instrumental rationality.[6] What should be noted, then, is that although MacIntyre and Taylor disagree in their evaluations of modern society, MacIntyre considering it bad and Taylor finding it potentially good, they agree on instrumentalism, or the manipulative tendency, as a characteristic symptom of disease in our society.

Take the simple example which both MacIntyre and Taylor give of such instrumentalism's confusion of means and ends, efficiency as an end in itself, or rather – the relation between efficiency and well-being. What is the means and what is the end? The aim of our endeavors must be the good society, characterized by well-being. It cannot be efficiency as such, which must be the means. There must be something wrong, a lack of meaning, in a society where people stress themselves to death in the name of efficiency; but how often we see efficiency set up, in both word and deed, as the ultimate goal.

Many would in reply point to a certain form of institutional compulsion, the "iron cage" referred to by Taylor. The logic, that is under which such institutions as the market, and the enterprise in the market function, compel one to become more efficient. So we appear to be trapped in a dilemma – but MacIntyre denies that any such dilemma confronts us. In his words, "What if effectiveness is part of a masquerade of social control rather than a reality?" [7] This shows MacIntyre to be writing within a tradition which has usually maintained that the links between social control and effectiveness are not necessarily so close.[8] Social control has been given such priority within technocratic structures, either because of a mistaken belief in close links, the assumption that control is a prerequisite for effectiveness, or because social control actually has higher priority than effectiveness, although it will constantly be claimed that control is being exercised for the sake of effectiveness.

MacIntyre adopts the former point of view: we have been living a fiction. His main point, however, is not the lack of connection between control and effectiveness, but that the scope for control or manipulation is limited. Systems based on the manipulation of persons through the subtle application of influence are therefore inefficient and brittle. Sooner or later, in some way or other, they produce resistance which renders them ineffective or simply breaks them down. Totalitarianism of the kind Aldous Huxley or George Orwell imagined is impossible, as he says.[9] MacIntyre deserves credit for having pointed out this fragility in totalitarianism, and that at a time when everyone believed that, although totalitarian regimes were repressive and economically inefficient, they at least possessed some social control and stability. Today we know that MacIntyre was right. We shall return to this point of better control through less "control" in the last section.

Our main concern here, however, is with the ethical problem of the manipulative attitude to one's fellow-men which follows from instrumental reason. People have to be "tricked" into adopting a particular life-style or "culture" precisely so as to promote effectiveness, the institution's objective. To quote a modern management specialist: "By management perspective we simply mean that personnel programs, procedures, skills and activities are all managed to accomplish organizational and unit objectives. Naturally, then, the objectives determine how human resources are managed." [10] In so far as we put a full stop there without modifying the argument, which is surprisingly often what happens, we are turning the world upside-down: man exists for the sake of the organization and not vice-versa. We can begin to guess why totalitarian regimes took such an interest in management research. What we need to think about, according to Taylor, and what modern society so often forgets, is the original moral inspiration underlying such things as the market or efficiency drives. That is to say, the moral inspiration behind the whole modernisation project, which was intended in its entirety to serve the interests of the good life.

In this connection it is very important to be aware of the unclarified ambiguity in feelings about work in modern society. Work is partly regarded as a necessary evil, as a hindrance to the real life lived outside the workplace, during leisure hours. For this reason any reduction in working hours would have to be a good thing in itself. The dream of full automation in industry means that the individual is to a great extent removed from manufacture. If this opinion is held about work, it becomes easy to argue that manipulation during working hours must be defensible in the interest of efficiency. [11] On the other hand we can see, particularly at the present time, that the one of the major problems with unemployment (which is, not least, a result of automation) is that, for most people, work does give meaning to their existence. This is exactly why manipulation in the workplace is such an important problem, because opinion is being manipulated.

We saw that the contradiction between MacIntyre and Taylor was a result of opposing views as to whether a common platform of norms exists in our society. This reflects a fundamental question in all ethical debate. Are there, for example, general and common ethical principles from which we can deduce rules for ethical behavior in special circumstances? Kant thought that there were, although later Kantian research claims to be able to prove that, even for Kant, institutions played an important role for the content and basis of morality. MacIntyre goes far to the opposite extent. [12] He thinks, in the first place, that norms are historically and socially determined. There have been, however, societies throughout history which have had common moral standards, but in the modern, traditionless society this common ground has been dissolved, and a chaos of individual attitudes has sprung up, making moral discourse difficult, if not impossible.

It is not necessary to assume any of these extreme positions, nor is it necessary to choose between general moral principles and the historically and socially determined norm. [13] Our point of departure will be that our moral life is lived in a state of tension between the general and special norms. We put ourselves on a level between these two, a level that is characterized by a mixture of general and situationally determined norms.

It is to MacIntyre's credit, however, that he insists that normative reflection based purely on general principles is bound to be lacking. As he points out, any ethic has its own sociology. Norms change, to a greater or lesser extent, between groups and over time. There are different norms for behavior towards one's spouse, one's subordinates and a business connection. There are also areas of tension between the various norm systems of different groups. There is, in other words, a norm struggle occurring in society, a competition for norm hegemony. It has been claimed that market norms are in the process of assuming a hegemonic position in our society. This means that when civil society disintegrates, the market's type of behavior towards others becomes dominant – even outside the market place. Perhaps one will begin to treat one's spouse like a business connection, by beginning, for example, to calculate profit and loss. . . . Contradictorily, it has also been claimed that the business world is in the process of losing much of its legitimacy with respect to society around it. It is not unusual, within the business world, to feel that one is fighting with one's back to the wall, that one is exposed to moral criticism without actually quite understanding the nature of the criticism. It is reasonable to regard this as a reflection of a socially determined normative struggle.

Much of what is today known as "business ethics" has put itself into the Kantian corner. The practitioners are, in other words, relatively disinterested in normative sociology and history. Their point of departure is primarily that there are general principles which can be assumed, and from which rules can be deduced or problems illuminated. As it has been said. "Other norms do not apply to the business world than to other areas of life."[14]

We will base our argument on the premise that even if there are some general or common principles somewhere or other, and this is a thought that we are reluctant to relinquish, it is a fact that when we descend to the trivial plane, norms change over time and between groups, e.g. between "the system" and the "life world", to use Jürgen Habermas' famous expressions. It is only by going more deeply into these contradictions and studying the dynamics of norm development that one can achieve an understanding of e.g. the business world's or management's general problems in giving itself moral legitimation.

A casuistry based on the belief of more or less general norms can be useful for an individual who wishes to reflect upon individual moral dilemmas, of which there are always enough, wherever one lives. This, however, gives us no understanding of the problems on the social level. The demand for ethics which is heard from so many directions today is thus, on the one level, a positive phenomenon which should lead to a higher degree of ethical reflection if the demand is met by a well informed supply. On another level this "demand" could be interpreted as a disquieting phenomenon which is important to understand in its social context. The capitalist behavioral pattern must be socially acceptable if the system is to function properly.[15] Does the demand for ethics means that something is lacking in this respect? Or does it represent a reaction to the view that modern society has finally been made complete by the victory of the instrumental rationality of the market in all spheres? In both cases, an individually oriented moral rearmament is insufficient to restore the system.

It is also important to understand the specific problems that arise for those who are caught in the various social institutions. Each institution (the market, the company, etc.) generates its own specific moral dilemmas for those working in the institution, and who are attempting to realize its intentions.[16] These problems can possibly be solved by changes in the organization. Much intellect has been involved in philosophizing over how society should develop its institutions in order to ensure the realization of more or less generally accepted moral aims. This is a central theme in political philosophy. It is, however, important to be aware of that which has already been suggested, that the institutions can generate their own norms for what is expected, or "correct" behavior. This is why (norm) history and (norm) sociology are so vital for ethical reflection.

To take an example; when one tries to "create a corporate culture," it can easily take the form of resolving moral problems by readjusting the behavioral norms. This is what so easily can assume the character of manipulation. Nor is it certain that it will solve the problem as intended. To the extent that this can be done within a limited constitutional context, it may lead to the problems being transferred to problems between the company and the surrounding society, resulting in the above-mentioned struggle for a hegemony of norms. It would perhaps have been better to have maintained the moral discussion within the institution.

Taking MacIntyre as a starting point, we have sketched a dichotomy between general principles and individual attitudes, or between common and special norms. We have, then, placed ourselves on a level between these, since we base our discussions on the assumption that our lives pass in a mixture of common and special norms. There is, however, another level, a fourth level which we shall return to, where ethics are suspended to the benefit of ethical assessment. As we have seen, it seems that manipulation presupposes suspension of the general ethical norms (whether they have been declared dead, as in MacIntyre, or are hidden away, as indicated by Charles Taylor). If one has come thus far, a total suspension of ethics cannot be very far away. One quite simply chooses not to choose between good and evil.

Self-image: The Generalizer as the Autonomous Manipulator

There are, without doubt, many competent managers in industry; hard working, decent human beings who manage to establish an atmosphere of mutual respect within the company. Many of them would also be capable of something MacIntyre meant was impossible in the modern society, to participate in a moral conversation – as manager. There are also, naturally enough, poor managers. The problem is that it is very difficult to get to grips with what makes a good manager a good manager, or to define the nature of management functions. It has also proved difficult to make general statements about management. The danger lies in the fact that the image that is built up is false, and that this can contribute to building up an erroneous self image in the good managers, who then can be misled into becoming poorer managers. There is thus no doubt that much management literature identifies the good manager with the good manipulator. To this extent the moral philosopher MacIntyre is on the right track.

Here we approach the question of the relationship between theory and practice, or between knowledge and action. This is a question which has attracted great attention within research on professions. The discussion concerning the character of the basis of knowledge has been specially heated about the engineering profession. There has been a clear tendency on the part of the profession to regard technology as applied knowledge. This is to say that the skills of the engineer lie primarily in an articulated, generalized science. In the discussion this view is challenged. There exist those who claim that the engineer is primarily a practical worker, for whom too much theory could actually hamper rather than assist his activities. Whether or not this applies to the engineer, it is clear that, with regard to management, the problem is exactly the distance, or lack of clarification between theory, or generalized knowledge and good practice. In such a situation the possibility is present that theory can ruin practice. There is also reason to note that the attempt to build up a generalized management science, "scientific management", grew out of the engineering profession.[17]

I referred above to Peters & Waterman's book. It is only one of the more successful examples of the flood of books on management which appeared in the 1980s. The genre itself was not new: its roots can be traced back to the engineer and consultant Frederick W. Taylor and his "scientific management." Although Taylor died in 1915, his ideas caught on in the inter-war years. Nor is the genre easy to define, and attempts to analyze it critically are few and far between. At first glance the genre appears to lack unity: the underlying premises vary, leading to widely differing "theories." Yet it does seem as if one can talk about a special type of literature, which functions in a special way in a special context. What I have in mind is the amorphous group of popular books with promotional covers which fill the shelves headed "management" in most modern bookshops.

Most of these books were written by people who work as consultants to managers, i.e. as general specialists in the field or, as it has been put, as planners for planners. A special sub-group consists of the autobiographies of successful tycoons. A characteristic of the genre is that it offers no analysis of managers themselves in their institutional contexts. He (or she) is not inserted into the patterns into which everyone else is supposed to fit. They are assumed to be autonomous; heroes exalted above everyone else in the organization. In other words, it is in a sense taken for granted that the manager is the manipulator, the person who constructs reality. The question, of course, is how well this assumption matches the true state of affairs.

In more academic organizational research, at any rate, one finds a different view of the manager. Sweden's Sune Carlson was one of the first to set himself the task of discovering what managers really do and, as he says in a frequently quoted passage:

Before we made the study, I always thought of a chief executive as the conductor of the orchestra, standing aloof on his platform. Now I am inclined to see him as a puppet in a puppet-show with hundreds of people pulling the strings and forcing him to act in one way or another.[18]

Following this up, organizational research has studied management in its institutional and social contexts, generally arriving at the contrary conclusion to what is assumed in management thinking. They have found that "managers mean practically nothing to the organization's results." [19] Typically, however, theories of this kind have had very little influence on management thinking,[20] founded as it is precisely on the image of the manager as orchestra conductor – a recurring metaphor in the genre. This discrepancy in relation to real functions is one of the main reasons why, in his examination of some leading management books, Staffan Furusten concludes that they must be regarded as "ideological tracts rather than centres of information of knowledge, and as such might have an influence on the process of social construction." [21]

This is in complete accord with Stephen Waring's more detailed study of American management literature.[22] Admittedly, Waring takes as his point of departure the huge spread of the genre, sometimes reflecting fundamental differences in underlying views of man. Broadly speaking, one can distinguish two rival traditions, the "bureaucratists" descended from Frederick Taylor, and the "corporatist" or "human relations" school deriving from Elton Mayo. The former emphasize centralized power and specialized tasks, while the latter seek to reduce conflict and create harmony by means of "democratic" procedures and participatory methods.[23]

Despite these differences, Waring sees a basic similarity in that they all base themselves on "the management theory of value." It is and must be the manager who defines the objectives, also according to the participatory theories. Even the so-called "job enrichment" ideas which broke with the "human relation" trend in the 1950s "reinvented Mayoism and merely proposed using participation to change despotic rule into hegemonic rule." [24] This is done, then, under cover of the notion that management is a separate profession with its own foundations in scientific knowledge, free from considerations of value. The problem which is ignored, then, is the fiction of value-free management. Or, as we have seen Charles Taylor maintain, there is a conspiracy not to debate the essential issue, which is instrumental rationality and the blurring of the dividing line between manipulative and non-manipulative relations which it entailed.

Waring's analysis is interesting, but we will argue that it has a weakness inspired by MacIntyre as there seems to be an a priori assumption that morally acceptable management is impossible in our modern society. Even the best intentions have to be perverted into manipulation.[25] Our argument is that morally acceptable management is possible, but difficult. One has to break out of the conspiracy to which Charles Taylor referred. In some of the democratic and participatory experiments one probably managed to come round the manipulation problem.

Another characteristic feature of this process of professionalization was the emergence of specialists in management, mandarins who, as Waring says, "commodified themselves" by becoming management consultants and selling often widely diverging theories and techniques, adapted to their various clients:

> ... the techniques were not value-free facts of nature, but rather value-laden devices developed and driven by managers and their will to power. So even if the techniques were practical, technical progress for managers and bureaucracy was not necessarily equivalent to moral progress for society.[26]

This situation gives rise to two problems, one practical and one moral. The first concerns the applicability of the theories in practice – given the manager's value assumptions. Do the theories contribute to the achievement of the desired type of effectiveness? The management consultancy profession can reasonably be expected to possess some real competence. Experienced managers can always give good advice. But on the whole there seems to be a gulf between the knowledge they claim for themselves and the knowledge they actually possess. To quote Torodd Strand (in translation):

> The subject area "management" is not a discipline, but a collection of bits of knowledge and recommendations from many disciplines, primarily American psychology as far as science is concerned, and business administration, epic biographies, and the gurus' books of worship where recommendations are concerned. The most widely read material, disfigured by a highly normative style, offers advice which is difficult to follow and has a validity which is very limited in time and space.[27]

Even given its own value assumptions, the system does not seem to function particularly well. A general overview of developments in recent decades invites the comment that the private bureaucracies, probably to a greater extent than the public ones, suffer from distinct incompetence, despite all the rhetoric. (Of course there are exceptions.) As Waring has shown, a confusing mixture of different techniques is also applied. As such, this accords with MacIntyre's analysis: the system is ineffective perhaps precisely because it is based on a mistaken view of the manager as autonomous and of man as more easily manipulated than is in fact the case.

The second, moral, problem originates directly in the discrepancy between what the theories claim to be and what they really represent. We can clearly see ideological elements dressed up as science. This is nothing new, but on the contrary a general characteristic of our modern society, but it does stand out especially clearly in our present context. A corollary to this problem is the one which is the theme of this article: that morally questionable manipulation is legitimized by its presentation as value-free science.

The Function: Management Theory as Legitimation

The next question is why these inadequate management theories have been so successful, and why there are so many management consultants? Are people so easily taken in? There are explanations along this line. What they say is that managers, in order to take the far-reaching decisions they so often must take, will have to simplify reality. They need to believe that the world is simple.[28] It is possible that there is such a tendency to self-deception in the popularity of this literature. It cannot explain however the particularly strong popularity in the last 10-20 years. Neither should one be fooled by the fact that managers act on the basis of "bounded rationality" into believing that they don't know that reality is more complicated.[29]

We will suggest another explanation of the popularity of the management theories and the consultancy functions, namely that these theories and functions satisfy a genuinely felt need, but a different one from the need for the knowledge or the techniques as such, or for the need for self-deception. What we are looking at is probably the general need of the management function for legitimacy in modern society. What has made this such a pressing problem?

The term "authority" is often used in connection with a manager's legitimacy. Its meaning should be kept distinct from the instrumental use of power, whether concealed or open, and from democratic procedures and rational argumentation – "compulsion by better arguments." Authority implies obedience to the manager without either sanctions or rational arguments. Authority is to be found in traditional structures, tied so to speak to the past, to tradition, to the grace of God, etc. It has been said that "There is always a sacred aspect to leadership." [30]

The paramount traditional embodiment of authority was the paterfamilias. Elements of similar traditional structures of authority have occurred in the business world, with managers regarded as father figures.[31] The implication is that the norms which govern interpersonal relations in a family have to some extent been transferred to business. In this connection one often hears talk of paternalistic management. In the old handicraft businesses in particular this was not uncommon.

It is sometimes argued that authority in this sense of the word is disappearing from our changeable modern world.[32] It is simply not so much left of the sacred and elevated of leadership. Our point in this connection is to suggest that one likely reason why manipulation has become so common – and "unproblematic" – is that old structures of authority have crumbled. That leaves a need for new kinds of control by use of power. That is the historical situation in which the distinction between authority and power is often lost. From a moral point of view, however, that is a very important distinction to maintain – just as important as the distinction between to convince and to manipulate.

Old-fashioned authority, then, can be replaced by power in some form or other. It is my conviction, however, that the pure exercise of power, in other words the threat of sanctions, is a poor basis on which to exercise management, not only morally but also from the point of view of effectiveness. Possibly the situation is somewhat different with respect to hidden power, or power exercised through the subtle application of influence. The latter may be more effective (though we have seen that that is by no means certain), but morally it is more questionable. The old hierarchic chains of command were in a way more honest since they did not pretend to be anything other than they were. Manipulation by means of subtle forms of influence is more doubtful because it contains an element of concealment, yet in our society it is, as a rule, considered less questionable because, as I mentioned, we have lost some of our capacity to distinguish between manipulative and non-manipulative circumstances. There is, characteristically, very little emphasis on power in management thinking.[33] Hidden power, manipulation, is not seen as the exercise of power once you are caught in the trap of instrumental reason.

The open or hidden exercise of power can thus replace authority, but power has a tendency to crumble unless it is combined with forms of legitimacy which go beyond the exercise of power itself. Trust is the other element which has taken over from authority as the basis for leadership in the modern society. This means that modern leadership has to be based upon the two conflicting foundations of power and trust.[34]

There is reason to distinguish between pragmatic and moral trust.[35] Pragmatic trust is trust based on factual criteria. The manager possesses competence which enables him to take the right decisions, so that the enterprise flourishes and its employees with it. Good results build trust, which then becomes the basis of legitimacy. But that presupposes agreement as to the purposes of the activity. Besides, the problem arises when results are not achieved. That is to say that trust as the basis of legitimacy is easily lost, and what can you do if you are confronted with a general loss of trust, of which there are some indications today? So far, however, we have yet to arrive at a specifically moral problem.

Moral trust is different in nature: it is non-instrumental, and it is not results that count but the feeling and belief that the manager is behaving decently and openly, and that there is a foundation of shared values which one can cooperate to realize. There is a definite tendency for moral trust and the exercise of power to be opposed. The essence of MacIntyre's critique is that in our modern society, dissolving as it is into a confusion of individual attitudes, the possibility of moral trust has decayed and with it the distinction between manipulative and non-manipulative social conditions. In a certain sense, manipulation through the subtle exercise of influence has become a necessity. On this point Charles Taylor takes the contrary view: the basis for moral dialogue and moral confidence does exist, though to a large extent unrealized, as a potential.

Though opinions may differ on how far moral trust can give a management legitimacy, what does seem clear is that the falling away of traditional authoritarian structures has created a legitimacy crisis. As we have seen, pragmatic trust can to some extent take over as a basis for legitimacy. Typically, however, attempts are made to extend that basis further than it will reach by hooking it onto the allegedly value-free science which modern society has adopted as its foremost source of legitimacy. Despite the large differences between them, management theories tend, at least until recently, to claim that management is a distinct profession with its own scientifically-based store of knowledge. As Waring concludes, the premises of Taylorism remain unquestioned, its dream of "scientific management" still underlying the management theories. The clearest manifestation of this is the emergence of a separate group of management consultants supposed to be pre-eminently the guardians of this particular knowledge.

What they deliver, however, is not only knowledge, but primarily ideology and legitimacy – in the guise of value-free knowledge.[36] It is reasonable to assume that the most attentive players in the game see through this, at least half-way. Operational managers who apply to consultancy firms often have a fairly clear idea in advance of what advice they will be given. What they lack is not so much knowledge as legitimization of the steps they themselves wish to take.[37] What they are primarily seeking, and what the consultants deliver, is – legitimacy. What I am suggesting, in other words, is that the general crisis in authority and legitimacy is the chief source of the huge crop of management theories and of the large numbers of general management consultants. The part played by those theories and those people in our society, then, and the moral dilemmas marking their activities, reflect a general problem in our modern society.

The Critique: Consultants as Post-Modernists

There are certainly many able consultants in the market, decent people with a real knowledge for sale which can help to solve business problems. In particular we have in mind some specialized groups with their own identities, like EDP consultants or auditors, but it applies even to more general management consultants. Their knowledge will however presumably be more experience-based than science-based. Nor should the possibility be discounted that the so-called "quality movement" of the 90s, with its faith in "qualitative methods, standardized tests, counting and measurement of results" may develop into something more substantial and helpful at a more general level.[38] It can be regarded as a direct extension of the Taylorist "scientific management" principles. But what the management consultancy group may have to contribute along these lines remains unclear and haphazard.

Today we can see a new trend, claiming that the whole notion of "scientific management" is or at any rate should be a thing of the past. The manager is neither as omnipotent as management theory assumed, nor as superfluous as organizational theory presupposed. We have simply failed to grasp the essence of the management function. Its core objective, according to this new trend, is "by negotiation to arrive at, and to symbolise, a social order, an institution, which has a virtually coherent conception of its own identity and appears of value to the surrounding world." To achieve this, the manager must "speak and act forcefully and comprehensibly." The new international buzz-word is "impression management."[39] Possibly this reflects a clearer understanding of the management function than its elimination in the old organizational theory. Perhaps the premises of management theory did contain certain elements of reality after all. Management is not without significance. (It is nevertheless important to recall that even if the manager succeeds in establishing social control, that is no guarantee that the enterprise, if what we have in mind is an enterprise, will survive in the market.)

The role of independent consultants is not likely to be less important within this new paradigm – on the contrary. James March sees no disadvantage in their inability to solve their clients' practical problems which, as we saw, they were not well suited to tackling.[40] What they can do is to help to legitimize the management by linking it to science and giving it the appearance of being more knowledge-based than it is. In addition, they can be helpful in that production of symbols which may be the manager's most important task. What consultants do is, to borrow a book-title, "act with words." Their products are "labels, metaphors and platitudes." [41]

So we have conceivably come closer to a true understanding of the function of management, of consultants' potential contribution, and of why the consultancy industry has swelled to its present proportions. At the same time, it needs emphasising that the moral dilemma has not been reduced. On the contrary: this latest dilemma brings out still more clearly the moral dilemma surrounding manipulation.

One characteristic of the consultancy business is its almost total independence:

> In contrast to managers and researchers, consultants seem to lack inhibitions where association, bisociation and creative tricks in general are concerned. Bosses may be afraid of being taken literally; for researchers they amount to bad manners. [42]

The message between the lines here is that, to a surprising extent, consultants do not need to assume responsibility for what they do or say. They keep no watch on the use made of their products. This responsibility problem must be at the core of consultancy ethics. The consultants are not governed by the ethical rules which apply in science, and they are outside the manager's moral universe. And this is a prerequisite for their usefulness in the production of symbols. This shows, as I suggested to begin with, that what we are concerned with is a struggle for the normative hegemony.

If post-modern society has moved as far as MacIntyre implies, and we have lost our common ground for moral dialogue, so that we are no longer able to distinguish between manipulative and non-manipulative conditions, the next step must be to discard ethics in favor of aesthetics. The labels, metaphors and platitudes supplied by consultants do not lend themselves to judgement by moral standards, but must be judged, as they say, in aesthetic terms. "The consultant's advice need not be 'true' or 'new': it should be beautiful." [43] Consultants accordingly tend to see themselves as artists in, as it were, a post-modern sense.

Charles Taylor has explained how art in post-modern society is understood as "creation", and how closely the modern concept of self-realisation has been drawn to creative art, at the expense of morality. Standard morality for its part has become associated with rigid convention. A value has become something of one's own making, which can give a feeling of freedom and power. Taylor points out how this understanding of value paves the way to "a love affair with power." [44]

We can now see the various pieces falling into place. Consultants belong to the power elite, which is why, as I mentioned, they never talk about power. But they are all the more useful to the manager. They can say what he can't say. It is precisely in his conspiracy with the consultant that the manager can boost manipulative competence. And this is a conspiracy in Charles Taylor's sense of the word, inasmuch as it is guided by instrumental reason and does not question it at all.

This "post-modern" aesthetic tendency is just a tendency. The dream of "scientific management" is not dead. The aforementioned tendency with its suspension of ethics seems, however, to be symptomatic of a certain change in attitudes in modern society, a change which is rooted in a relinquishment of general norms. It also clarifies the moral dilemma which forms the theme of this article: It is not as simple as just choosing not to choose between good and evil. Søren Kierkegaard writes on this point:

> Either, then, one is to live aesthetically or one is to live ethically. In this, as I have said, there is no question yet of a choice in a stricter sense; for someone who lives aesthetically does not choose, and someone who, once the ethical has become apparent to him, chooses the aesthetic, does not live in the aesthetic sphere for he sins and comes under the category of the ethical, even if his life must be described as unethical. [45]

Modification: The System in a Specific Context

The so-called "Kenning tradition" has had great influence in Norway.[46] It is typical that the moral dilemma we have discussed here has not been thematically discussed in this tradition. On the contrary, Ragnvald Kalleberg has for instance pointed ed out that Kenning opens up for manipulation. The Kenning tradition should, therefore, be fairly typical. A central argument in Kalleberg's analysis is thesis 29 (of, in all, 31) which states "Most people wish, and have often felt the need, to be told what is expected of them. They require assistance, attention and advice from their superior." With organizational research this "unrealistic view of Man" is, according to Kalleberg, replaced by "images which presuppose that Man seeks self-control and meaning (the self-determining Man) or with conceptions about the complex individual who reacts according to the situation, and who is able to learn throughout his or her life." [47] In contrast to management theory in the Kenning tradition, organizational research has taken as a theme the manipulation problem, according to Kalleberg. The ideal within a part of this research is, characteristically enough, the rational, normative argument where one simply yields to the" force of better arguments." [48]

There are, of course, examples within the management literature where manipulation has been taken as a theme (even if it is not typical). Henri Werring has pointed ed out that in business one can often gain the impression that "adult education can approach the level of assault, a frightening scenario." He also refers to reaction from labor organizations, – something "that we who are involved in personnel indoctrination for the companies must, to a great extent, take ad notam." [49]

The conception about engagement in "personnel indoctrination" is symptomatic. Just as interesting is the reference to labor organizations. There has generally been a tendency to attempt to transfer American management theory, relatively uncritically, to Norwegian conditions. [50] One of the contexts where Norwegian conditions differ relatively strongly from American, is exactly the strong position of organized labor in Norway. According to management thought, which is based on the "management theory of value," there is a tendency to regard interests within a firm as concurring, making labor organizations surprisingly absent, or in the best scenario, into elements of disturbance, or "a problem." [51] Odd Viggo Nilsen has, in his examination of the organizational development at Årdal Verk since 1985, pointed out that in the management theories and consultancy reports which formed the basis of the developments, "the understanding of opposing parties in the workplace is absent." [52] This would not necessarily exclude successful operations, although it would seem that success would occur more despite, rather than because, of the theories that are applied.

Consensus building is an important part of the strategy in management thought. Symbol production is expected to contribute to consensus, and consensus is seen as being vital for efficient operations. Consensus building is, as we have seen, doubtful from a moral point of view as it can easily lead to manipulation. Nor is the idea of consensus as a precondition for efficiency without problems, if we are to believe MacIntyre. Also from the viewpoint of efficiency it can be favorable to build into the structure an organized and fundamental criticism.

The need for criticism or opposition is an admission which is built into our liberal democracies, but which is remarkably absent from management thought. We would bring to attention a subject touched on introductorily, that of the popularity of management thought in the totalitarian regimes. It became apparent there that manipulation did not result in the intended control. The consequences were catastrophic. Nor have management theories shown to be obviously viable in the context for which they were originally developed. In liberal political theory consideration has been made for the fact that power both corrupts and deceives.[53] Systematic and continual critical discussion of both the ends and means of the organization should be applied for the sake of both efficiency and morale. Such a discussion would not gain from an atmosphere of consensus. In such an atmosphere discussion is silenced. We refer back to what we said about the need for what can be understood as moral discussion within the institutions, in other words a discussion concerning ends and means. Why is this obvious point so systematically ignored? [54] It is difficult to see any other explanation than the old one: Social control was more important than efficiency and morale.

Strong labor unions have, basically, a potential for the representation of such a critical element, as mentioned above. In this way they would be able to represent an interesting resource for the organization. Management would be forced to use them as partners in a discussion arising from an admission of the existence of a mixture of common and conflicting interests. We are probably not so far from the truth if we regard this as an accurate description of conditions in many companies.

There are those who will claim that, as far as company management is concerned, there is at present a tendency to introduce a form of symmetry in interpersonal relations. It is not so unusual to treat employees as individuals. The ideal of democracy in Mayo-inspired organizational research has achieved a fairly strong foothold in Norway, as expressed by the 1977 Working Environment Act.[55] It is also interesting to note that Kenning claimed to have observed a certain unwillingness among Norwegian managers to be managers, at least the sort of manager that Kenning meant, and that they felt uncomfortable about this. So it is an open question how far the manipulative tendency has gone.

How should the modern manipulative tendency be met? What is the alternative to this extensive use of hidden power? We have implied it earlier, but will repeat the main points. It is vital to establish moral discussion, as Charles Taylor recommended. In reality, it could be a question of moving into the institutions, into the company, for example, as a part of a real democratization. There is, at present, an unfortunate tendency for this dialogue, to the extent that it actually takes place, to be between business and industry, on the one hand, and the surrounding society on the other. It can easily degenerate in this context as dialogue and assume the form of a struggle around the hegemony of norms.

The most important way to meet this manipulative tendency is to accept it as the moral dilemma it is, and not to pretend that no moral problem exists. This admission, in itself, gives a form of humility which will color practice. In this connection it may be apt to remind oneself of the fundamental rule of the ethics of virtue, that moral acts are performed by moral individuals. As far as difficult moral choices in a complicated world are concerned, there is no other alternative than to rely upon the intuition of a morally educated person.

Some would claim that "manipulation" is a negatively loaded word, and that it should perhaps be replaced by the more neutral "influence." Is it not true that we all go round influencing each other? We do, of course, but when it becomes, in exactly the management situation, a moral problem giving reason to use the word "manipulation", it is because there is a fundamental asymmetry in the relationship between manager and managed. As manager, the manager has significantly more power than the managed, and this is why the influence he exerts will so easily assume the character of exploitation.

A manager must, of course, also lead, in other words use power. This is not, per se, immoral. The question is how it is used. It must be used overtly, not least when objectives are to be made clear. The manager must also be able to accept criticism, which is also a part of knowing when not to act as manager, or use the power inherent in the position of manager. Power alone is not sufficient. It must be balanced against its counterpart – trust. This is, in itself, a difficult art as wielding power can easily destroy trust. Pragmatic trust is not, in itself, so much of a problem. A basis of legitimacy is built up by making correct decisions. The foundation of moral trust is more difficult to grasp. Its function is a reminder of the old authoritarian condition where it was neither a question of sanctions, nor of discussion. The manager was simply accepted. It is impossible to give any strategic indications as to how this sort of trust should be built up. There are certain things in this life which cannot be achieved simply by aspiring to them.

Notes

1. For a more detailed analysis of this matter, see Sejersted, F., Marked og moral. Om det gode samfunns avhengighet av moralsk tvilsomme handlinger, (Market and morality. On the good society's dependence on morally doubtful acts), in *Demokratisk kapitalisme*, Universitetsforlaget, 1993.

2. Peters, Thomas J. and Robert H. Waterman Jr., *In Search of Excellence*, New York, 1982. For a brief analysis of the book, see Furusten, Staffan, Knowledge or Ideological Tracts – a Case Study of Three Popular Management Books, in his *Management Books – Guardians of the Myth of Leadership*, Uppsala Univ. Dept of Business Studies, 1992. See especially p. 41 on the need for both "shared values" and "strong leadership."

3. MacIntyre, Alasdair, *After Virtue*, London, 1981, 1985, pp. 23 and 30 ff. "The manager represents in his character the obliteration of the distinction between manipulative and non-manipulative social relations; the therapist represents the same obliteration in the sphere of personal life. . . . Neither manager nor therapist, in their roles as manager and therapist, do or are able to engage in moral debate" (p. 30).

4. Ibid., p. 74. I shall be returning to the problem of legitimization, which I consider of central importance in the present context.

5. Taylor, Charles, *The Ethics of Authenticity*, Harvard U.P., 1992, Ch. I, especially p. 5.

6. Ibid., p. 96.

7. Op.cit., p. 75.

8. This applies especially to Marxistically-inspired literature. Cfr. for instance Braverman, Harry, *Labor and Monopoly Capital. The Degradation of Work in the Twentieth Century*, Monthly Review Press, New York, 1974; and Noble, David, *Forces of Production. A Social History of Industrial Automation*, Alfred A. Knopf, New York, 1984.

9. Ibid., p. 106.

10. Baird, Lloyd S., *Managing Human Resources*, Homewood Ill., 1992, p. 15.

11. The "Fordist" system is characterized by all attempts at legitimizing the system being moved out of the factory and into the consumption of the manufactured product. Cf. Sissel Myklebust, Dagens teknokratidebatt sett i lys av teknokratiske retninger i perioden 1900 – 1945, Ms. TMV, 1993 p. 22.

12. MacIntyre, op. cit.

13. Martha Nussbaum, Virtue revived, *Times Literary Supplement*, 3 July 1992. In this article Nussbaum makes a conditional criticism of Macintyre.

14. Kai Dramer, Næringslivsetikk (Business ethics) in Jon Bing and Kai Dramer, *Etikk i næringslivet* (Ethics in the business world), Hjemmets bokforlag, 1990, p. 110.

15. This is emphasized, e.g. by Talcott Parsons in Talcott Parsons & Edw. Shils (eds), *Towards a General Theory of Action*, Cambridge, Mass., 1951.

16. Robert N. Bellah et al., *The Good Society,* New York, 1992, p. 303.

17. Sissel Myklebust, Teknologi og vitenskap i 'ekspertsamfunnet' (Technology and science in 'the expert society'), in TMV, series of working papers 1993. The basis of knowledge of the engineering profession is discussed here, and also the relationship to management theories. It should, perhaps, be emphasized in this connection, with a view to consultancy activities within the field, that practical experience can, naturally, be communicated, although not as pure theory, but in connection with action in specific situations.

18. Carlson, Sune, *Executive Behavior,* Stockholm, 1951, p. 52.

19 Strand, Torodd, Ledelse, noe som virker eller noe vi tror på? (Management: something that works or something we believe in?), in Strand, Torodd, (ed), *Ledelse kan læres* (Management can be learned), Bedriftsøkonomens forlag, 1992, p. 30.

20. Furusten, Staffan, op. cit. p. 17.

21. Ibid., p. 2.

22. Waring, Stephen P., *Taylorism Transformed. Scientific Management Theory Since 1945,* Chapel Hill & London, 1991.

23. Ibid., p. 7. Waring places Herbert Simon in the Taylor tradition and Peter Drucker in the Mayo tradition, to take two of the most influential "mandarins."

24. Ibid., p. 133.

25. This point of view is not uncommon. Cfr. Tian Sørhaug, *Leadership: The Sociology of the Personal. Organization, Power and Magic,* The Work Research Institute, Oslo, 1992, p. 17: "A leadership can never count on being in ethical equilibrium." And p. 33, ". . .we face a parallel situation to that of agent 007's famous "licence to kill", namely to give leaders a right to act immorally."

26. Ibid., pp. 202-203.

27. Strand, op. cit. p. 29.

28. Sørhaug, op. cit. p. 2: "this literature offers a promise to manage the leader's impossible task." cfr. ibid. p. 22.

29. The concept of "bounded rationality" is taken from Herbert Simon, Rational Decision Making in Business Organizations, *American Economic Review,* 1979, p. 501.

30. Sørhaug, op. cit. p. 12

31. Cf. Sørhaug. op. cit. p. 21 and Werring, Henri, Det etiske ansvar ved opplæring (Ethical responsibility in the provision of training), in Werring, Henri, (ed), *Etikk for ledere. Selvmotsigelse eller utfordring?* (Ethics for managers. Self-contradiction or challenge?), Godbok, 1987, p. 103 (in translation): "In Norway, too, we find managers today frequently speaking of their employees as a "family" – implying that the closeness and permanence which link biological relatives also apply to the company's personnel, and that they have the same kind of concern for their employees as parents have for their children." Werring rejects this as empty rhetoric.

32. Arendt, Hannah, What is Authority? in her *Between Past and Future,* Penguin, 1978. Arendt emphasizes among other things the distinction between totalitarian regimes based on power and authoritarian regimes based on authority. It can be argued that authority can also be founded in "charisma." No doubt the charismatic leader as described by Max Weber is also to be found in modern society. But according to Weber charisma provides a very transient basis for the exercise of leadership.

33. Czarniawska-Joerges, Barbara, *Att handla med ord. Om organisatorisk prat, organisatorisk styrning och företagsledningskonsultering,* Carlssons, Stockholm, 1988, p. 121, where (in translation) "discreet control" is described as "more effective and more difficult to

resist than traditional visible organizational control", and p. 47 where, with a reference to G. Morgan, *Images of Organization*, Sage, London, 1986, she notes how characteristic it is for "bosses and others in positions of power to tend not to pay attention to power as a phenomenon." Sørhaug, op. cit. p. 28: "Contrary to organizational theory which "only" looks aside, we can say that management literature had a sad tendency to lie about the most painful things concerning power and trust."

34. Sørhaug, op. cit. p. 6

35. Nielsen, Torben Hviid, Moralske Verdier (Moral values) in Marked og Moral (Market and morality) (Næringslivets Hovedorganisasjons serie *Næringsliv og etikk*, no. 1, 1992) (-series on business and ethics published by the Confederation of Norwegian Business and Industry).

36. Halvorsen, Kjersti, *Noen linjer i bedriftsrådgivningens idehistorie* (Some trends in the history of business consultancy ideas), LOS-senter Notat, 92/39. She quotes Waring, but in the present connection attaches at least as much importance to Andrew Abbott, *The System of Professions. An Essay on the division of expert labor*, The University of Chicago Press, 1988. He sees an imbalance among management consultants between practical labels and transcendent abstractions, which leaves them lacking in substance (Halvorsen, p. 25).

37. This has been pointed out in many connections, e.g. Czarniawska-Joerges, op. cit. p. 45.

38. Halvorsen, op. cit. pp. 13 ff. and 23.

39. The quotes (the first two translated) are from Strand, Torodd, op. cit. An important book representing this new trend is Eccles, Robert G. and Nitin Nohria, *Beyond the Hype. Rediscovering the Essence of Management*, Harvard Business School Press, 1992.

40. March, James, Organizational Consultants and Organizational Research, *Journal of Applied Communication Research*, Vol. 19, Nos. 1 & 2, June 1991. Cf. Halvorsen, Kjersti, op. cit., p. 26.

41. Czarniawska-Joerges, op. cit. p. 43.

42. Ibid. p. 44.

43. Ibid. pp. 119 and 123.

44. Taylor, Charles, op. cit. pp. 62-67.

45. Kierkegaard, Søren, *Either/Or. A Fragment of Life*, Penguin Books, 1992 p. 486.

46. After the American author George Kenning. Cfr. Nils Schjander, *Hvis jeg bare hadde en bedre sjef. George Kenning om ledelse*. (If I only had a better boss. George Kenning about management), Hjemmets bokforlag, 1991, first edition 1987. This book has been published in an edition of tens of thousands, and has been discussed with a number of central Norwegian leaders of industry.

47. Ragnvald Kalleberg, Kenning-tradisjon i norsk ledelse (The Kenning tradition in Norwegian management), *Nytt Norsk Tidskrift*, 3/1991, pp 218-244, p 226.

48. Ibid p. 237. Kalleberg refers here to Bjørn Gustavsen, Workplace Reform and Democratic Dialogue, *Economic and Industrial Democracy*, Vol. 6, 1985.

49. Henri Werring, op. cit. pp. 106 and 108.

50. The Kenning tradition is an example of exactly this. Cfr. also Furusten, op. cit. chap. 2, "Swedish Managerial Thinking: A Shadow of America" for a comparable observation under Swedish conditions.

51. Czarniawska-Joerges, op. cit. p. 93. Cf. also Judith A. Merkle, *Management and Ideology* (1980) and Myklebust, op. cit. p. 64 f. for a discussion of Merkle. Management theories of the Taylorist variant are analyzed as techniques for oppression of class conflicts. The

struggle between work and capital must be transcended by management control of both workers and owners.

52. Odd Viggo Nilsen: *Miljø og Organisasjon. Årdal Verk 1985-1992* (Environment and Organisation. Årdal Verk 1985-1992), TMV working paper report no. 67, 1993, p. 38.

53. That power deceives has, interestingly enough, been discussed by Torodd Strand in a management context, op. cit. He has not, however, discussed the moral problem that results from the corruption.

54. Some would say that it is not ignored. On the contrary, it is a trend which represents a sort of anti-organisational ideal – chaos bringing out innovation. Cfr. Michael J. Piore and Charles F. Sabel, *The Second Industrial Divide,* Basic Books, New York, 1984, p. 247. Such analysts as Waring (op. cit.) would reply that this is a fiction,it is at best a controlled chaos, in other words that it does not go outside the trap of instrumental reason – chaos is used instrumentally.

55. Sejersted, Francis, Demokratisk kapitalisme (Democratic Capitalism) op. cit. p. 199. The same chapter puts forward the argument that the technocracy movements have had difficulty in breaking through in Norway, even if the tendency has also been clear there.

2

The Use of Consultancy
– Ethical Demands and Requirements

Paul Batchelor

The last decade has seen phenomenal growth in business consulting. Major firms like mine have more than doubled in size. Our role has become a focus of public interest because the use of consultants has become a fundamental element in the way management problems are tackled in both private and public sectors in almost all European countries.

During the same period, interest in and debate about business ethics has grown sharply in Europe within the business community, academic, government and regulatory circles. Not surprisingly, given our enlarged role, consultants have featured in this debate both as a subject for scrutiny and as a source of ideas on how to deal with some of the major ethical questions which business faces.

In this chapter I will focus principally on issues concerning the ethics of the consulting process but I should like to touch first upon the nature of business ethics, the changing nature of the ethical issues facing top management and the framework within which I believe these issues need to be addressed. This provides a useful backdrop against which we can review the role which consultants can properly play and the ethical issues to which the use of consultants can give rise.

What Do We Mean By Business Ethics?

Until quite recently, the very nature of what we mean by 'business ethics' was unclear. Some extreme elements of observed business behavior – fraud, deception, false claims about product performance, wanton exploitation of 'indentured labor' and the like – were clearly unethical in just about everyone's eyes, but there was no underlying set of values or philosophy against which more normally-observed individual or corporate performance could be readily and objectively assessed. Although the legal framework in most countries provides some boundaries beyond which behavior may not acceptably stray, there has been a growing sense that some of what is strictly legal may not be generally accepted as ethical. In other words

H. von Weltzien Hoivik and A. Føllesdal (eds.), Ethics and Consultancy: European Perspectives, 27-37.
© 1995 *Kluwer Academic Publishers. Printed in the Netherlands.*

there is a gap between the strictly legal and the ethically acceptable: this grey area gives rise to most of the ethical problems which managers have to address.

Academic attempts to define a robust framework for business ethics were recently reviewed in a very interesting article by Andrew Stark[1] in the Harvard Business Review. He argues that, when business ethics first became a formal discipline, the few writers who touched upon the subject equated 'business ethics' with a sense of 'corporate social responsibility'. Their basic assumption was that the market would ultimately reward 'ethical' or 'socially responsible' behavior.

Research quickly showed that this comfortable congruence between ethics and business interests is not always evident in the real world. Ethical behavior does not automatically allow businesses to secure their objectives and, when such a conflict arises, managers are often unclear as to the right course of action – not wanting to be 'unethical' and yet strongly desiring to 'do the best' for their firm.

In the continuing search for an appropriate framework, some writers turned to the insights offered by moral philosophy and concluded that, quite contrary to the notion that 'ethics pays', there was a fundamental conflict between ethics and self-interest: they argued that a manager's motivation could be either altruistic (and therefore ethical) or self-interested, but never both.

I am not a moral philosopher nor a specialist in business ethics, but I do share Professor Stark's conclusion that both these lines of argument, what I might call the 'ethics pays' and 'only altruism will do' approaches, are naive and unrealistic. In both private sector business and public sector service, the real world is one of moral and material dilemmas. It is a world of mixed motives, conflicting objectives, difficult trade-offs and hard choices. But this does not mean that the real world has no place for ethics. Rather I believe business ethics should provide mechanisms and standards which allow managers to wrestle with these conflicting interests, assess the financial, economic, social and moral impact of different options and decide on the appropriate course of action without being guided only by the legal limits of permissible behavior.

Some may find this approach too pragmatic. They may argue that, forsaking the moral high ground of altruism, is inherently unethical. In my view such argument fails. The real task of business ethics is to provide the guidance needed by real-world managers faced with resolving real-world dilemmas and conflicts.

What Are The Ethical Issues Facing Top Management?

Let us now briefly examine the way the ethical issues facing top management are changing. I will not attempt to be comprehensive. Time does not permit that. I will develop one or two lines of argument which will be helpful when we come to consider the role of consultants. I will focus on private sector business.

It is often taken as the point of departure that businesses are about profit maximization measured in terms of returns to shareholders. Regardless of whether this is indeed the primary objective that most businesses actually pursue, few would dispute that business managers now feel that they must also respond to the demands and aspirations of other stake-holders – particularly employees and customers – and that they must give recognition to the external impact of their activities on the environment and society at large. Many of the current ethical challenges confronting business arise from these divergent stakeholder interests and the way in which the balance between these interests is shifting. Let me explain.

For much of the post-war era the principal perceived choices which managers faced were between maximizing shareholder returns and satisfying the demands of organized labor, particularly in areas of skill shortage. Some European countries were quicker than others to recognize employees as legitimate stakeholders and to meet their demands particularly for health and safety measures, for fair and non-discriminatory pay and for reasonable security of employment – by providing legal safeguards in each of these areas. Some managers claim that, in certain countries, these safeguards have since gone too far and that deregulation is required. It is not my task here to argue this case but I would simply note that where such deregulation is occurring it is creating new ethical challenges for business. Recent events surrounding the closure of the Timex factory in Scotland illustrate this point.

As unemployment has risen, the demands of labor have abated only to be replaced by a new management preoccupation – the demands of customers. Much of current management literature is based on helping businesses become more 'customer-focused'. Some go as far as to say that 'what is good for the customer is good for the business' – (echoes of the corporate responsibility school – that 'ethics pays'). While this is a good slogan for re-enforcing the importance of meeting, perhaps even exceeding, customers needs and expectations, it does not take sufficient account of the hard choices that managers have to make and the trade-offs involved between achieving lowest cost, best quality, least time and superior service – and maximizing profits. It is simplistic to argue that these are never in conflict particularly over the short time horizons by which management performance is often judged.

The same lines of argument can be advanced with regard to environmental issues and the social impact of business. I am very conscious of the acute environmental problems which some businesses inflict on society – sometimes across borders – but in an intensely competitive world, (and one operating on a far from level playing field) it is not surprising that the high costs of environmental compliance create real ethical dilemmas for some managers. On a recent visit to Canada I witnessed the struggle going on between a major timber company and its employees on the one hand and environmental interest groups on the other regarding permits for logging in an attractive part of British Columbia. The immediate impact of full environmental compliance will be the loss of several hundred logging jobs in an area of severe unemployment and potentially it could undermine the viability of the company. Clearly management – and others – are faced with a real ethical dilemma here arising from complex and conflicting objectives.

I would suggest that the complex ethical issues facing top management arise principally from this shifting tide of stake-holders' interests and consequent difficulties managers face in answering, unequivocally, four questions:

- What really are we trying to maximize?
- Whose interests are we seeking to serve?
- What are the external consequences of what we do?
- How do we manage the choices and tradeoffs involved?

The practical consequences for business lie in facing up to the personal and corporate dilemmas to which these four inter-dependent questions give rise, almost every day and in almost all the important business decisions we have to take. Business ethics therefore is not about some separate frame of reference or occasional safeguard against gross misconduct, it is a fundamental element of the way we need to behave and make decisions.

The Role of Consultants

Turning now to look at the role of consultants, let me begin by looking at the nature of the consultant's role and some of the ethical issues which can arise in using consultants. For the purpose of this discussion I will divide the work of business consultants into four broad categories:

- information gathering
- analysis
- the provision of advice, and
- assistance in implementation

A single engagement may involve one or more of these broad categories, sometimes all four. Ethical issues can arise in all of them.

Information Gathering

In many consulting engagements the information which has to be gathered is readily available within the client organization or in the public domain externally. In other instances it has to be gathered specially. For information obtained internally, the most common ethical issues concern questions of disclosure of personally – sensitive data – on the performance of an individual manager for example – and the risk that information may be manipulated by the provider in order to enhance or protect his or her point of view. These are long-standing ethical issues for which most major firms now have well-established rules of conduct to protect individual confidentiality and to verify the quality of information sources.

As regards external information gathering, few ethical problems arise in relation to publicly-available information – though the need for independent verification or evaluation of its accuracy is often important. Where however, information is to be specially gathered from other organizations, acute problems can arise. Some clients specifically seek to use consultants as a means of securing confidential information about their competitors in a covert way. This is clearly unethical. But the current interest in 'benchmarking' is indicative of the close interest which individual businesses are showing in how their performance compares with that of others.

Particular safeguards are necessary to chart a way through this potential ethical minefield. In particular there is need for

- protection of the confidentiality of suppliers of information;
- appropriate disclosure of both the purpose for which information is being collected and its ultimate recipient(s);
- assurances regarding future re-use of such information.

Provided there is sufficient transparency of purpose and protection of confidentiality, many businesses conclude that participation in benchmarking exercises is worthwhile. Most importantly however, given the proper disclosure and safeguards, they have an ethically robust basis on which to reach such a decision. I would however express some concern about the growing re-use of such information and in particular the development of 'benchmarking data-bases'. Very careful safeguards will be needed here.

Analysis

The second main role of consultants is in the area of analysis. Here the major ethical issues relate to completeness and bias. Rather simplistically, I would argue that one of the principal differences between much of the work of consultants and that of academic analysts, lies in our need to try to focus our analysis on what is essential to reach a decision rather than what is relevant and interesting. However we constantly have to recognize the dangers of over-simplification and have an ethical duty to disclose to our clients areas where the scope of our analysis is limited and the potential shortcomings which may thus arise. Perhaps more subtly, we have to take steps to remedy the bias which might arise from the selective focusing of our own work as a result of political pressures within the client organization to reach the 'right' decision. It is thus absolutely critical that consulting work is properly scoped and the context properly understood before the terms of reference for an engagement are finalized. Time and financial pressures on both sides may militate against this but any reputable consultant must recognize the great danger of posing the '-wrong' question in order to reach the 'right' answer in the client's eyes and know that the consequences can be severe.

Provision of Advice

The provision of advice often involves the definition of options, the exercise of judgement and the formulation of recommendations. Very often this process takes us to the very heart of the areas where our clients are facing ethical dilemmas as they struggle with the complex questions to which I referred earlier. We can bring to that process not only our information gathering and analytical skills but also our objectivity and independence. These valuable attributes can allow us to stand apart from the political processes which may be taking place within the client organization or in its dealings with third parties. It would, however, be naive to argue that it is as simple as that. While many clients can and do respect our objectivity, some will seek to engage us in their political cause and, at the very least, most will rightly question our analysis and our advice as part of the process of reaching sound decisions. It is therefore crucial that our consultants understand these pressures, have the robustness to withstand them and the speed of action to seek advice when the pressure to 'take sides' threatens to become too great.

Given the importance we attach to objectivity and independence it is worth making reference to two important ethical questions which most major firms of business consultants have had to face in the last decade or so.

The first of these concerns what I call 'advocacy consulting'. By this I mean situations where clients wish to enlist our help to argue their side of a case. Let me cite a well-publicized example: My firm was engaged by the Association of Metropolitan Councils in Britain some years ago to help them make the case against their own abolition. It was the first time we had faced such a question and we had a very lively debate before accepting the assignment. The conclusion we reached was that it was appropriate to accept provided three crucial safeguards were made:

- first, our role was transparent – all interested parties knew what it was we had been asked to do;
- second, we would only associate ourselves with recommendation based on sound factual evidence and objective analysis;
- third, we disclosed to our client, at all times, both the weaknesses as well as the strengths of their case.

My second example concerns the difference between 'independence' and 'integrity'. For many years, one of the main streams of work which firms like mine have undertaken is to help clients select the most appropriate software for a particular systems requirement – accounting, inventory management, personnel information or whatever. Typically this involves a carefully-structured process of understanding the users' needs, specifying the requirements in detail, identifying potential suppliers and evaluating their offerings. We provide independent advice in this process. In recent years however as more and more systems requirements are met by software packages we have come to question the validity of this approach for two reasons:

- first, in many instances we know, to a high degree of probability, which package is most suited to a particular set of needs;

- second, many of our clients expect us to know what is 'best of breed', to tell them and to allow implementation to begin speedily.

In some respects you could argue that to persist with total 'independence' in such circumstances is something of a charade which costs the client time and money when we know the likely answer all through the process. We have therefore decided that the appropriate ethical course is to give the client the choice either to proceed with a full independent assessment or to accept our judgement that a particular solution is workable and is based on our knowledge and experience of what is currently the best in its field. This is a good illustration of how ethical questions arise even in quite basic day-to-day decisions and how transparency helps provide an answer.

Assistance in Implementation

Returning now to my main theme, the fourth main aspect of the role of consultants is in providing implementation support.

For those who are not familiar with the structure of the consulting industry I should perhaps say that for every dollar spent on information, analysis and advice, probably ten dollars are spent on implementation support and, with the shifting boundary of consulting activity to include 'facilities management' and 'outsourcing', this multiple is probably increasing.

The very scale of the implementation task – and the opportunities it represents for consultants – does in some senses directly give rise to ethical issues. Perhaps most fundamental is the risk that the objectivity and independence which should attach to analysis and advice may be compromised in an effort to shape and secure a major implementation engagement.

Other ethical issues arising from implementation concern accountability to stakeholders. Particularly as regards work in implementing strategy and handling major processes of corporate change, concerns are expressed about the risk of consultants usurping the role of management and of their securing the authority and influence of management without ultimate accountability. As more and more of the work which consultants undertake relates to very complex problems and assisting companies with long-term processes of change – and my firm is one of those in the vanguard of this trend – we need to pay particular attention to this area.

The Nature of Engagements and Client Relationships

Having focused on four elements of the consulting process – information gathering, analysis, advice and implementation – I would like briefly to mention two other aspects which I do not have time to develop in detail but which I should also like to emphasize as important in identifying potential ethical problems.

First is the nature of the engagements which consultants are asked to undertake. Illustrating this from the perspective of my own firm, we identify three broad streams of work:

- setting long-term strategic direction,
- enhancing competitive capability, and
- improving the efficiency and effectiveness of current operations.

As a broad generalization, consulting engagements aimed at helping clients improve the efficiency and effectiveness of existing operations are less likely to give rise to major ethical issues than those concerned with enhancing competitive capability and setting long-term strategic direction. There are two principal reasons for this. First, projects of a more strategic nature are likely to bring consultants directly face to face with the major ethical issues facing top management itself. Second, such projects frequently involve the search for commercially sensitive insights and the provision of competitively sensitive advice. Issues of conflict of interest are therefore more likely to arise and appropriate safeguards must be put in place to try to avoid them. The growth of 'benchmarking' however has brought new ethical sensitivities into the area of work on efficiency improvements.

The final aspect of the role of consultants to which I should like to refer briefly concerns the relationship between consultant and client and, where they are involved, other third parties (such as financing institutions). Others will be dealing with this aspect in much more detail than I have time for today. I would however like to make three observations relating to the process of consultant selection in which all three parties are often involved.

First, I would urge caution regarding the often-assumed effectiveness of competitive selection processes as a means of combatting some of the unethical practices which they are designed to alleviate. While there is, quite clearly, a need for a robust process of choice which is seen to be objective, there is a danger that this single process will be seen as the panacea and will be used to try to achieve too many ends at once. Given the complexity of many of the engagements for which consultants are currently being retained it is very doubtful, in my view, that a single stage process will achieve:

- effective scoping of the engagement, and
- appropriate rapport between the prospective client and adviser, and
- reconciliation of conflicting views within the client organization, and
- appropriate balance between the expectations of the client and interested third parties, and
- 'fair' allocation of work between competing firms and different countries, and
- the best cost-benefit profile,
- etc.

The very process which is designed to achieve probity may, at times, undermine it. Clients therefore need to be more sophisticated in their selection processes and not rely on a simple notion that competition will achieve all their aims.

My second observation is that an effective consultant selection process is not just about ensuring ethical behavior on the part of the consultant. There are equally important ethical requirements of the client and any third party, where political and personal objectives may otherwise be pursued.

Third, it is important that differing views within the client organization and between prospective client and third-party financing institutions should be resolved as far as possible, or made transparent, before the consultant selection process begins. Otherwise this may give rise to serious conflict at a later stage.

An Ethical Framework Outline

I should like to conclude by suggesting some of the key elements of a framework to deal with the ethical issues which I have raised.

Professional Standards

First there is need to increase the extent to which the ethical standards governing our profession are understood and observed. Some of the ethical concerns relating to consultants stem simply from the fact that 'consultant' is a much-abused term and management consulting is still a rather poorly-regulated profession. Sadly, as the recent recession has swelled the ranks of unemployed executives, there has been a marked growth in the number of independent consultants who have no previous consulting experience and are not bound by appropriate professional standards. Considerable efforts are being made by the efforts of appropriate professional bodies – the Institute of Management Consultants in the UK, FMK in Denmark and the Swedish Association of Management Consultants for example. We need to strengthen them and ensure that the standards which they set are known and adhered to by clients as well as practitioners.

Corporate Programs

A second crucial element lies at the corporate level – both in business at large and in consulting firms in particular. During the last decade for example my firm has invested substantial amounts of money and a huge amount of time in developing, gaining adherence to and sustaining a set of corporate values and patterns of behavior which underpins our activities both internally and in our relations with clients. These steps include:

- the development, publication and repeated communication of our statement of values;
- the publication and reinforcement thorough training of a guide to professional ethics;
- substantial investment in training related not only to achieving technical excellence but also to achieving a thorough understanding of the consulting process and the management of relations with clients based on sound ethical principles;

- a quality assurance program based on total quality principles extending to all aspects of the conduct of our business and supported by continuous monitoring of compliance as well as compulsory feedback from clients;
- strict guidelines on internal consultation to ensure that all potentially difficult situations are quickly identified and appropriate advice sought.

Each of these items is of importance because the achievement of high ethical standards is not just about avoiding major problems or preventing serious misconduct it is about the multitude of decisions we take day by day involving judgement and choice. Each element of our corporate program seeks to reinforce high standards.

Individual Behavior

The third crucial element is of course the individual. Some of the steps needed to secure high standards of behavior are well known. Clearly the employment selection process is of critical importance. So too are the important 'role models' provided by project leaders, managers and partners.

But perhaps most important of all for the individual is to recognize that, since business is about competition and choice, we face very tough decisions and there are potential ethical components in each decision-making process. The dilemmas arising from divergent interests and values are real. By creating a culture of openness, a commitment to consultation and a passion for objective analysis of the relative costs and benefits involved for different interested parties we can help improve the quality and transparency of decision-making which I believe is at the heart of ethical behavior.

Fundamental Values

Each of these components of the ethical framework – professional, corporate and individual – needs however to be underpinned by an appropriate set of values. Despite the efforts to date of those who specialize in business ethics I believe that there is an urgent need to promote a wider debate on the appropriate framework of moral, economic and social values which should govern business behavior. We need to combat the 'moral muteness' which allows certain types of behavior to go unchallenged as if ethics did not exist.

I will end by echoing the words of Sam Brittan the distinguished journalist, who, in a recent article entitled 'How Economics is Linked to Ethics' says:

What is needed is more critical scrutiny of widely-accepted moral beliefs and the moral implications of widely-advocated economic policies. The idea of technocratic value-free economics has had its day! [2]

So too, I would say, has value-free business decision making, devoid of moral principles.

Notes

1. What's the Matter with Business Ethics? Andrew Stark, *Harvard Business Review,* May-June 1993.

2. How Economics is Linked to Business, Sam Brittan, *The Financial Times,* Sept. 2, 1993.

3

Ethics and Interventions in Business
Moral Issues in Consulting and Economic
Systems Design

Jan van de Poel

The Subject is Business

As a business man and an academic, I have been on both sides of the consultancy table. But never before did I have to express in public my thoughts about the ethical problems involved. When preparing this chapter, I had to recall and rethink my entire career in order to find elements and episodes that could be used to construct a relevant point of view. To be honest, I found this preparation process rather difficult and at times painful. Not only did I recall situations in which certain people I know quite well were engaged in unethical behavior, but I also had the unpleasant experience of recalling bad things for which I was responsible.The only good thing was that I did not need the help of outside consultants specializing in ethics. Just a few of my closest friends would do. And this simple fact turned out to be the best synthesis of the experiences I reflected upon: friends you need.

I have tried to condense and reconstruct a number of episodes and reflections. To pin down the subject, I have chosen the present day top executive who leads a relatively large organization as the main character whose behavior may need to be judged. In the business environment we can clearly observe the consultant whose business is to profit from selling advice to this poor, ignorant creature. Many more actors can be seen, but I'd like to restrict my view so as to offer you some ideas of mine that make at least some sense.

Let me issue a warning first: I am not a trained philosopher nor an academic expert in ethics. My knowledge of the subject is limited to the reading of the Dutch classic Henk van Luijk (1993) and the introduction by Velasquez 1992. Without even trying to evaluate these well-structured textbooks, I fully agree with both of these authors when they try to avoid a type of philosophical discourse which certainly is remote to the practicing manager's perception. Clearly, we should realize

H. von Weltzien Hoivik and A. Føllesdal (eds.), Ethics and Consultancy: European Perspectives, 39-47.
© 1995 *Kluwer Academic Publishers. Printed in the Netherlands.*

that it is not sufficient to broadly discuss the evils of modern business and jump to a classic debate among philosophers. In my opinion, we have to define three distinct areas for application of ethical reasoning that can easily be recognized by practitioners.

The first one is systems ethics: How do we define and restrict the behavior of entrepreneurs and businesses? The question is: How much leeway do we give to executives whose first priority is to profit and gain from designing and drawing up contracts to exchange and cooperate with others? Even before we start thinking about details, we know that there is a trade-off problem involved in this: giving too much leeway, will result in casualties and many victims, but tight control leads to other dysfunctional behavior. Evidently all legislators at the national and international level might be interested in results from analyzing this trade-off problem.

The second domain regards the decision making of our main character the top-executive. When we come to think of this domain, we realize that it should be split into a couple of sub-domains which are more or less homogeneous. Hence, there is an area called planning and organizing with the following basic question: At what moment or phase in the process of contemplating new activities and strategies, could we best intervene with ethical reflections?

Next, there is a sub-domain concerning exchange relationships. The basic question in this area is: How much may be gained from an ignorant other party? Why would a business partner voluntarily give up certain gains? The economic side of this question is: can we gain in the long run from giving up in the short? After all, many ethical considerations or moral reasoning can evidently be reduced to self-interest seeking in the long run.

The third sub-domain is the ethics of information systems. Here we have issues like: How honest and reliable should internal and external reporting be, to what degree can biased and strategic information be accepted? What is the role of lawyers, auditors and tax advisers? Should internal specialists such as controllers be instructed to ethically judge the decisions made by their superiors?

The final domain regards, of course, consulting, that is the sale of advice to executives. Because this is one of the main topics for this conference, I will go into details shortly. But before I do, let me concentrate on systems ethics first.

Systems Ethics: Why Capitalism and How Much Leeway?

Ethical issues in the business context have always interested business leaders, lawyers, politicians, priests, philosophers, consumers and many more. The question always was: how to protect the sorry lot of naive, innocent, honest, and goodwilling people who run the risk of being exploited by the masters of the liberal-capitalist system of laissez-faire economics. I strongly believe that no change of nature of this basic problem has occurred since ancient times. If we had kept our old pagan faith in many gods, we would still have one single god for both business owners and thieves.

It took many centuries before mankind even started to think about the possible advantages of free enterprise. And even today, we find many nations wrestling with the problem, for example Russia. Nevertheless, in all societies, regardless of their degree of development, business operators are closely watched and never fully trusted.

Yet, we are witnessing a fundamental change in application of the capitalist system. The centrally planned economies of Eastern Europe and China are in transition and moving towards systems which have more in common with Adam Smith's first attempts to understand how an unrestricted economy might work than with the present Western mutants which are the results of centuries-long trial-and-error. We have come to believe that our present system is the result of curbing primitive profit-seeking, because that is the sequence of historic events we observe. However, in many cases, this idea is completely wrong. Examples from the Dutch industrial development can be found in Wennekes' (1993) history of founding fathers, many of whom were engaged in social programs of all kinds. We can safely conclude that, more often than not, codification was the last action in a sequence of events that started with altruistic experiments.

From the history of individual firms we can learn that in the very beginning many entrepreneurs were trying to cope with social problems that were not the result of industrial development as such, but of the older society. For example, the company I have been working for during the last three years, was founded in 1834 by a man whose reputation in Dutch history books is little better than that of a criminal. Yet, he paid higher wages to his workers than the landowners who employed these workers before they went to the city. He tried to solve the social problems caused by a substantial migration process, while the city officials were not interested at all in solving these problems. This man, Petrus Regout, single-handedly implemented systems to civilize the work force, to stimulate education, to reward willingness to cooperate with peers, to provide social security, housing and leisure. Each of these systems had to be invented, there were no precedents, no regulations, no models, no social chapters whatsoever. For more details, see Van Iterson (1992).

Legislation came later, when government officials, politicians and trade unions had discovered that industry was going to stay. By then, the industrial pioneers felt insulted because they had done the work alone and law-making turned out to be nothing but codifying what was already accomplished.

Codification seldom brings progress. Compare for example the German and the British attitudes vis a vis the social chapter of the Maastricht treaty. There are two interesting points to make. First, the present German social policy, which is so alien to the British soul, was installed by the British Labour government after the second world war. What Labour could not accomplish at home was forced upon the Germans. Secondly, more than 95 percent of the social chapter is simply describing the existing situation in most European countries, Britain included. I think codification is alien to the British soul, not the things being codified. But then of course, other European nations will never do without codes, particularly the French. Cultural differences cause many problems for Europe. Geert Hofstede's (1983) well-known study provides useful insights into this type of problem.

The first lesson is that codification is a delicate matter because some like it and some don't. Secondly, codification is always after the fact and therefore not always essential. Thirdly, we have to recognize the importance of altruistic behavior when we focus on the way capitalism works. This seems to me an important lesson for Eastern Europe. In the West we have just begun accepting that our economies and their effectiveness in producing good outcomes, are based upon widely differing cultural arrangements which we do not fully understand. This makes it difficult to harmonize our laws, let alone to instruct newcomers in the capitalist arena how to design their own systems. Even if an Eastern European government decides to imitate a Western economy, they still have to choose a particular version. Only one thing seems certain: merging different elements from different systems will produce a Frankenstein. Yet, this seems exactly the policy of most Eastern states.

In summary, capitalism was never as pure as academic analysts and legislators thought it to be. Many of the pioneers of early capitalism have experimented with social policies so as to improve the conditions under which their employees had to live and work. As a rule, codification took place later and in a wide variety of forms that seem to depend heavily on national and regional culture. In some cultures, entrepreneurs enjoy more freedom than in others. Yet the results of these different arrangements do not always vary significantly. Apparently, there are many alternative solutions to the same problem as Aretz (1993) observed. How these different systems work, though, is badly understood. This fact is clearly illustrated by the present problems confronting Eastern Europe. It also complicates ethical analysis and moral reasoning to a considerable degree, even if the scope of our analysis is restricted to sub-cultures which are all part of the larger culture of the Christian world.

Consultancy – How To Preserve Independence

When discussing consultancy, the first thing to realize is that in the present economic context, no development can take place without the intervention of at least one consultant. Any significant change in business is either initiated, supported or controlled by armies of consultants. Secondly, and related to the theme of the 1993 EBEN Conference in Oslo, consulting always concerns ethical issues because the clients of this consulting are in doubt, not so much about what to do, but how to implement and communicate their intentions. This evokes the risks of resistance, which – in the end – are always based upon ethical reasoning.

Consulting is too broad a label for too many activities which only have a few things in common. We need a richer framework. I therefore propose to distinguish style, value and efficiency in the context of rational decision making (Ackoff, 1972). Style refers to the preference for certain means without a necessary relationship with efficiency or value. This is the aesthetical aspect of decision making. Efficiency refers to the probability that a certain means, course of action or tool, will realize a given objective. While value denotes the utility of objectives in terms of still higher goals and ideals, this is the ethical aspect, which, together with the aesthetical aspect, denotes at macro-level the cultural dimension which appears to be so important when we discuss the implementation of capitalism in Eastern Europe.

Consulting can now be defined as any outside intervention which intends to change a given decision-making context. Such change implies any combination of style, value and efficiency. As pure types we have information, instruction and motivation. Information is simply confronting clients with a new alternative which they did not know before and which they may like or dislike. Instruction is teaching clients how to apply certain means and thus improving the efficiency with which they pursue objectives. This type of consulting is technical; its proper name is engineering. Motivation is helping the client choose objectives so as to better live up to ideals. I think this is the true ethical reasoning; its domain is strategic planning, corporate identity and mission statements. All of these terms are now widely recognized in the corporate world.

Note that conventional wisdom defines consulting as improving efficiency only, thus neglecting the other two dimensions. In practice however, the ethical and aesthetical aspects often dominate the problem for whose solution consulting was sought. Also note, that in addition to the ethical component, there is an equally important aesthetical one which never attracted much attention from consultants and scholars who try to explain managerial behavior.

A first conclusion could be that experts in ethical reasoning have no contribution to the engineering type of consulting. When the client is pretty certain about goals and is interested in better ways to accomplish them, there is no opportunity to bother with ethics. Well-defined, almost perfectly programmed activities such as exist in the technical domain seem to me of no importance for ethical experts. Although, I should add, that in some cases there is doubt as to the degree of engineering. There are, of course, situations where the problem is not merely to improve efficiency, but to achieve a better fit with existing ideals. However, as a rule I would say that consultants should rest their case until there are clear signs of ethical needs. All long-range planning and corporate strategy are, however, better candidates for ethical reasoning. If you are a consultant, you´d better concentrate on these issues.

Consultants can do many stupid things without having to pay for them. After all, others are responsible for what happens when advice is put into action. Once consultants have built a reputation, they more or less are allowed to make a mistake every now and then. The only serious problem is that they have to balance independence and commitment. Clients never worry about independence, but they definitely want commitment. In fact, clients would often like to see a little more dependence, at least in the short run. In the long run, clients need of course independent consulting; they need truly honest and reliable advice in the longer run, but, for a while, they may be interested in opportunistic commitments. So let me try to analyze some of the problems related to keeping this balance.

First, why is there at one moment in time a contract between a specific client and a specific consultant? The true reason is the reputation of the consultant for solving a certain type of problem in a certain way. Consultants believe in the solutions they have previously developed in other client-organizations. Hence, clients select them because of this solution. There is a huge ethical problem involved in this routine: the client knows what (s)he wants and therefore hires this consultant. The consultant, however, thinks that (s)he is chosen because of technical skill, while in fact, the reason is the predictability of advice in a given context of problems.

Second, a well-known problem is that most consultants are interested in finding out who is in favor of the boss and who is not. By knowing this, they can more easily build a winning coalition when it comes to implementation. This strategy is widespread, I have never seen exceptions and its dark side is an ethical problem of the first degree. What is more, the consultant is exactly behaving as the client; opportunistic behavior with adequate commitment to the cause of the client, but not a lot of independence. This raises an interesting problem: Should the consultant be more aware of ethical problems than the client? I think so, but if you are not convinced, I have to admit, I can't prove it.

Third, selling more than one service to the client often reduces the outside experts' independence because they are always on the watch for new opportunities to do business and may manipulate advice to this end. In many cases, it's obvious that experience with one problem in the client's environment can be used efficiently for another. A well-known example is the auditor who not only verifies the client's external reporting, but also has expertise and client-specific knowledge in related fields such as internal control and tax. As a client, I have seen many cases of this nature and I seldom refused to engage in them, because as a client you observe a reduction of independence which leads to strong commitments to the client's cause. Serious problems exist, however, when consultants engage in manipulating their reports and advice so as to get new jobs. I therefore tend to reject most of these combined consulting projects. It's a little more costly, but it keeps things straight. A less radical alternative would be to introduce better communication between clients, consultants and other stakeholders. More disclosure, more ability to explain, more interaction, may be helpful in this respect, as Schilder (1992) argues.

Finally, I would like to present to you a real meta-problem, which I think is the most urgent to solve. It goes like this: the more problems are solved by external experts, the more the client, as a manager of the organization, has to rely on political skill and internal network in the organization. The more consulting is applied, the less reasoning is performed by the manager; the reasoning function is, so to speak, sourced out to a considerable degree. A typical client's reaction is "I never had this idea myself, but if this famous consultant makes these proposals, they must have a point and we'd better implement the changes involved." As a result, the internal debate about problems and their alternative solutions is driven out of the organization. The negative side effect is the suppression of dissenting ideas and an organization that only consists of a political system allocating power to some of its members without an intelligence of its own. In the end, the client is completely dependent on outside help, while the staff is not allowed nor is used to thinking or discussing other issues than those regarding power. I have seen several examples of this bad habit. In my opinion, this is also an ethical problem of the first degree.

There may be many more ethical problems in consulting than the ones I have presented to you. I have focused almost entirely on behavior on the part of consultants rather than on moral issues for which clients are responsible and which might be interesting opportunities for consultants to make some money. I do realize that many consultants are aware of such problems and I personally know several experts who accept the consequences. On the other hand, I strongly believe that ethical problems that may arise from consulting ought to be put on our agenda. If consultants would not be aware of them, how could they expect their clients to be interested in theirs? Consultants can only be independent if they are committed to support their clients in their search for better objectives vis a vis their ideals. Such an attitude combines commitment and independence, not because of semantics, but because it represents the only moral option in consulting. The implication, however, is that consultant and client must have a very special, personal relationship, or else they will not accept each others concerns.

Friends You Need

Both consulting and economic systems design consist of interventions in dynamic systems. Consulting regards mainly the change of organizations, while economic systems design is a task that most governments as well as supranational authorities have set themselves. Governments intervene mainly through legislation, at least this is the case in modern capitalism. Both types of intervention have become very important for the daily life of millions of people. Both are concerned with moral issues, some of which have been described above. In some cases, decision makers who intend to intervene are in need of ethical support, in other cases, the consultants who give them advice are.

What everyone is looking for is someone who is both committed and independent. Let's not think about this too long; the ideal consultant is a friend. Friends are the only truly independent and committed persons by definition. Friends are the only experts in ethical reasoning. The problem, however, is that in many situations friends cannot be found. Take for example the case of Eastern European economic transition. Can a personal friend be engaged in such a process? Or do we need to extend the definition of 'friend' so as to include institutions and organizations? I honestly don't know. Some nations have older and wiser colleagues who help them out, but I don't know whether this is the same as it is between individuals. Sometimes, two institutions or organizations maintain friendly relationships at all possible personal levels. Maybe that's as close as you can get to a personal friendship.

Long-standing relationships between a client and a personal advisor are, of course, possible and helpful. If the consultants stay around long enough, they may be disciplined by the prospect of watching their ill-advice in the future. Thus they will be interested in honest and reliable consulting for a particular client. Even some risk-sharing can do no harm, but I know that in many countries there is no room for the old system of 'no cure, no pay'. After all, the American legal tradition is a frightening example to the rest of the world. 'See you in court' is not everywhere in the world the same old routine. Hence the least we can conclude is that it is extremely difficult to separate ethical behavior from economic decision making. Decisions may seem altruistic in the short run, while, much later, they appear to bring useful results for the one who took them. On the other hand, we should not be worried too much about this impossibility to separate. Ideals – by definition – are long run objectives. So if something works, why bother about the rewards?

The more I thought about the subject, the more I discovered that our capitalist economy depends on ethical behavior and ethical reasoning. I also came to realize how difficult it must be for newcomers like Eastern Europe to copy this successful model because of that. The difficulty is that we do not know the secret of this system. Part of the secret is the tradition of what I call altruistic experiments. Actions are deliberately taken to improve the fate of those who suffer. Particularly the early entrepreneurs whose reputations have always been very low were engaged in this. These experiments are terminated either when the problem is solved because the victims can take care of themselves, or when the actions happen to have no significant effect. This process is still alive, although at a lower level since legislators began to intervene. The economic system, however, remains viable and does not allow mere rituals; its basic principle still is quid pro quo, but we have discovered many other aspects and principles that are equally important. Among these is altruism in its many forms. As a consequence, the system motivates learning, change and improvement. In fact, the present capitalist system has so many built-in mechanisms for learning and change – also in ethical terms – that there will probably be never something else. The system not only allows its own change, it also stimulates it.

In classical economic models capitalism is easy to understand, but the more we have learned about neglected aspects and variables, the more we realize that we hardly know why this system works. We will probably have to continue studying this system forever without experiencing much progress in our understanding of its functioning.

References

Ackoff, R. L. 1972: *On Purposeful Systems*. Chicago and New York: Aldine Atherton.
Aretz, E. M. 1993: Efficient Law, Limburg University dissertation, no. 93-13, Maastricht.
Hofstede, 1980: *Culture's Consequences*. Beverly Hills: Sage.
Iterson, van A. 1992: "Vader, raadgever en beschermer" Petrus Regout en zijn arbeiders 1834-1870. Maastrichtse Universitaire Pers.
Luijk, van H. 1993: *Om redelijk gewin*. Amsterdam: Boom.

Schilder, A. 1992: Auditor independence: A real issue? *Business Ethics, A European Review,*
Volume 1 number 4, October, pp. 257-263
Velasquez, M.G. 1992: *Business Ethics.* Englewood Cliffs: Prentice Hall.
Wennekes, W. 1993: *De aartsvaders.* Amsterdam: Atlas.

4

Consultancy in the EU Arena

Stanley Crossick

No clear theme distinguishes consultancy in the European Union from national consultancy – it is more an extra dimension to be taken into account when looking at the use of consultancy and its ethical demands and requirements. This chapter highlights some of the differences which apply, drawing on experience of working together in the Union which enables us to learn from each other.

Although my views are, of course, personal, they come from 15 years' experience of practice in Brussels and 25 years' experience of the structure and organization and culture, as well as the politics of the legal and other liberal professions at the EU and international level.

The Meaning of Consultancy

When discussing in particular ethical demands and requirements, it is important to distinguish between an activity (regulated or unregulated) and a profession (regulated or unregulated).

First, however, it is important to examine the use of the term 'profession', which in English means a regulated profession, best translated into French by 'profession liberale'. The French word 'profession' means occupation. To avoid confusion, I will use independent profession to denote profession in English and profession liberale in French.

There has been much confusion in EU legislative activity because the distinction between a regulated profession (e.g. lawyer) and an activity (e.g. consultancy) is not always clearly made or understood. Independent professions are regulated as to title and as to some, but not necessarily all, of their activities.

Needless to say, the regulation of independent professions, including which activities are regulated and how such activities are regulated, varies according to different member states. Thus, judicial/contentious activity of lawyers is regulated everywhere but legal advice/juridical consultancy is rarely regulated.

The structure of any particular independent profession frequently differs between Member States and sometimes and independent profession is regulated in one mem-

H. von Weltzien Hoivik and A. Føllesdal (eds.), Ethics and Consultancy: European Perspectives, 49-52.
© 1995 *Kluwer Academic Publishers. Printed in the Netherlands.*

ber state but not in another. So we have a multiplicity and a diversity which both enrich and complicate.

Consultancy is obviously not an independent profession but an activity carried out by members of independent professions and others. As the world becomes more and more interactive and interdependent, distinctions between activities of independent professions themselves frequently blur (e.g. tax advice by accountants and lawyers).

Myths and Mystique of Regulated Professions

The activity of consultancy is practiced by individuals who may or may not belong to a regulated profession. It is a myth that only members of regulated professions put the interests of their clients first. No business will survive long unless the interests of the client/customer are paramount.

However, if members of regulated professions break the rules, they risk being deprived of their livelihoods, although the risk varies according to the profession and to the country. But it does instill into the professional the importance of two fundamental ethical principles, namely confidentiality and conflict of interest.

Everyone likes to surround themselves with their own language. Knowledge is power and the use of words not understood by the recipient gives power, or at least a feeling of power. At the EU level we are all guilty, not just in using jargon but also acronyms, made even more complicated by their being different in different languages.

But clients pay their consultants to clarify and not to confuse. Clearness of expression is all the more important in a multi-lingual and multi-cultural society. We must banish forever statements such as:

"I have a meeting with an A2 in DG XV to discuss a B point on next week's COREPER agenda." This is translated as:

"I have a meeting with a senior Commission official, Directorate General for Internal Market, to discuss a controversial point on the agenda for next week's meeting of the Committee of Permanent Representatives."

Use of Consultancy at the EU Level

We consultants are here to serve our clients. We must, therefore, quickly adapt to changing needs and, above all, anticipate the present and future needs of our clients.

What does this mean at the EU level? The EU both represents the aggregate of its currently 12 constituent member states and something more. It exaggerates the differences and, paradoxically, also leads to a convergence of behavior. Today's Union combines the power of the center (up to 80 percent of national economic decisions begin in Brussels) with the reality of subsidiarity and proportionality.

Subsidiarity dictates that action at the EU level must only be taken when it is best taken at such a level, i.e. that there is sufficient value added. Subsidiarity, however, does not apply while the Union has exclusive jurisdiction. Proportionality governs the way in which policies are implemented and in some ways is more important than subsidiarity. Thus, self-regulation is to be preferred to legislation, framework legislation to detailed legislation and so on. Both concepts require the maximum delegation to Member States of implementation and enforcement.

These factors make life more complicated for our clients. Interaction grows regularly, not just between the center and the Member States, but also between the Member States. The "habit of cooperation" (a phrase coined by former US Ambassador George Vest) should not be under-estimated. Daily contact at public and private levels in the EU 12 and the EFTA 7 and beyond makes it harder to follow what is happening but produces trends which become clearly discernible later.

Most clients understand the national arena in which they operate but few understand the theory – let alone the practicalities and the dynamics – of Union decision-making. This melting pot of languages, cultures, politics and economics requires much greater multi-dimensional consultancy, i.e. multi-national and multi-disciplinary. The EU can enrich or impede and communication is both more exciting and more complex. Different consultancy offices in the EU arena frequently offer different approaches to solving the same problem – whether they be the approaches of lawyers, accountants, engineers. . . or French, German, British.

Finally, a word a bout the use of consultants by the EU Commission itself. Everyone who has had the benefit, or burden, of working on consultancy contracts of the Commission will know that, with the best will in the world, the Commission is not very good at instructing consultants. There are a number of complex and historical reasons for this. The current situation is, however, untenable and decreasingly cost-effective. The commission badly needs help from consultants to overhaul its system and it is in the interest of consultants to help the Commission do this. Above all, the Commission must shake off its reputation of being such a slow payer (ironic as the Commission is currently promoting the need for prompt payment legislation).

Ethical Demands and Requirements at the EU Level

It is beyond the scope of this chapter to enter into the sensitive issues of multi-national and multi-disciplinary professional partnerships and practice. Practicing consultancy at the EU or international level shows how unworkable many of the ethical and monopolistic rules are that operate at national levels. EU and international businesses have different requirements from their consultants than national businesses. It is, however, difficult to separate rules for cross-border activity and yet, if national rules are adapted to reflect international considerations, they may not suit domestic circumstances.

There is, of course, a particular need in the Union because of the creation of the Single Market. Perhaps we need a new approach and to create some kind of international consultancy profession which is open to members of regulated professions who practice exclusively or predominantly outside their own country. Professions must be better organized across borders. As there is no international profession of consultants, clients have to deal with a variety of qualifications and nationalities to perform similar jobs. The conduct of consultants differs according to their profession and/or nationality. However, the onus is always on the consultant to make sure that the client fully understands. There needs to be transparency in rules and, in particular, in fee calculations.

EU Regulatory Approach to Consultancy

Despite the existence of the Single Market, the Commission in 20 years has only succeeded in regulating at the Union level some medical professions, lawyers' services and architects. Despite the policy change from harmonization to mutual recognition of national norms, there has still been very little progress, even though professional services are an increasingly important component of the economy, they facilitate business and help the completion of the Single Market.

The underlying issues are complex, the Commission has not been effective and the vested interests of the professions themselves have impeded progress.

Conclusion

The European Union arena is only an extra dimension to the use of consultancy and its ethical demands and requirements. Despite the importance of the independent professions in the development of the EU in general, and the Single Market in particular, there has only been limited harmonization of professional requirements. There is a need, therefore, in light of the increasing complex and inter-dependent world and the rapidly changing requirements of clients, for there to be a fundamental rethinking. Independent professions must subordinate their vested interests to those of their clients, who must always come first.

5

Ethical Issues in Consultancy

J. Wessel Ganzevoort

There is nothing either good or bad, but thinking makes it so.

– William Shakespeare

Introduction

When talking about ethical issues one talks about the behavior of people. Too often ethical issues are considered to be a matter of behavior. Only the analysis of behavior brings us to a full understanding of what ethics really mean. This means that ethics are a dynamic phenomenon in society. Ethics are created in everyday life and this process of creating values and rules is a process of power and coalition. Looking at this process is of much more relevance than the outcome of the process. We have to be aware that we create values and rules in a society, or in a profession like consulting or within a company, to protect ourselves against others and that also means that rules and values are often rooted in fear.

The rules themselves tend to be static, they are just the outcome of the process and they make people lazy and unconscious of their fears and black sides. That is why I believe that every individual has the duty to re-examine every value, every rule, every law and look within him or herself where these values are rooted. Complying to values and rules is only legitimate when they are related to examined feelings. But no rule, no value, not in a society, in a company or profession can be taken for granted: those who trespass can be criminals and innovators at the same time.

I will now go through the business process of a consulting firm and try to spot some ethical dilemmas consultants or the management of a consulting firm finds on their way.

First is the definition of the firm's strategy, defined as the set of decisions taken by management and the actual behavior of the firm aimed at achieving a certain future position and result in its environment. Then I will deal with the marketing activities of the firm, defined as activities that enhance the buying process of intend-

H. von Weltzien Hoivik and A. Føllesdal (eds.), Ethics and Consultancy: European Perspectives, 53-59.
© 1995 *Kluwer Academic Publishers. Printed in the Netherlands.*

ed clients. Furthermore I will make some remarks on the ethical issues during the selling process and during the process of conducting a consulting engagement.

Strategy

There is a major issue in defining the mission or the objectives or vision of a consulting firm. As far as profit is concerned, a few questions spring to mind. Should a consulting firm go for maximum profit, should it go for the benefit of its clients or for the desire to produce added value? By the way, what is the definition of profit?

In my experience, people working in consulting do this because of the intellectual challenge, the need for personal recognition and fun. Doing consulting just for money, like in any other developed profession, is always a failure, but profit is one of the most important measures for our clients' appreciation. Therefore profit is of importance, as a yardstick, not as an objective.

Another issue is the choice of clients. There is a dilemma whether we should only accept clients who have the money or all clients that need our help. It is remarkable that other disciplines like medicine and law have so-called "pro-bono" rules that ensure that all clients can purchase their services. Consultants do not have these rules and it is about time to think about that issue in the consulting industry. For the time being I would prefer the 'publishers model'. This is the model of a private publishing company that has the policy to make money on the one hand, with commercial editions which enables the company to publish those novels and poems of high quality which the publisher really believes should be published albeit for a limited number of consumers. It is a form of cross-subsidizing which one sees in more companies. Consulting firms in particular need to take a closer look at this model.

The definition of the portfolio or scope of services of a consulting firm is another strategic issue with interesting ethical dilemmas. There is a widespread notion that consulting is driven by client needs and of course, if you want to sell your services in the market place, there needs to be a desire with clients to buy your services. But, if you compare the type of services we are selling today to our clients, with the services we sold ten years ago, you can see significant change, and that change has not only been driven by the changing needs of our clients. It is to a large extent driven by innovation. Innovation in academia, innovation in the MITs, the Stanfords and the Harvards of this world. This means that academic inventions come first, that they are consequently translated into technologies and methodologies that can be used by consultants and finally be applied with the clients. Ninety percent of the services we sell now were not available ten years ago. This has not caused the changes in the portfolio of consulting firms and was not driven by client needs but by innovation. Innovation means new services, and new services means that there is a lack of experience.

One of the most important reasons why a client asks a consultant is experience. In everyday practice you see that those consultants who are applying new technologies do not have the experience and thus are "learning by earning." The ethical question here is whether a consultant has the courage to say to his or her client that he does not have any experience at all, and that he or she, for that reason, will lower the price considerably. A great number of consultancies, however, apply the principle of "learning by earning."

Another strategic issue is competition. Do we look upon our competitors as dangerous animals that need to be killed as soon as possible, or do we look upon them as actors who challenge us to be better? I do not believe in cut-throat competition. I do not believe in a market place where you win when the other party loses. Of course, in the short run there should be the fiercest possible competition when a consultancy is trying to win a proposal or a new client. On the longer term however, consultancies should help each other with improving their professionalism and quality, thus improving the reputation of the industry as a whole.

Marketing/Image

Unlike hardware or consumer goods consulting is not a tangible product that can be described before you buy it, nor can it be compared to other products. Clients virtually do not know what they buy when they choose a consultant. The transparency of the consulting market is very, very limited because, on the one hand, no single client issue is the same and, on the other hand, there are as many solutions as there are consultants. Clients base their decisions to a large extent on image, reputation and on the firm's employees. Consultants are pretty smart in creating an image. They use free publicity, publish articles, give lectures, write books, etc. However, all these activities to improve their image do not necessarily improve their quality. In their publications they frequently talk about their successes. They would help clients and their profession if they would be prepared to talk much more about failures.

Since there is no concrete deliverable in consultancy, and a low degree of market transparency, client relationships are of paramount interest not only for a consulting firm, but also for a client. Consultants tend to be 'job hoppers' and also some clients seem to go from one consultant to the other as well. Enduring relationships are beneficial for both the client and the consultant. However, the coin has two sides. On one side it is beneficial for the client if the consultant knows the client's culture and environment, has the client's trust, has previous experience with the implementation of recommendations and also takes responsibility for the implementation. Moreover, an existing relationship is much more efficient because of the fact that there is no need to collect data which are already in the consultant's file or mind. The other side is that the consultant might sell services to his or her client for which he is not the best qualified person.

Of course there are certain technical criteria for the quality of consulting work. However, acceptance by the client, the level to which the client really understands what the recommendations are, and responsibility for the implementation are of paramount interest. A technically perfect solution which is not implemented by the client is of no value. Whilst balancing these two sides one will come to the conclusion that an enduring relationship is beneficial for both the client and the consultant.

Another aspect is that consultants who have a relationship with the client will, in certain cases, sell services that the client does not really need. This happens in practice, but, if a relationship is open, and if there is good feedback between client and consultant, this risk is only limited.

Selling

Let's first look at what type of sellers we have. Based on a typology of David Maister[1] we can see three types of consultancies: the pharmacists, the surgeons and the sports physicians. A pharmacist consultant is a consultant with a shop and all kinds of products, and if the client comes to the pharmacist and says: "I have a headache, I need aspirin," the pharmacist will sell it, or in terms of a consultancy, if the client says: "I need a new logistics system," the consultant will build and implement it.

A surgeon however, makes a thorough diagnosis first, conducts all types of tests and then finally decides on the remedy. A surgeon is someone who operates a patient when the patient is ill.

A more productive model is the 'sports physician' consultant who looks at the condition of a client and tries to improve it, he compares the condition of the client with that of its competitors and trains the client all the time in order to get better results.

During the selling process it is extremely important that both the client and the consultant understand what the buying motives of the client are and thus what type of consultant the client needs. A client may only need resources and resources mean that the client does not need any diagnosis, nor an intensive process of analysis, recommendations and implementation, nor complicated project management. The client may just need a second opinion in order to give the client the certainty that he has taken the right decisions. A client may need experience, in other words, a solution that has been found with other clients already. Or a client may need a completely new and innovative perspective.

Finally the need of a client can be to keep his hands clean. Consultants are sometimes hired as snipers or mercenaries.

All these motives or needs can be perfectly legitimate but the ethical demand is that a consultant finds out exactly what the real motives of the client are and confronts these with the type of consultant he is. Otherwise the consultant can never render services at the right level or with the right objectives. An interesting ethical question in the selling process is: "Are we able to deliver the best quality to this client, are we the best consultants for this problem?" And, like in any other industry, commerce makes people corrupt. I am afraid that in certain cases, even when a consultant is aware that he or she is not well qualified to do the job, he or she still accepts it.

A principle debate in consultancy is (or should be): What is it that we are selling? Consultants do not sell time, they do not sell know-how, they do not sell reports, they do not sell advice, they do not sell recommendations. In my view consultants should sell improvements. Improvements in the organization and the results of a client. This implies that a consultant should be committed not only to submit a report but to be involved in the implementation and to commit for certain results. In many countries consultant are, legally speaking, not committed to do more than their best.

Nowadays there is a clear tendency that consulting firms commit themselves to results. That leads us to the questions of whether a 'no cure no pay' condition in a contract or whether contingency fees are allowed. Generally speaking, I am not in favor of 'no cure no pay' conditions and contingency fees. The reason being that in many cases it is so hard to define the result and all the conditions needed to create that result, that there is always the danger of conflict between consultant and client. Only in cases where the deliverable for the client and the conditions under which this result has to be delivered, can be defined very, very clearly can one use a 'no cure no pay' or a contingency condition in the contract.

In almost all circumstances the number of causal connections between the result and the variables that are influenced by both the consultant and the client is so high that it is very often almost impossible and dangerous to do it. The tendency nowadays is to agree with the client about a lump sum which is paid for a certain well defined result and to define the client's obligations much more precise than consultants used to do in the past.

Conducting the Engagement

First and foremost consulting is much more an art than a kind of engineering. This means that fact-finding at the beginning of a consulting engagement is important but that feelings, perceptions are as important. An interesting dilemma here is that the findings of the consultant can be based more on feelings than on facts, in other words that the consultant is not able to find evidence for his recommendations. During the engagement one comes to the question whose side are you on? Do you serve the interest of management only or of all people concerned? Do you take into account what the employee council or the unions think about your job?

My answer to these questions is that, within moral and legal boundaries, the consultants should serve the interest of the party that pays him or her. Of course it can contribute much to the final success of a consulting engagement if other people are involved, if the voice of employees is heard and if the consultant is accepted by other parties within the clients' organization. But in the end the interest of the party who pays should be served by the consultant.

Another question in the approach of a client problem is: Shall we just solve this problem or should we go for continuous improvement? In other words, should we give the client a loaf of bread or should we teach the client how to bake the bread? Seemingly it is commercially interesting for a consultant to sell a loaf of bread time and again, but nowadays modern consultants try to teach their clients more and more how to solve their problems, they try to act as coaches and trainers for their clients thus enabling their clients to solve the problems themselves.

Finally there is the problem of quality. There are two aspects in consulting quality. One is the technical, professional aspect and the other one is the aspect of client satisfaction. Client satisfaction is relatively easy to measure and it is important from a commercial point of view. Consultants can focus on either making clients feel better or making clients be better. The over-emphasizing of client satisfaction nowadays may push consultants into a direction of making clients feel better, knowing that the objective of a consultant should naturally be making clients be better. The technical quality of a consulting engagement is difficult to measure. It is therefore of even more importance that the outcome, the deliverables of a consulting engagement are defined very clearly at the beginning of the process and are measured at the end, if this is possible. An essential element of the quality control process during the engagement is a continuous feedback between client and consultant about both objectives and the actual work that the consultant is doing.

For many consultants it is hard to put questions like: "Am I doing what you expected me to do? Am I delivering the results you wanted? Are you doing what you promised to do Mr. Client? Are you meeting the terms and conditions we defined before we started with the engagement?" Continuous and open feedback is a prerequisite for quality care of an engagement.

During the last two or three years, the debate about certification based on the ISO9000 standards has arisen. In my view certification of a consultancy has to a large extent commercial purposes and does not enhance the quality of consulting.

After sales

As mentioned before, consultants tend to be job hoppers. That means that once they have closed an engagement they turn their back to go to some other place. For professional reasons, instead of commercial reasons, consultants should go back to their clients and establish whether the process they started is still going on, whether the improvements they advised to their clients have been implemented, whether the results they have achieved are still improving.

Consulting as an Intervention or as a Process

In too many cases consulting has been considered as an intervention and not as a process of improvement embedded in a continuous relationship between consultant and client. A feature of this process is that it is a limited rationality. Images, feelings, perceptions play an important role. This implies that objective measures for the quality and the results are often hard to establish. Nevertheless clients and consultant need to be as explicit as possible about the desired outcomes of their efforts. During the consulting process a continuous feed back about expectations and actual outcomes must take place. This is the best assurance for quality.

A permanent relationship and communication between client and consultant also reduces the risk of commercial exploitation of the client by the consultant. In order to maintain the relationship between client and consultant the desires, expectations and motives of the client should be made explicit and the consultant needs to be clear about his or her abilities, skills and feelings. Consciousness of roles and sincere communication about added value of the consultant is a prerequisite.

Finally, both client and consultant should be aware that both players in this process are vulnerable.

Notes

1. Maister, David 1993: *Managing the Professional Service Firm*. Boston: Maister Associates, Inc.

PART II

General Issues

6

Management Consultants
– The Danish Experience

Flemming Poulfelt and Adrian Payne

Abstract

This chapter examines the Danish management consulting industry from the perspective of the consulting firms' managing partner and the client organization's chief executive officer. It examines the principal motives in clients' use of consultants and their buying behavior, as well as clients' perceptions of consulting firms and their experiences in working with them. The results confirm a number of basic beliefs regarding the value of using consultants, but question some of the consultants' capabilities and ethical behavior. The chapter also addresses the challenges facing consultants and clients in improving both their relationship and assignment effectiveness.

Introduction

The global management consulting industry has grown at a rapid rate over the past decade. On average growth rates have been estimated at between 15-40% per annum throughout the 1980s. However, growth has taken place in cyclical patterns which have fluctuated in different countries and practice areas.

This growth can be explained by a number of factors. Managing large companies is an ever more complex task and the increasing need for specialized know-how has made it necessary for more and more CEOs to make use of external consultants in their management process. Some clients use external consultants to solve particular problems, some because they need an external impartial view, and others because they have found that they are compelled to involve consultants because of a crisis. Also, the pressure on reducing costs in client organizations has had a positive impact on the consulting industry as fixed staff costs can be converted into variable costs through the use of external consultants.

H. von Weltzien Hoivik and A. Føllesdal (eds.), Ethics and Consultancy: European Perspectives, 63-81.
© 1995 *Kluwer Academic Publishers. Printed in the Netherlands.*

The use of consultants can also be seen as a direct way to improve profitability through a variety of techniques. Today, clients are in a better position to understand their business and, if they do not have the answers, many at least know where and what to ask for. Further, they are exhibiting greater confidence in selecting and evaluating consultants. This is in line with the notion that understanding the consulting industry and where consultants can add value is an important management task (Payne & Lumsdon, 1987).

Not only should corporate clients have a good understanding of the management consulting industry, but also the form and nature of cooperation between clients and their consultants is also critical for a successful relationship. While the consultant-client relationship often is one of unequal power, ethical behavior of the consultant is a key issue (Gallessich, 1982).

Despite the management consulting industry having experienced rapid growth, many criticisms about practices in the industry have been made (The Economist, 1988). However, a trend towards more professional use of consultants by their clients can also be observed. In fact, the expansion of the management consulting industry is an indicator of more sophisticated clients, demonstrated by the fact that repeat business has represented an increasing part of many consulting firms' total revenues – a comment made by a number of larger consulting firms we surveyed. A different aspect of the greater sophistication of clients in their use of consulting firms is reflected in their dissatisfaction with consultants' efforts (eg. Wilderom, 1990) and a demand for higher quality work.

The focus of this chapter is on the market for consulting services in Denmark. Whilst a number of studies have been conducted on the market for consulting services in other countries, little is known about the Danish consulting market. In fact, within Scandinavia as a whole there has been very little research published on the consulting market. Of the studies that do exist (Berg, Hansen & Poulfelt, 1990), these tend to have been based on a limited number of issues and have focused primarily on issues from the consulting firm side and have not explored relationship-based issues which requires an examination from both the consultant and client perspectives.

The objective of the study was to examine a number of specific issues regarding the Danish consulting market. These include:

1. The Extent of the Consulting Market

Within Europe, there are major differences in the supply and use of consultants (Hunt, 1993). The research sought to identify the size of the Danish market in terms of revenues, numbers of firms, number of consultants and range of services offered. Further, the Danish business community, overall, is fragmented (Kristensen, 1992). The study also sought to determine to what extent this was true of the consulting market in Denmark.

2. The Motives for Using Consultants and Factors Used in Their Selection

There are significant differences in what clients ask consultants to do across European countries (Hunt, 1993). The research sought to examine the motives in the Danish market for use of consulting firms and the factors used in selection, from the perspective of the CEO of client organizations.

3. Client Experience and the Client-Consultant Relationship

The different and often negative views and experiences of companies working with their consultants in studies in other countries suggest a number of interesting issues to research, including; what are Danish clients' experiences in working with consultants, what are clients' perceptions of consultants, and what are consultants' perceptions of clients? As relationship building has been a feature of Danish industrial development (Kristensen, 1992), the study sought to gain an understanding of the degree to which such relationship building exists between consulting firms and their clients, particularly as evidenced by client satisfaction and agreement on the motives for carrying out assignments.

The importance of relationships between suppliers and buyers is receiving considerable attention in academic writing and research. The topic has been described under various headings such as relationship management (Levitt, 1983), network interaction theory (Ford, 1989, Håkansson & Johanson 1992) and relationship marketing (Berry 1983; Grönroos, 1989; Christopher et al 1991; Gummesson, 1994). Whilst relationships have been the subject of much research in industrial companies and service companies, they have largely been ignored in professional service firms and particularly in management consulting.

Because of the importance of relationships in consulting, and the lack of previous research on them, the research focused on the Danish consulting industry from both the client and consultant perspective. The research sought to gain some insight into how the consultation process and the client-consultant relationship can be improved. In contrast to other studies such as Covin & Fisher (1991), which focused on consulting from a consultant perspective, or Shenson (1990), which studied the client perspective, this study adopts a more integrated approach by simultaneously considering the perspectives of both client and consultant.

In this study, the research focused on examining the client organizations and consulting firms and their relationships from a *strategic* perspective. As a result, and to make the study manageable, the views of the most senior person in the organization – the chief executive officer of the client organizations and the managing partner in the consulting firms – were investigated.

Method

This chapter is based on research into the Danish management consulting business undertaken between 1990 and 1992. The research is divided into two major parts. The first part of the study focused on management consulting firms. A list of firms were compiled from the yellow pages in the telephone directories covering all the regions in Denmark. This list was cross-checked with the major Danish business directories and the member list of the Danish Management Consulting Association. This resulted in a list of some 300 consulting firms. A questionnaire was designed, piloted and then sent to the managing partners of these firms in order to obtain quantitative and qualitative data about their business, nature of services, revenues, profitability, and number of consultants employed. In addition, the questionnaire explored the managing partners' perceptions of their clients as well as their views on the future of the industry.

The response rate from firms which were classified as management consultants and for whom consultancy was their core business was 60%. Some 92% of responses were from the managing partner or equivalent position (including titles such as CEO, managing director and chairman). Among the non-usable returns were responses from firms not meeting the definition of management consulting (described in the next section) and firms no longer in business. The respondent group was highly representative for large and medium-sized consulting firms. Only one of the ten largest firms did not respond (and this was followed up by a personal interview) and an estimated 80% of the top 25 firms responded. It thus represented a reasonably high proportion of the Danish consulting market in terms of number of employees and total revenues.

The second part of the study focused on client organizations from the perspective of the chief executive officer. Questionnaires were sent to the CEOs of 200 organizations – 150 in the private and 50 in the public sector. This split was based on the estimated proportion of consulting work derived from the private and public sectors. This proportion was identified in the first part of this study. The list of companies and organizations was generated from a number of business directories and directories of public sector organizations in Denmark. A stratified random sample was selected to represent different industries and size of organization. This included large corporations, medium-sized companies, small companies as well as public sector organizations in Denmark.

The questionnaire sought information on the type of assignments undertaken, frequency of use of consultants, the value of the work, and their experience and perceptions of consultants. Additionally, questions were included regarding their expected use of consultants in the future.

The questionnaires were piloted and then sent to the CEO and had a 45% response rate. In the survey, we emphasized that we required a response from the CEO. A very high number of responses received (97%) were from the CEO. This request may have reduced the number of responses but it did ensure a very high proportion of the responses came from the level we desired – the CEO. An examination of non-respondent and respondents did not indicate any obviously strong structural bias. A similar proportion of private and public sector organizations responded, although a slightly higher proportion of larger organizations were represented. Of those responding, 88% had used consultants in the last 3 years whilst the remaining 12% had not used consultants in the last 3 years or had not used consultants at all. Based on these proportions, respondents using consultants may be over-represented as those with experience of using consultants may have been more likely to respond. However, as information was sought on their experience in the use of consultants this was seen as an advantage rather than a disadvantage.

Although a larger sample of respondents would have been desirable, a response rate of 45%, with 88% of these using consultants in the last 3 years, was considered a reasonably high response from busy CEOs. This compares favorably with some studies undertaken in other countries, which requested responses from CEOs, and where response rates varied from 8% to 42% (Payne, 1989). (The highest response rate of 42% was achieved only after an extensive telephone follow-up of the questionnaire and re-mailings).

In order to make direct comparisons between the survey of the clients and the survey of the consultants, a number of questions were identical or designed in a way which made it possible to make appropriate comparisons and cross-analyses.

Before proceeding with the results of the research, a brief qualification of the findings is appropriate. There may be some sensitivity when it comes providing specific data on consulting firms and success in the use of consultants by client CEOs. Accordingly some bias could be reflected in the answers provided. The research was designed to minimize any potential bias in the construction of the questionnaires. The comments provided by most CEOs were very frank and, overall, any such bias was not obvious. Where it is considered that bias may exist, a comment is made on this at the appropriate point in the chapter.

The Danish Consulting Market

For the purposes of the study, after an examination of several definition of management consulting, the definition used by the Féderation Européenne des Associations de Conseils en Organization (FEACO) was adopted:

Management Consultancy: The rendering of independent advice and assistance about management issues. This typically includes identifying and investigating problems and/or opportunities, recommending appropriate action and helping to implement those recommendations.

This definition, in common with others examined, is fairly broad and not totally satisfactory. To make this definition more operational, a list of sixteen widely accepted practice areas in management consulting was developed, based on those used by FEACO and Greiner & Metzger (1983), and used this in the questionnaire to determine which respondents should not be classified as consultants and not be used in the study.

Using this definition it is estimated that the size of the Danish management consulting market is approximately US$250 million, and that the management consulting business in the early 1990s grew at an average growth rate of 14% per annum. These figures were derived from the individual responses of firms and included an estimate for non-responses. As a high level of response was obtained from the 25 largest firms, this is considered a reasonably accurate estimate. The growth rate in Denmark has been slightly lower than in other parts of Europe and the US where growth rates of typically 20-25% were experienced (FEACO, 1989; ACME, 1990; Hunt, 1993).

With respect to future expectations of growth, it is of interest to note that within specific consulting firms there appears to be a strong correlation between past performance in terms of growth rate, and expected future growth rates. Firms which experienced a higher growth rate had similar expectations concerning the future, whilst firms with a flat rate of growth only expected moderate increases in the future.

The number of management consulting firms in Denmark is estimated to be around 250. The Danish consulting industry is a fragmented one characterized by relatively few large firms and a large number of small ones. In this regard it follows the general pattern within Danish industry (Kristensen, 1992) – but what is the extent of this fragmentation? The study surveyed the distribution of these firms by size and found that 70% of the firms had less than five consultants, 20% between five and fifteen consultants and 10% of the firms had more than fifteen consultants. Some 75% of the total revenues in the consulting industry were accounted for by 25% of the firms. The research suggests a total of around 1,400 full time consultants are employed in the industry with a total number of approximately 1,900 employees, including administrative staff.

The survey found that the Danish management consulting firms offer a wide variety of services and the profile of many firms is broad-based consulting. Although it is to be expected that larger firms have this broad-based profile, because of a full service philosophy, it was noticeable that many of the small players offer a fairly wide range of services. Although some small firms are highly specialized in both the services that they offer and the market segments that they serve, others serve smaller companies need the approach of a generalist. However, it was apparent from some of the responses that some small firms' ability to offer a broad range of services must be questioned. This finding raises the issue as to whether some of these small firms have the professional capability to offer such a wide range of services. The ability to offer broader based services depends, however, not just on size, but also on the knowledge, experience and capabilities of people within the consulting firm. It was evident that a number of respondents considered the smaller consulting firms they had retained did not have consultants with such capabilities.

The consulting firms surveyed identified three dominant success factors: satisfied clients; solving the problems of the clients; and high quality work and professionalism factors which all are essential in conforming to consulting codes of professional conduct. Successful consulting firms are highly focused on servicing the interests of clients. However, whether clients perceive consulting firms deliver high levels of service quality is an issue to be examined later in this chapter.

Motives for Using Consultants

Based upon this current research, previous studies into the use of consultants (Gattiker & Larwood, 1985; Wilderom, 1990) and the consulting literature (eg. Askvik, 1991; Kubr, 1986; Greiner & Metzger, 1983), six motives for using consultants were identified and used in this study. As the same questions regarding motives were used in both the questionnaire to the consulting firms and the client survey, a direct comparison of the responses from them was made possible.

The analysis in Figure 1 shows that there was remarkably close agreement between clients and consultants in their beliefs as to the specific motives driving the use of consultants. This indicates that consultants, in general, have a very clear understanding of the reasons why clients seek their services.

FIGURE 1. Motives for Using Consultants

Motives	Clients' Responses	Consultants' Responses
1. To provide expertise, knowledge and new methodologies	21 %	21 %
2. To provide additional resources	13 %	13 %
3. To present new solutions to the organizations problems	21 %	21 %
4. To act as an external catalyst and moderator	24 %	24 %
5. To bring an independent and neutral perspective to the organization	18 %	16 %
6. To legitimize results and for political motives	3 %	5 %

The distribution of responses in Figure 1 shows the relative importance of the various motives for using consultants in the Danish market and emphasizes the consultant as a provider of expertise and new methodologies; a party bringing an independent and neutral view point to client assignments and a change agent and catalyst. The use of consultants to provide additional resources was not so important which implies that switching fixed staff costs to variable costs though the use of consultants is not widespread.

When the responses are separated into responses from clients in the private sector and the ones in the public sector, the most important difference is that clients from private firms emphasize "additional external resources" more than clients from the public sector, whereas political motives are more important to clients in the public sector.

Political motives cover a broad range of more specific reasons, including hidden agendas, but were not ranked as a motive of importance by respondents. These issues are often related to consulting ethics. Political issues are evident in a number of consulting projects within the public sector in Denmark where consultants have been criticized for taking on assignments with a questionable agenda (Sorensen, 1993). Political motives are, however, highly sensitive and are difficult to elicit in written questionnaires. Further, consultants may be unaware of the "real" motives and clients may be unwilling to reveal them. Thus their importance may be under-represented in this study.

An analysis was also carried out of the motives for use of different sized consulting firms. An assumption could be made that the major consultancies are primarily used as providers of knowledge and to develop new solutions, while smaller consulting firms act more on a process consulting basis. However, an analysis of these three groups did not provide any support for this assumption and suggested that the motives for using consultants were very much the same regardless of their size.

The client CEOs were also asked about their purchasing behavior in selecting consultants, including the factors of greatest importance in the buying process. Specifically, they were asked to evaluate the relative importance of nine factors. These factors were selected on the basis of preliminary research involving in-depth interviews with 15 consulting firms and a small number of clients in Denmark, an examination of previously research, and buying behavior examined in other studies of the management consulting market undertaken in the UK and Australia.

The results of this analysis are shown in Figure 2 which illustrates the specific factors and their relative importance. Care was taken in choosing the phrasing of questions relating to the buying factors to avoid contentious issues or leading questions. An examination of responses showed no obvious evidence of respondents answering with "what they considered proper."

FIGURE 2. The Client CEO's Buying Factors

Buying Factors	Unimportant	Some importance	Very Important
Previous experience	3 %	24 %	73 %
Professional competence in the field	0 %	14 %	86 %
Specific industry and/or sector knowledge	10 %	56 %	34 %
The consultant's formal presentation was highly convincing	5 %	25 %	70 %
The consulting firm's reputation	0 %	29 %	71 %
Knowledge of specific people in the consulting firm	20 %	49 %	31 %
The consultant's style and appearance	20 %	60 %	20 %
The level of fees charged	10 %	78 %	12 %
Membership of FMK (The Danish Management Consulting Association)	92 %	8 %	0 %

Figure 2 shows clearly that the management consulting firm's professional competence in the field is of the most important factor. Previous experience, the consulting firm's reputation and the quality of consultant's presentations are also important. This illustrates that well developed inter-personal skills and a high level of professionalism displayed during an assignment, play a crucial role.

On the other hand, specific industry and sector knowledge does not seem to play such a prominent part in the Danish market. This is an interesting finding considering the emphasis many management consulting firms have placed on specific industry knowledge as a means of competitive differentiation. In fact, creating industry specialization has been suggested as an important factor in the operations of large consulting firms (FEACO, 1989). This was confirmed in the analysis of the survey on consultants where they placed more emphasis on this factor. However, the variation may be based on different perceptions in the meaning of "industry knowledge". For consultants it may be seen as equivalent to the services offered whereas clients may see industry knowledge as a prerequisite.

Considering a widely held view that trust and personal chemistry are decisive factors, it is notable that greater importance is not attached to the consultant's style and appearance in initial interactions with clients.

Whilst only 10% of clients considered fees were unimportant, only 12% stated they were very important. Interviews with clients and other research we have conducted point to a higher importance of fees, than the results shown in Figure 2. The lower emphasis on the level of fees charged might reflect a discrepancy between "theories in use" and "espoused theories" (Argyris & Schon, 1974).

Finally, it is notable that membership of The Danish Association of Management Consultants (FMK) is considered totally unimportant from a client perspective. This is not unexpected, given the Association's weak positioning in the Danish business community and public sector. This is similar to the situation in other countries where professional organizations representing the consulting industry do not play a prominent role (Berg & Poulfelt, 1986).

Client Experiences With Consultants

An important part of the survey involved examining clients CEOs' experiences with management consultants. An interesting conclusion, contrasting with research undertaken in other countries (e.g. Payne & Lumsdon, 1987; Wilderom, 1990) was that Danish users of consulting services generally have had favorable experiences in using consultants. The study shows that 88% are satisfied when using them and approximately 40% were very or totally satisfied. Only 5% were totally dissatisfied. The results are shown in Figure 3 and illustrate CEOs' satisfaction in the use of management consultants.

FIGURE 3. The Clients CEOs' Satisfaction Index

1.	Totally satisfied	7%
2.	Very satisfied	32%
3.	Satisfied	49%
4.	Less satisfied	7%
5.	Totally dissatisfied	5%

Several factors in the Danish consulting market help explain this finding. First, the consulting industry in Denmark has evolved to a higher level of professionalism during the last ten years which is also reflected in the clients' attitude to their consultants. The notion of "being aware of your company working style – and choose your consultant type accordingly" (Nees & Greiner, 1985) seems to have become well accepted. Second, the clients' response should also be seen as an expression of the improved service quality amongst consultants. The clients' increasing demands and involvement in consulting projects generally have sharpened and stimulated the quality of consultants' work and their emphasis on professional development. At the same time it should be noted that clients are becoming more selective in the use of their consultants and are not buying external advisory services unless they believe they will yield good value. The notion of consultants using high pressure selling tactics to prospective and existing clients was not evident in this study.

It could be argued that below average performance in a consulting assignment may be covered up by a certain degree of subsequent post-assignment rationalization by managers (Festinger, 1957). A client company spending a significant amount on a consulting assignment may have difficulties in admitting that it has not been worth the money, as this may reflect weak managerial ability. However, this assumption is not supported by research undertaken in other countries where managers are most candid with respect to the failings of their consultants, e.g. Payne & Lumsdon (1987).

The view that clients are increasingly discriminating is supported by the consultants' responses. Some 70% of the consultant firm managing partners surveyed indicate that their clients have become more demanding. Figure 4, below, illustrates the consulting firms' experience with clients, based on their responses to a number of statements in the survey.

FIGURE 4. The Consultant Managing Partner's Perception of Clients

Consultants' Perception and Experience	Agree	Disagree
1. Clients have become more demanding	70 %	30 %
2. Clients want to involve themselves more in the consulting work	55 %	45 %
3. Clients have become better at identifying the key problems	47 %	53 %
4. Clients transfer too much responsibility to their consultants	22 %	78 %
5. Clients are not competent enough in their use of consultants	38 %	62 %

As shown in Figure 4, the consultants are finding that clients are seeking more active involvement in the assignment. However, although some managing partners consider their clients have become better at problem identification, the majority of consultants surveyed (53%) do not hold this view.

Finally, it should be noted that 62% of the consultants disagree with the statement that clients are "not competent enough in their use of consultants". This suggests that the users have become more sophisticated – even if they should place more attention on how they formulate consulting projects, undertake problem definition and their approach to implementation of projects. This is in line with Czarniawaska-Joerges et al (1990) who argues that "it is not the consultants, but their clients who must professionalize". It is highly evident that most consultants (78%) believe that clients do not transfer too much responsibility to consultancy firms.

Client Perceptions of Consultants

In addition to questions regarding the degree of satisfaction, the client CEOs were also asked to respond to a number of statements in order to get more specific data on attitudes and key issues regarding cooperation between consultants and clients. In Figure 5 twenty statements are shown together with the distribution of clients' responses.

An examination of client CEOs' responses in terms of different sized firms and different sectors (both private and public) showed no marked differences.

A number of the results in Figure 5 are of particular interest. The perception that consultants are very competent at structuring complex situations and problems is confirmed, just as the clients' experiences indicate that consultants, in general, are results-oriented. Further, consultants' appreciation of the process elements in the assignment is emphasized including their ability to manage projects. It is notable that consultants are not perceived as often "over promising" with respect to results, with 50% not agreeing with the statement relating to this. However, one fifth of the clients believe that this is the case. From a services marketing and "word of mouth" point of view this indicates that many managers still have a mixed view of what consultants offer and how much added value is delivered.

Figure 5 also illustrates that the consultant's approach, when it comes to the client's specific situation and how to approach it, is not as customized as many consultants claim. It is noticeable that 25% of the client CEOs consider that consultant do not adapt their problem solving enough to the specific client environment. This finding is of relevance in the context of the current debate regarding the customization versus the standardization of consulting services. If a more standardized approach is adopted by consultants, it is likely to create further problems, from the client's perspective, regarding the relevance for the services offered.

The figure also shows that consultants in Denmark are not perceived as being very internationally-oriented in their approach. This is in agreement with another part of the research which confirmed that only a small portion (approximately 2%) of the total industry revenue stems from assignments abroad. Consultants are, therefore, not gaining international experience and are not having an opportunity to develop their international expertise.

Even though some of the client CEO respondents have mixed views regarding the consultant's ability to specify the benefits of a specific assignment to the clients, the overall results of the study illustrate that, in general, consultants appear to add value to the client organizations. This result corresponds with the client satisfaction index in Figure 3. It is also worth noting that the view that consultants are expensive is more strongly held by companies who do not use consultants. One of the most frequent reasons for not using consultants, among companies in the non-user group, is that they are too expensive. Other reasons for not using consultants are prior bad experiences from using them, no specific need for external advisers, and a perception that consultants do not provide value.

FIGURE 5. Client CEOs' Perceptions

Statement	Disagree	Partly Agree	Totally Agree
1. Consultants are good at understanding the specific problem of the company	2 %	65 %	33 %
2. Consultants are competent of structuring complex situations	0 %	33 %	67 %
3. Consultants know how to specify the added value/benefits of an assignment	16 %	66 %	18 %
4. Consultants always adapt their problem solving approach to the specific client situation	25 %	50 %	25 %
5. Consultants meet deadlines and work plans	9 %	49 %	42 %
6. Consultants know how to establish good co-operation conditions	10 %	55 %	35 %
7. Consultants are exact in their analyses	9 %	77 %	14 %
8. Consultants appreciate the importance of the process	0 %	41 %	59 %
9. Consultants know how to manage a project	2 %	56 %	42 %
10. Consultants are good at balancing conflicting interests	9 %	74 %	16 %
11. Consultants are very focused on implementation	14 %	63 %	21 %
12. Consultants have a well-developed political intuition	22 %	60 %	18 %
13. Consultants are very result-oriented	5 %	38 %	57 %
14. Consultants are international-minded	20 %	75 %	5 %
15. Consultants are expensive	5 %	37 %	58 %
16. Consultants are focused on forces resisting changes	18 %	74 %	8 %
17. Consultants often promise more than they can keep	50 %	29 %	21 %
18. Consultants are creative in their problem solving approaches	7 %	70 %	23 %
19. Consultants are focused on what is best for the client	5 %	51 %	44 %
20. Consultants are professional in their efforts and approach	5 %	52 %	43 %

The Client and Consultant Relationship

A key issue and an explicit reason for undertaking an analysis of consultants, from the client perspective, is to generate data for identifying key issues for better understanding the consultant-client relationship. The underlying logic and structure of the twenty statements in Figure 5 reflects five key issues for consultants in the consultant-client relationship. These are:

1. Proposal writing   (statement 1, 2, 3)
2. Problem solving & client cooperation   (statement 4, 6, 8, 9, 18)
3. Results of assignment   (statement 7, 13, 15, 17)
4. Focus on change   (statement 10, 11, 12, 16)
5. Professional conduct   (statement 5, 19, 20)

The scale used in Figure 5 was: totally agree, partly agree, and disagree. Even though clients tended to be cautious placing a mark in full agreement (unless the statement is a criticism), partly agree and disagree can be seen as possible areas for improvement. Therefore, if a majority, i.e. 2/3 of the answers within the categories disagree or partly agree this can be seem as areas for potential improvement. Based on the results in Figure 5, a number of conclusions can be drawn.

Proposal Writing

Consultants received credit from their clients for their ability to structure the problems when writing a proposal. However, the ability to understand the specific problem of the company seems less apparent. This can be characterized as "missing business empathy". It is interesting that a study of consultants' perceptions of effective and ineffective consultant behavior (Covin & Fisher, 1991) emphasizes that effective behavior is stimulated by empathy and that ineffective behavior, among other things, is caused by "preconceived ideas about the client and his industry".

Another conclusion about proposal writing is that there is often a failure by consultants to translate the benefits of their experience into tangible results for their clients. Greater industry knowledge and business insight is, therefore, in many cases a necessity in order to respond to a company's specific needs. Greater preparation and research, including background reading, research on the client and a deeper study of the relevant industry should take a higher priority on the consultant's agenda.

Problem Solving and Client Cooperation

The most critical issue in the client-consultant working relationship is the absence of adaptability of the part of the consultant. For instance, Covin & Fisher's study (1991) emphasized that effective behavior is based on a consulting effort where the consultant "did not impose a solution, but sought collaboration" and developed a program content that met the requirements of the client. This represents an interesting question: Why is there is a misfit between the messages in customization typically sent out by consultants and the clients' perceptions, and what can be done to close this gap? One assumption could be that when there is increased standardization of services, there is a risk of conformity in the problem solving process. Another assumption is that the adjustment of mutual expectations has not been given sufficient attention – not only in the early phase of a project – but also during the whole assignment. This could also imply that consultants often exaggerate the focus on clients' specific needs, while clients at the same time have an unrealistic expectation of the actual meaning of customized services. However, it is still the task of the consultant to ensure the correct balance is achieved. The process of communication and client education is, therefore, a critical element.

There is a mixed view when it comes to the ability of consultants to create a constructive and collaborative climate. Thus there appears to be a greater need to focus on process skills. This finding is supported by the view expressed in "Profile of an International Executive Consultant Today and 2000" (Kienbaum, 1990) which emphasizes process elements as being the most necessary skills which need to be strengthened in the profile of existing consulting firms. O'Connell (1990) also emphasizes this issue.

To a degree, the limited ability to create a stimulating work environment is in contrast to the findings that consultants understand the importance of the process. However, one explanation may be that many managers of today are conscious of the impact of the process in a project and that this answer might reflect their own attitude and not necessarily their specific perception regarding the consultants' focus on the process.

Results of Assignment

From the analysis it can be learned that clients, in general, are satisfied with the results-oriented working style of most consultants. However, it should be noted that the study also shows that consultants should be more precise when communicating the findings of their research. This observation corresponds with earlier views of consultants as professionals who deliver vague conclusions (*The Economist*, 1988). This issue is emphasized by researchers who argue that the ability to communicate successfully can have a great impact on the overall result of an assignment.

Focus on Change

The most important task for a consultant is to create change (Schein, 1990). The role of consultant as a change maker or change agent is frequently emphasized. In examining the clients' perception of the consultants' change role it is notable that clients would prefer a more distinct profile. More attention should also be given to the consultant's position as a mediator and to their political role. Both these elements are extremely important in the change process (Margerison, 1988; Mastenbrock, 1986; Schein, 1987).

Implementation issues in relation to change are also of critical importance. The client CEOs' responses in our survey shows that a strengthening is needed by their consultants in the focus on implementation. Consultants claim on one hand that they are focused on implementation and yet on the other hand claim that clients often do not allow them to participate in the recommended changes. Therefore, some redefinition of the implementation concept may be needed and greater clarity given to its meaning.

Creating change is the desired outcome of most assignments, so a key challenge for consultants is to find a balance between technical issues with those that are political and emotional.

Professional Conduct

In general, client CEOs perceive consultants as being professional in terms of their commitment to solving the client's problem, meeting deadlines and agreed workplans, and their professionalism and work style. This is confirmed by the client satisfaction index in Figure 3.

The Danish findings on professional conduct are in some contrast to other studies. Wilderom's (1990) study of 300 large and medium-sized Dutch companies and their satisfaction with the use of management consultants concluded that 50% of the respondents did not think highly of management consultants. This is different to consultants' views on the value of their own business -in a pilot survey of 26 Dutch consulting firms almost 75% of consultants considered the projects to be highly successful. This may portray complacency or over-confidence on the part of Dutch consultants in their professionalism. In a study of 150 UK companies, one quarter were not wholly happy with the outcomes of their consulting assignment (Payne & Lumsdon, 1987). A small Swedish survey (Dagens Industri, 1989) had very similar results with respect to the proportion of dissatisfied clients. In any event, it is clearly a critical issue in the development of an ongoing consultant-client relationship.

In a study of 610 buyers of consulting/professional services Shenson (1990) outlined the ten most frequently mentioned issues which clients felt consultants "– should have communicated about". Among these were ethical issues, conflict of interest, confidentiality, non-performance and time management, expenses, and use of subcontractors. Many of these issues were raised by respondents in this study.

Conclusions and Future Research Opportunities

This study sought to gain some understanding of the relationships between consulting firms and their clients. Relationship building through personal networks, "tying persons across boundaries of individual firms to each other as friends and colleagues... and thereby also creating trust" has been a feature of Danish institutional development (Kristensen, 1992). Unlike the large western economies and its close neighbor, Sweden, Denmark has relatively few large industrial companies. In the absence of raw materials much of its manufacturing and other activities are in smaller companies frequently operating in niche markets and often with advanced technology. Such companies have made up for a lack of size through exploiting such niche markets and through innovation. In such a competitive environment relationships between consulting firms and their clients are clearly crucial to help continually improve performance. Management consulting firms play an important part in this process. Payne (1987) argues that, from a microeconomic perspective, consultants make a contribution to the economy, greater than might be expected. Management consulting enables unique sets of skills and abilities to be developed, and efficiently allocates these scarce resources of highly skilled professionals to those organizations purchasing their services.

Relationships, a principle of complementarity and subcontracting out specialist activities have been pointed out as attributes of Danish industry. Also stability and trust among business partners have been emphasized as a Danish characteristic (Kristensen, 1992). These attributes may also be reflected in this research which indicates that there is a general high satisfaction among client CEOs using consultants in the Danish consulting market. As discussed in the previous section of the chapter, this level of satisfaction is higher than that found in studies undertaken in some other countries. It is also worth emphasizing the strong fit between the perceptions of client CEOs and consulting firm managing partners on a number of issues.

Satisfactory completion of an assignment, in most cases, needs a joint effort from the consultant and the client. This requires both parties to be aware of their expectations, roles and potential contribution, not only in the initial stage, but during each step in the assignment. How to screen consultants or clients, establish, and develop a professional relationship are, therefore, key issues.

This study provides evidence that more focused effort should be made by clients in defining the basis for an assignment, the project itself and the participation required in the assignment. The absence of strong client commitment is often a major reason for less successful assignments (Margerison, 1988). Even though it is the task of the consultant to ensure client involvement, clients would often benefit more by reflecting on their role and how they might complement the role of the consultant. In addition to setting out more realistic expectations, clients also have to consider the dilemma of being committed whilst at the same time accepting analysis which may criticize the existing management, either directly or indirectly.

Among the challenges facing consultants are issues relating to client adaptability including balancing customized and standardized services. More attention should also be given to the role of the consultant as a change maker and to implementation issues. The role of the consultant needs to be balanced to reflect the requirements of business knowledge, process management skills and functional expertise (O'Connell, 1990).

An important issue in a professional client-consultant relationship is knowledge transfer based upon mutual trust and ethical behavior. The study has shed light on some elements which influence this relationship. However, more research should be undertaken in order to understand more clearly the dynamics of the client-consultant relationship. In the case of often very sensitive assignments involving business, political and emotional issues, the relationship management task in consulting differs in complexity from the general framework of relations between sellers and buyers (Hedaa, 1991). This complexity should be recognized in research projects focusing on client-consultant relations.

While much has been written about consultancy, this is usually based on generalized observations. There is a need for more systematic research including longitudinal study of protracted consulting assignments. Another area for further research is the study of the key success factors in consulting projects focusing on "best demonstrated practice", including identifying key characteristics of such consulting firms, their consultants and their clients.

This study has focused on consulting in a strategic context – ie. what are the perceptions of the client CEO and the consulting firm managing partner. The study has been concerned with a view from the top of the client and consultant organization rather than identifying opinions of people throughout the organization. There are, however, differences of perception within both client and consulting organizations. For example, within a client firm, Schein (1987) discusses four categories of client: contact, primary, intermediate and ultimate. Work the authors have undertaken elsewhere showed a variance between the perceptions of the results achieved by leading strategy consulting firms when seen by the chief executive and when seen by mid-level managers. Future research could examine these differences and explore their impact on issues such as implementation success.

A comparative study between consulting styles and methods in different countries is also worthy of examination. In particular, how does the business environment, leadership style and culture impact the consulting process? Also, more research on ethical issues from a consultant and client perspective could enhance the insights into how to further professionalize the consulting relationship. Even though codes of ethics and standards of professional practice exist (e.g. those of ACME and FEACO – see Kubr 1986), such standards are often too abstract or absolute for encompassing many consulting situations. Additionally, the ethical codes are primarily related to the behavior of consultants. Focus on ethical issues and dilemmas should include both parties and their relationship in the consulting assignment.

References

ACME, Management Consultants' 1990 World Conference, New York, 1990.

Argyris, C. and D. Schon 1974: *Theory in Practice: Increasing Professional Effectiveness.* Jossey-Bass

Askvik, S. 1991: Rådgivning, rutine eller ritual? *Tidsskrift for samfunnsforskning,* årgang 32, pp. 249-268.

Berg, P.O., Hansen H.H. and Poulfelt F. 1990: Management consulting – an analysis of unregulated professional markets – the case of the Scandinavian management consulting markets. CBS.

Berg, P.O. and Poulfelt, F. 1986: Professionalizing a profession: Increasing the competence of management consultants. *Consultation,* Vol. 5, No. 4, Winter, pp 258-273.

Berry, L.L. 1983: Relationship Marketing. In Berry, L.L., Shostack G.L. and Upah, G.D., (eds), *Emerging Perspectives of Services Marketing*, American Marketing Association.

Christopher, M., Payne, A. and Ballantyne, D. 1991: *Relationship Marketing*. Butterworth Heinemann.

Covin, T.J. and T.V. Fisher 1991: Consultant and client must work together. *Journal of Management Consulting*, Vol. 6, No. 4., pp 11-19.

Czarniawska-Joerges, C. Gustafsson and Dag Björkegren 1990: Purists vs. pragmatists: On protagoras, economists and management consultants. *Consultation*, Vol. 9, No. 3, Fall, pp 241-256.

Dagens Industri 1989: Klagomål på konsulter, October.

The Economist 1988: Management Consulting, February 13.

FEACO, Management Consultants' 1989 World Conference, Copenhagen.

Festinger, L. 1957: *Theory of Cognitive Dissonance*. Row Peterson.

Ford, D. (ed) 1990: *Understanding Business Market – Interaction, Relationships, Networks*. Academic Press.

Gallessich, J. 1982: *The Profession and Practice of Consultation*. San Francisco: Jossey-Bass.

Gattiker, U.E. and Larwood L. 1985: Why do clients employ management consultants? *Consultation*, Vol. 4, No. 2, pp. 119-129.

Greiner, L. and Metzger, R. 1983: *Consulting to Management*. Englewood Cliffs: Prentice Hall.

Grönroos, C. 1989: A relationship approach to marketing: The need for a new paradigm. Working Paper 190, Swedish School of Economics and Business Administration.

Gummesson, E. 1994: *Relationship Marketing: From 4Ps to 30Rs*. Stockholm University.

Håkonsson, H. and Johanson, J. 1992: A model of industrial networks. In Axelsson B. and Easton E., *Industrial Networks – A New View of Reality*. Routledge, pp. 28-36.

Hedaa, L. 1991: On Interorganizational Relationships in Industrial Marketing, PhD thesis, Copenhagen Business School.

Hunt, J. W. 1993: Some observations on the European consulting scene. *Journal of Management Consulting*, Vol 7, No 3, Spring, pp 2-3.

Kienbaum and Partnere, 1990: *Profile of An International Executive Consultant Today and 2000*. New York.

Kristensen, P. H. 1992: Strategies against structure: Institutions and economic organizations in Denmark. In Whitley R., *European Business Systems*. Beverly Hills: Sage.

Kubr, M. 1986: Management Consulting, ILO.

Levitt, T. 1993: After the sale is over. *Harvard Business Review*, September-October, pp 87-93.

Margerison, C. 1988: *Management Consulting Skills*. Gower.

Mastenbrock, W.F. 1986: The politics of consultancy. *Journal of Management Consulting*, Vol. 3, No. 1, pp 20-26.

Nees, D. and Greiner, L. 1985: Seeing behind the look-alike management consultants. *Organizational Dynamics*, Vol 13, No 3, pp 68-79.

O'Connell, J.J. 1990: Process consulting in a context field: Socrates in strategy. *Consultation*, Vol. 9, No. 3, Fall, pp 199-208.

Payne, A. 1987: A European view of management consulting. *European Management Journal*, Vol. 5, No. 3, pp 154-62.

Payne, A. 1989: Strategic Management. In Samson, D. (ed), *Management for Engineers,* Longman Cheshire.

Payne, A. and Lumsdon, C. 1097: Strategy consulting – a shooting star. *Long Range Planning,* Vol. 20, No. 3, pp 53-64.

Schein, E. 1990: What do organizations of the 1990s need? *Consultation,* Vol. 9, No. 4, pp. 261-276.

Schein, E. 1987: *Process Consultation, Vol. II, Lessons for Managers and Consultants.* Reading, Mass.: Addison Wesley.

Shenson, H.L 1990: *How to Select and Use Management Consultants.* University Associates.

Sorensen, H. 1993: Fokus på managementkonsulentrapporter. ISF.

Wilderom, C.P.M 1990: Management consulting in the Netherlands – professional issues and prospects. *Consultation,* Vol. 9, No. 1, pp 51-61.

7

Nepotism, Politics and Ethics in the Purchase of Organizational Consultancy Services – Two European Cases

Patrick Maclagan and Collean Evans-de Souza

Introduction

In this chapter we are concerned with client managers' motives in the purchase of consultancy services for organizations. After an initial theoretical discussion, two real European cases are outlined and analyzed. Some conclusions and recommendations are then offered in the final section.

We view our focal concern (nepotism and self-interest by client managers in the purchase of consultancy services) as a specific type of a more general class of managerial action; namely the abuse of their authority to spend moneys and procure resources. Other, analogous, situations can be envisaged; for example, purchasing decisions in industry (e.g. Pettigrew, 1972). Thus, while the implications for consultants themselves are not excluded from consideration in this paper, our main focus will be on the behavior of those in client organizations who buy in consultants' services.

We hope to show that the extent to which such situations raise ethical issues depends on the circumstances in any particular case. It is reasonable to argue that the procurement of inappropriate or unnecessary resources amounts to a clear misuse of organizational finances, which may well be condemned on consequentialist grounds. If one is to engage in moral evaluation of such situations, however, one also needs to understand the motives and beliefs behind buyers' actions and the precise circumstances which may have constrained them. It cannot be assumed that deliberate favoritism or bias was involved. Similarly, what appears at first sight to be improper practice as a means to procuring resources, may be justified if such resources were essential and unattainable otherwise.

In working on the two cases we have become increasingly conscious of the ambiguity of much behavior in organizations. We have tried to cope with this by offering a taxonomy of client buying behavior, which may be used to assess the eth-

H. von Weltzien Hoivik and A. Føllesdal (eds.), Ethics and Consultancy: European Perspectives, 83-92.
© *1995 Kluwer Academic Publishers. Printed in the Netherlands.*

ical status of such conduct. In so doing, we have become aware of the complexity of the issues involved, and recognize that many questions remain unanswered (and probably unasked).

Understanding Managerial Behavior

There are various explanations which may account for what looks like questionable practice in resource procurement or in the award of contracts, and some of these explanations point to the possibility of mitigating circumstances. As a general observation, the area of enquiry indicated opens up a potentially vast agenda for discussion, which clearly we cannot pursue here. However we would draw particular attention to decision-making in organizations (Simon, 1947; March & Simon, 1958) and aspects of social and cognitive psychology (Staw, 1980).

First of all, it is possible that, at the time a decision is taken, a manager may genuinely believe, on the basis of available information, that the particular choice of supplier or consultant is the most suitable. So, if this is a source with which one is already familiar, even to the extent of apparent nepotism or patronage, and the choice is believed to be rational for the organization, then this would seem to be justifiable provided that it really is the outcome of a thorough search and consideration of alternatives.

This rational decision-making perspective can be put in context by considering the substantial literature on the nature of managerial work, ranging from Fayol (1949) through Stewart (1967) to Mintzberg (1977) and, of particular relevance to this discussion, Jackall (1988). This literature offers us contrasting perspectives. On the one hand, we have a picture of managers calmly engaging in (and who, it is claimed, "ought" to engage in) organizationally rational planning and decision making (Fayol, 1949). On the other hand, we find stressed individuals in politicized milieux, harassed by interruptions, mountains of paper and endless verbal exchanges (Mintzberg, 1977) but who, nevertheless, are still attempting to pursue some sort of continuous, consistent, agenda, some sort of rationality (which admittedly may reflect personal, political, rather than organizational goals) (Sharifi, 1988). Mintzberg's research suggests that managers do not always have time to search for the most appropriate resource, or solution to a problem; or, indeed, even to define the problem adequately. To use Simon's metaphor, such managers do not search for the sharpest needle in the haystack, but settle instead for the first needle they find which is sharp enough to sew with; what he termed "satisficing behavior" (March & Simon, 1958, p 141). Is this unethical, or just not very competent? Or defensible because of informational and time constraints?

Processes of rationalization, self-deception and dissonance reduction are such that people will usually seek to justify their actions ex post facto in any case. Discussing politics in organizations, Burns & Stalker (1966, p. xiv, 145) noted how decisions are rationalized in terms acceptable to the manager's audience. Such decisions are made to look sensible and acceptable in relation to unquestioned societal values and organizational goals. Similarly, Staw (1980) observed that managers may feel under pressure to "justify or demonstrate the rationality of previous allocations of resources." This may be viewed as face-saving behavior. The ambiguity of such behavior can make it doubly difficult to accuse individuals of malpractice or incompetence.

The Purchase of Consulting Services

Most of the sources in which the ethics of consulting is discussed refer to the behavior of consultants themselves (e.g. Gallessich, 1982; Greiner & Metzger, 1983; Maclagan, 1989). Many of the issues discussed in such sources are essentially the same as those with which we are concerned here; the match between consultants' particular areas of expertise and the problem in hand, or their employment in the context of ethically questionable political machinations in client organizations. Where the responsibilities of client managers are discussed, it is often implied that the potential for moral wrong lies with the consultant, rather than with the client. In Kubr (1980), for example, mention of the client's contribution to consulting ethics is confined to the manner in which clients can facilitate, monitor and report on the conduct of the consultant, adding that the choice of consultant is particularly important. Some sources, however, do begin to address the kinds of issue with which we are concerned, in that they deal with the whole question of problem definition as an outcome of interactions between clients and consultants (e.g. McLean et.al., 1982). The reality of such processes calls into question the nature of rationality in what, as already noted, is frequently a politicized organizational arena. For example Jackall (1988, ch 6) vividly describes the way in which consultants may be employed to legitimize unpleasant decisions which managers have already decided upon. Who better to call in than consultants with whom one has built up good working and personal relationships?

This said, there is a significant difference between the actions of a manager or administrator engaged in some sort of private reciprocal arrangement with a consultant (who would, for example, in return for the contract, provide convenient evidence supporting a personal, 'political', decision by the client) and the organizationally rational choice of a familiar source of help when faced with a problem, because one believes this to be the best available in the circumstances. After all, it is often important that the consultant should know and understand the client organization. Satisficing behavior (March & Simon, 1958), where the client manager lacks the time or resources to seek a better alternative, is an attempt at this ideal, and while some might argue that it demonstrates a lack of competence on the part of the client, it is not obviously unethical behavior.

The fundamental ethical issue which we are addressing concerns the role of management and administrators as trustees for other stakeholders in an organization. These could be shareholders, taxpayers, other employees, indeed anyone who bears the opportunity-cost of inappropriate spending. The idea of trusteeship as an ethical concept is rooted in the deontological principle of promise keeping. Promise keeping could, however, enter into the client consultant relationship also. Could not nepotism or patronage result from earlier promises made by client manager to consultant? If so, would the award of contracts under such circumstances be morally less blameworthy than when done in more immediately mercenary or self-interested circumstances? This possibility, which we may label as loyalty to the consultant, suggests a third type of action in addition to those suggested above. However it raises the question of whether the client manager was entitled to make such a promise to the consultant in the first place. Presumably, obligations to pre-existing stakeholders such as shareholders and employees should take precedence. The organization does not exist to provide work for the consultant! Lastly, in many situations ex post facto rationalizations are also likely to be presented. Persisting with the same consultant over time may reflect this, perhaps as face-saving.

A Basis for Ethical Analysis

At this juncture we shall summarize the main points arising out of the preceding theoretical discussion. This will provide a basis for the analysis of the cases. To facilitate such analysis the points are presented as questions.

(i) Who is the client? The answer to this is not always clear cut, as our second case will demonstrate.
(ii) Is the consultancy resource appropriate for the organizational situation? If not, in what respects is it inappropriate?
(iii) Into which category or categories of client behavior does the case appear to fall?
   a. Familiarity with the consultant/Satisficing
   b. Loyalty to the consultant/Keeping a promise to the consultant/nepotism.
   c. Reciprocity/Seeking a political resource.
   d. Face saving/maintaining an appearance of rationality vis-a-vis earlier decisions.

Questions (i) and (ii) are important, but for the purposes of this chapter we lack the space to elaborate on them. They are derived essentially from discussions of consultant (as opposed to client) ethics. (See Maclagan, 1989). The issues raised will, however, enter into our case analyses in the next section.

Case Studies

Case A

In the first case the client was a major multi-national firm, MNC, consisting of several distinct divisions engaged in related activities. The consultancy firm was hired by Goodman, the manager of the European region of a major division of MNC, to evaluate the effectiveness of its organizational structure. The particular area of concern was a collection of small countries geographically spread out across the region, each similar in market size, each with a national manager. These national managers reported to Lessing, who in turn reported to Goodman. Other countries in the European region were major markets and each of these also had a manager reporting to Goodman.

With regard to Lessing's area of responsibility, the divisional head, Burton, was concerned about the effectiveness of a management area which included several culturally diverse and geographically dispersed countries. Burton had thus approved the idea of an evaluation of the organizational structure, expressing interest in a more streamlined, rational design.

Goodman was personally insecure about the extent of his skill to manage the region, and therefore usually acted according to his perception of Burton's wishes, believing this to be a safer course than trusting his own judgement. Accordingly, Goodman hired the consultants to investigate and evaluate the comparative merits of leaving the regional structure as it was, or of breaking the area down and assigning each of the countries to the neighboring major market country, for example, Belgium to France.

The consultancy firm was North American, with no experience in Europe. Goodman knew the firm well and was personally acquainted with its directors. They adhered strongly to a particular philosophy of management and organization which stood in opposition to MNC's existing European regional and area structure, but was consistent with Burton's inclination, and with the suggested reorganization.

The consultants conducted their investigation and evaluation by interviewing personnel in the countries reporting to Lessing, Lessing himself, the major market countries reporting to Goodman, and central regional staff. The outcome was that the reorganization, entailing the break-up of Lessing's area, was proposed.

The countries within the area were opposed to these changes, with one exception, for the following reasons. Lessing had held the post for about eighteen months. Previous to this, the area had been managed by individuals of limited experience and competence, and, as a result, the area had not performed well. Under Lessing, sales had increased by approximately twenty-five percent, with strategic plans supporting continued similar growth. This growth was largely due to the specific attention which Lessing had given each country within the area, and to his acknowledgement of cultural diversity in the various markets.

Lessing's approach had two beneficial consequences for national managers in the area. First, it increased their prestige and importance within the company. Second, staff in the various countries felt more valued, due to the attention and respect which they now received from senior management. This, in turn, increased productivity and sales.

However the management in the major market countries within the region supported the consultants' recommendations. Their sales had seen a slight but consistent downturn over the same period, and the acquisition of a new market promised to boost their financial figures and sales performance. There would also be a small saving with the elimination of Lessing's salary (Lessing was guaranteed another post within MNC). On the other hand, financial losses were possible if major market countries did not meet the targets set for the area in strategic plans. More significantly, the national managers within the area had warned that loss of morale in their countries would be serious if the reorganization went ahead.

In response to these findings, Burton announced that no organizational changes should be made in the following year, because of the negative impact which this might have on morale and sales. However, despite Burton's caution, the consultants continued to argue that reorganization would be sensible, justifying their position by reference to their own theory of management. Significantly, they were supported by Goodman. Indeed, even when it became apparent that staff morale in Lessing's area was declining in anticipation of the changes, Goodman did not terminate the consultancy contract.

Analysis of Case A

Here we refer to the basis for analysis offered earlier. At risk of oversimplification, the client was Goodman, acting for the European region and, less directly, for the division and MNC as a whole. The consultancy resource was not obviously appropriate from an official, corporate, viewpoint. Their experience to date had been with small companies within a single nation, not with the diverse, regionalized operations of a large multinational. Also, they adhered dogmatically to a one-best-approach to organization, which in this case ruled out the status quo.

Turning to the categorization of client behavior, Case A highlights the distinction between the initial choice of consultants and the subsequent decision on whether or not to accept their recommendations. Using the categories offered earlier, we shall consider the initial choice of consultants by Goodman.

a. Familiarity, reliance on an already known source, perhaps involving a satisficing decision, would have been a plausible explanation for Goodman's choice of consultants in the face of pressure to show Burton that something was being done. This would also be compatible with

b. Loyalty to the consultants, whom he already knew well at a personal level.

c. An entirely plausible explanation is understood in terms of reciprocity. That is, Goodman gave the contract to the consultants in exchange for their assurance (or at least the probability) that they would recommend changes which would help him in a political struggle. Such an explanation could be reconciled with Goodman's deference to Burton at the initial stage (since Goodman had the discretion to choose consultants who would be relied upon to support him). The political struggle arises as follows.

Lessing had been very successful in managing his area. This was an irritation, if not a threat, to the other less successful major market managers; and it was a threat to Goodman himself (recall the earlier reference to his insecurity). Goodman would clearly benefit in more ways than one if he could be seen as responsible for initiating changes calculated to remove Lessing and partition his territory. This political argument is strengthened when one considers Goodman's decision to align himself with the consultants after they had made their recommendations. This was in opposition to Burton; it does not look as if, as suggested earlier, he was invariably deferential to Burton.

Nor, unless he genuinely believed the consultants to be technically correct, does it suggest an overriding concern for the performance of the organization. It could have been loyalty to his friends in the consultancy organization (an explanation not unconnected to a belief in the competence of the latter and also compatible with the political interpretation).

However the two most likely explanations for Goodman's behavior, once one considers the whole story, are reciprocity/political, as already just outlined, and face-saving. In other words, when he supported the consultants' recommendations, Goodman might have been trying to justify his original choice of consultant by demonstrating consistent belief in their competence. This face-saving behavior could be in addition to reciprocity/political and/or loyalty as explanations.

Case B

Our second case concerns a joint initiative between a government ministry in a European state and an inter-governmental organization (IGO). The project entailed the procurement of consultancy resources to advise the Ministry on the selection, design and implementation of programs funded by the IGO. This would include the placement of two senior advisors in strategic positions in this important and sensitive Ministry. The value of the project, including support staff, would be substantial (in excess of $1 million).

The IGO insisted that not only was it important that the two senior advisors performed their tasks well, but that they should also be known to the IGO as persons who could be trusted to provide it with early and regular analyses of the internal workings of the Ministry. This would enable the IGO to evaluate its funding allocations in relation to the Ministry's effectiveness in the implementation of the projects.

Thus, before any invitations to bid were prepared, steps were taken within the IGO to identify two individuals for these positions. A senior official in the IGO office in the host country, Mr. Roget, conferred with an official in the IGO headquarters, Mr. Purdy. Roget advised Purdy that he knew of two suitable persons for the job and the availability of these persons was subsequently confirmed. The selection of these two was based not only on their competence for the tasks envisaged, but also on their knowledge and experience of the IGO's procedures and decision-making processes. The fact that they were known personally to Roget, so that Roget could trust them to meet IGO information needs, was also important.

One of these individuals, Dr. Nystrom, acting in a consultant capacity, was asked to assist with the project preparation and became known to the host Government. Meanwhile, Roget took it upon himself to make an informal approach to a consultancy firm, Colpat plc, to see whether it would be interested in bidding for the contract. Roget chose this firm on the basis of its solid, well-respected, reputation in the eyes of the IGO, for whom it had done work previously. He did not consider other consultants. On confirmation of Colpat's interest, it was given the names of both the individuals. Colpat then established contact with these two persons and commenced initial negotiations for contracts with them. All this was before any formal invitation to bid for the consultancy contract was issued.

Knowing that he would be in a position to gain personally, Dr. Nystrom leaked information to Colpat on the aims and objectives of the project. Colpat was then able to prepare in advance its response to the anticipated invitation to bid.

Four such invitations were issued and three bids were received. These were evaluated by Purdy, his colleagues in the IGO, and representatives of the Ministry. The evaluation grid showed that Colpat scored highly, both for the individual competence of the proposed personnel, and for the level of understanding of the project objectives. Colpat was awarded the contract.

Analysis of Case B

Identification of the client is more complex in this case, being a combination of the Ministry and the IGO. The main point for present purposes concerns the role of Roget and Purdy, key members of the IGO. They took steps to plant Dr. Nystrom and the other advisor in the project team. Furthermore, Roget deliberately, and privately, helped Colpat to secure the contract by putting it in touch with those two individuals. So the choice of both the advisors and of Colpat was, at first sight, questionable; perhaps a case of nepotism or some other form of loyalty to them.

However, unlike Case A, the choice of both the two advisors and Colpat seems to have been the result of genuine feeling by Roget that they would do a good job on the project; that is, for the client institutions. In other words, both of these choices represented attempts to procure appropriate consulting resources for the project. If we consider Case B in terms of the four categories of client behavior (familiarity/satisficing; loyalty to consultant; reciprocity/politics; face-saving) both the advisors and the consultants selected were already known to Roget, and so these choices may be seen as instances of familiarity, at least. With regard to the choice of Colpat, the fact that Roget did not seriously consider other consulting organizations puts that decision in the satisficing category.

This explanation would appear to rule out, to varying degrees, the other categories of client motive. There may have been an element of loyalty, but reciprocity and face-saving seem unlikely. However, although in terms of consequences the choice of consultant appears ethically acceptable, questions remain concerning the means used. The official procedure was to invite consulting firms to bid for the contract. These bids would be evaluated by a group representing the Ministry and the IGO. Roget had acted in an unauthorized manner, making sure that Colpat had an advantage in the competitive bid.

Conclusion: Summary of Ethical Issues

In discussing consulting ethics Maclagan (1989) identified two main issues. First, obligations to the client, defined as matters of professional competence such as proper diagnosis. Second, sensitivity to organizational power and politics, and the implications of intervention and change for various members of the affected system.

These issues, and particularly the second consideration, signal the possibility that those who procure consulting resources may not be primarily concerned about adequate diagnosis or the consequent appropriateness of particular approaches to intervention in terms of some putative corporate rationality. Rather, they may be concerned with some other private rationality. Examples are nepotistic commitment to close friends; winning political struggles in the organization; or preserving an impression of good judgement and refusing to admit that existing consultancy services are less than adequate, by insisting on renewal of that contract.

Leaving aside the very real objection that the goals and activities of client organizations may themselves be ethically questionable, we may for this argument regard the acquisition of consultancy resources in genuine pursuit of corporate goals as ethically unproblematic. Conversely, nepotism, political motives and knowingly procuring inappropriate consultancy services, would be ethically questionable. However the argument is complicated when one recognizes further possibilities. First, apparent nepotism may be justified if it ensures that appropriate, competent, consultants are brought in, as in Case B. Here the end may justify the means. Second, the often ambiguous nature of organizational goals can sometimes mean that politically motivated managers may actually be sincere in their claims that they are acting in the corporate interest. In Case A, do we really know that this was not true of Goodman when he brought in the consultants?

Thus the moral evaluation of client behavior when purchasing organizational consultancy services is not always straightforward. Such evaluation is itself ethically problematic. One has to appreciate motives and intentions, limits to persons' rationality, and other circumstances. This is often impracticable, if not impossible.

As already noted, however, consultants should be alert to client motives in so far as they can identify these. But of equal importance is the lesson for client managers themselves, since there is a moral demand on the buyers of services to examine their own motives. This is not an unrealistic proposition. Such clients could be essentially well-intentioned, yet their consciousness has not been raised on particular occasions. Thus their decisions regarding the use of consulting services may reflect lack of thought for others' interests, lack of concern for their official responsibilities to the organization, and lack of foresight concerning their own reputation.

References

Burns, T. and Stalker, G.M. 1966: *The Management of Innovation, Second edition.* London: Tavistock.

Fayol, H. 1949: *General and Industrial Management,* (trans. C. Storrs; first published in 1916). London: Pitman.

Gallessich, J. 1982: *The Profession and Practice of Consultation.* San Francisco: Jossey-Bass.

Greiner, L. and Metzger, R.O. 1983: *Consulting to Management.* Englewood Cliffs, N.J.: Prentice-Hall.

Jackall, R. 1988: *Moral Mazes.* Oxford: Oxford U.P.

Kubr, M (ed.) 1980: *Management Consulting: A Guide to the Profession.* Geneva: International Labour Office.

Maclagan, P.W. 1989: Methodology choice and consulting ethics in management science. *Omega: the International Journal of Management Science,* Vol. 17, 5, pp. 397-407.

McLean, A., Sims, D., Mangham, I. and Tuffield, D. 1982: *Organization Development in Transition.* Chichester: John Wiley & Sons.

March, J. and Simon, H.A. 1958: *Organizations.* New York: Wiley.

Mintzberg, H. 1977: *The Nature of Managerial Work.* New York: Harper & Row.

Pettigrew, A.M. 1972: Information control as a power resource. *Sociology,* Vol. 6, pp. 187-204.

Sharifi, S. 1988: Managerial work: a diagnostic model. In A.M. Pettigrew (ed), *Competitiveness and the Management Process.* Oxford: Basil Blackwell.

Simon, H.A. 1947: *Administrative Behavior.* New York: MacMillan.

Staw, B.M. 1980: Rationality and justification in organizational life. In B.M. Staw and L.L. Cummings (eds), *Research in Organizational Behavior,* Vol 2, pp 45-80. Greenwich: JAI Press.

Stewart, R. 1967: *Managers and Their Jobs.* London: MacMillan.

8

Occasional Ethical Consultancy

Antonio Argandoña

Abstract

In business, it is very common for people to ask others for advice, in a more or less formal manner, on an ethical matter, almost always in the form of a brief, unpaid consulting. This chapter studies the nature of this ethical consultancy, its content and nature as occasional advice, and the differences with respect to ethical "teaching" (in a broad sense of the word teaching). The chapter also analyses its quasi-contractual nature, based on trust, which is a key element of occasional ethical consultancy; the obligations that each party must fulfil, and the many forms that, in real life, this type of consultancy may take. The prudential content of occasional ethical consultation and the criteria for choosing the consultant is also discussed, closing with a few remarks on occasional consultancy within the company.

Introduction

"Hi, how are you? Can I bother you for a few minutes?"

"Of course! What's it about? Take a seat."

"Thanks. Look, I've got a problem and I wanted to ask your advice, as a friend and expert. I know you have sound moral criteria and are very familiar with the kind of matter I want to ask you about. Well, to get to the point..."

This type of dialogue is common in private life and in business. I would say that fortunately it is common because it is unlikely that a person would be able to take meditated decisions alone on major ethical and technical problems without the help of others.

However, occasional advice is by no means trivial, because it means helping someone to make a good decision, work for the good of the advice-seeker and society as a whole, and sharing responsibility for a decision. Therefore, the advice should meet certain conditions with regard to the person asking for the advice, the person giving it, the subject, the circumstances and its consequences.

The purpose here is to analyze the nature of occasional ethical consultancy and

93

H. von Weltzien Hoivik and A. Føllesdal (eds.), Ethics and Consultancy: European Perspectives, 93-107.
© 1995 *Kluwer Academic Publishers. Printed in the Netherlands.*

advice-giving, the nature of the relationship formed between advice-giver and advice-seeker, the advice-seeker and advice-giver's duties to the prudential content of ethical consultancy and the question of choosing the advisor. It will conclude with a few remarks on the importance and functions of occasional ethical consultancy within the company. Being normative, the chapter does not seek to establish hard and fast rules but rather to offer guidance on an important activity in everyone's ordinary and professional life and propose possible subjects for discussion. This will help the reader to understand better the importance of the function of advice or consultancy in ethics and in the company. Although a large part of the following discussion could be applied to any consultation or advice in general, we will concentrate mainly on those that have an ethical content.[1]

The Nature of Occasional Ethical Advice

According to the New Webster's Dictionary, advice is "information or opinion given to aid the judgement or actions of another." It thus involves the action of two people, the advice-giver and the advice-seeker, concerning the taking of a particular decision.

The difference between advice and "teaching" in a very broad sense is the fact that the latter is aimed at conveying certain knowledge or criteria, but not to guide directly towards a specific action. However the criteria transmitted in a class may be used for decision-taking. Thus, the important point in the difference between "teaching" and advice is in this process of guiding towards a specific action, which is defined with relation to agents, purpose, goal and circumstances. A "lesson" or a "teaching" answers generic questions, such as "What is the appropriate ethical criterion regarding bribery?" or "What do you think about whistle-blowing?" Advice, however, answers questions such as "What should I do in this case?" or "What would you do if you were in my situation?"

In any case, it is very difficult to establish a clear dividing line. Sometimes, people ask questions couched in impersonal terms, without any reference to specific situations, but which are basically asking for advice. There are questions asked in the third person ("A friend of mine has this problem") when really the person asking the question is asking for himself. And there are "lessons" which have all the features of advice; for instance, when the teacher says to his students, "Whenever you find yourself in a situation like this, follow this course of action." Therefore, whoever gives a "lesson" or offers a general criterion should accept a certain degree of responsibility (moral, not legal), just as if he was giving advice. But only a certain degree of responsibility because nobody can pretend that that criterion is applicable to all possible situations.

For this reason, the person giving a "lesson" should clearly state all the relevant criteria, even if this only be generically. And as this is not always possible – because a class must finish by a certain time, because an article can only have a certain length or because of the intrinsically informal nature of an interview or a conversation in the local bar. It is only natural that the "lesson", even though it possesses some of the features of advice, does not offer the same depth or precision and, therefore, cannot bear the same degree of responsibility. (In any case, one should not forget the responsibility taken on, in a wide sense, by people invested with a certain degree of authority – parents, teachers, managers, etc. – for the words they speak and the actions they perform, which are basically a way of "teaching". The sales director who pulls a wry face when a salesman tells him that he used unethical means to win a sale is transmitting a"lesson" to his subordinate.)

Strictly speaking, ethical advice or consultancy deals with a decision's ethical content. However, when it involves a specific decision, it is no longer possible to separate the decision's ethical content from its technical (economic, financial, commercial, etc.) content. Sometimes, the consultation addresses specifically and solely an ethical problem, for example, "May I use racial discrimination as an argument for an advertisement?". Although the advice given requires a consideration of the technical details – nature of the product, nature of the campaign, target audience, media used, duration, etc. – it does not involve any marketing consulting. On other occasions, the advice asked is of a technical nature – "Which of these arguments seems to be most effective to you for an advertising campaign?" – but the answer contains ethical advice –"I find this argument unacceptable for moral reasons; this other argument seems better to me from the technical viewpoint and has no ethical drawbacks". Sometimes, the consultation is generic –"What arguments can I use for an advertising campaign?" – and the content of the answer should be both ethical and technical. And, of course, there are lots of situations that lie in between the two extremes.

Ethical advice may or not be given in answer to a prior consultation. Sometimes, the consultation is implicit, for example, when someone relates their professional problems to a friend or superior, it is obvious that they expect to receive advice. On other occasions, the situation is one of an unilateral action by one person who offers moral advice to another. As ethical advice implies a certain relationship, with reciprocal rights and duties, it is wise to clearly establish the title of the unelicited advice, by reason of which that relationship is created. Because, to a certain extent, the advice-giving implies a quasi-contractual relationship, although without any legal effects. Therefore, there must be a cause, a reason in the advice-giver and the advice-seeker, as there must also be in the case of unelicited advice.

The subject of this chapter is occasional ethical consultancy or advice. The advisor is not an ethics consultant (and therefore does not act as such) nor is a formal legal relationship created. There is no contract for the provision of services, or payment of a fee. However many of the criteria that will be discussed here are also valid for formal consultancy. Occasional means non-professional (not a professional of ethical consulting, although it is by no means a task for amateurs). Therefore, it is free, although it may give rise to a gift, in gratitude for the help given, and, if appropriate, payment of the expenses incurred by the advice-giver. However, occasional does not mean short-lasting or not repeated. A consultation such as that considered here may be lengthy, or repeated over time, on the same subject or others, precisely because it establishes a relationship of mutual trust, as we will see later on.

The Relationship Established in Occasional Ethical Consultancy

As we have already said, occasional ethical consultancy implies a quasi-contractual relationship between advice-seeker and advice-giver. The fact that this relationship has no legal status recognized by law nor does it create rights and duties which would stand up in court does not mean that it has no moral content and, therefore, that it does not create ethical rights and duties.

We say that the relationship is quasi-contractual because the advice-giver undertakes to provide to the advice-seeker a criterion or advice on a decision, to the best of his knowledge (and probably without any obligation to dedicate resources exceeding those normal resources that are immediately available), while the advice-seeker acquires a certain commitment to listen to and consider the advice received. It is not a fully-fledged contract as there is nothing having legal validity that is given in exchange for this advice (since occasional advice is, in principle, free). In this sense, it has more in common with a donation, which also implies duties for both parties.

Perhaps the aspect that best defines occasional moral advice from the ethical viewpoint is the relationship of trust built up between the two parties which enables one to state a problem and the other to offer advice. Both parties' duties are defined, to a considerable extent, by this relationship of trust and the advice-giver's consequent loyalty and the advice-seeker's gratitude. Without pretending to be comprehensive, the following pages discuss these rights and duties in greater detail.[2]

Duties of the Advice-Seeker

For our purposes, the advice-seeker is a person who, on his or her own behalf or on behalf of others (a company, etc.), must take a decision (or series of decisions, or adopt a criterion that will help decisions) on management issues. This decision contains an ethical component and the advice-seeker seeks guidance in the taking of the decision and not just theoretical knowledge or criteria (or, if this knowledge is sought, it is to form a criterion with a view to future decisions).

Some of the requirements that the advice-seeker must meet in order to satisfy the ethical requirements of advice are the following:

1 To seek an advisor who can really help, due to his/her technical and moral knowledge, experience, moral calibre and closeness to the advice-seeker. To have a wish to learn and take correct decisions.
2 To act in good faith, with a genuine desire to seek advice, and not for other purposes (such as trying to obtain information from the consulter, or to obtain reasons for accusing or discreditation, or use the acquaintanceship later for

personal reasons, etc.). The advice-seeker should not look for an adviser who will tell them what they want to hear but rather one who gives the best ethical device, in the same way that a patient will not look for a physician who will be reassuring, or say they are in fine shape, but someone who will speak frankly and who can affect a cure.

3 To state clearly the purpose and scope of the consultation, so that the other party is freely able to accept or reject it.

4 To tell the truth, clearly stating all the relevant details about the case, separating, as far as possible, what are personal impressions or feelings from hard facts. However, one may partially or wholly conceal data that are clearly irrelevant, that could only address the advice-giver's personal curiosity, or which may reveal the identity of people that it is preferred to keep anonymous. For example, one can give an approximate figure, or a range of figures, instead of the exact quantity, or simply call "a salesman" the person who committed a certain immoral act. In short, in such cases, the general rules on the obligation to tell the truth, but not necessarily the whole truth, are applicable. However, by virtue of the relationship of trust with the advisor, the need to tell the truth is particularly important here as part and parcel of the request for advice.[3]

5 To give the advice-giver complete freedom, first, to accept or not the consultation; second, to state the conditions considered appropriate (time, information required, etc.); and finally, to give appropriate advice. However, this does not mean that the advice-seeker cannot ask for further explanation or reject the advice, if it is considered unsuitable.

6 To give the necessary time to study the matter, although pressing for a prompt answer, if the case so requires.

7 To listen to the advice received, paying attention to it and taking it into consideration – which includes the possibility of rejecting it. Unless it is superficial or trivial, it was precisely to receive advice that the person approached the advice-giver in the first place.

8 To personally take the appropriate decision, which may or may not be in line with the advice received. The advice-seeker is completely free to follow the advice received or not because, in the final analysis, it is the advice-seeker, not the advisor, who will bear responsibility for the decision.

9 To not unload responsibility for the decision or its consequences onto the advisor. The decision must be taken by the advice-seeker alone, unless agreed otherwise in the consultancy "contract" (e.g. because the advisor, being the advice-seeker's superior, takes the decision that normally the latter should have taken). Consequently, the advice-seeker may not detract from the advisor or be critical of the advice, nor place upon the advisor the responsibility or loss of prestige implied by actions in the eyes of third parties.

10 To never use the advice against the person who gave it, if they acted in good faith.

11 To keep discreetly secret the advice received, depending on its confidentiality

(explicit or not). Obviously, there are types of advice that can be made known to others, at least insofar as they are concerned with general criteria or rules for judicious behavior, and the advisor's name may lend greater credibility and acceptance to the advice given. There is also the alternative of revealing the advice while keeping the advisor anonymous ("an expert told me one day that. . . .").

12 To express proper gratitude. This will often be the only sign given in exchange for the advice.

13 To compensate the advice-giver, if applicable, for the expense and bother which has been reasonably incurred. And if the advisor named a price and the advice-seeker accepted, pay it.

Duties of the Advisor

The advisor or consultant asked to provide moral advice should act in accordance with the following rules: [4]

1 Upon receiving the consultation, the advisor should consider whether or not it is possible to give it suitable consideration. For example, consider whether the availability of the necessary technical and ethical knowledge, whether there is enough time, and whether there is the necessary freedom of judgement and cooperation (which would be adversely affected, for example, by a professional relationship or otherwise with the person seeking advice, or the possibility of using insider information, etc.). If these impediments arise in the course of the consultation, the advice-seeker should also be notified of this circumstance and, if appropriate, the advice should be discontinued (although this should be assessed in light of the degree of commitment involved).

2 In particular, the advisor should have the necessary general or specific ethical knowledge required to take the decision. Should advisors not have this knowledge but they undertook to provide the advice, they should acquire such knowledge by the most suitable procedures. This obligation will be more or less compelling depending on the nature of the commitment taken on, the importance of the consultation and its implications, etc. Lack of the necessary knowledge is a more than sufficient reason for rejecting a consultancy task, as it would be senseless to blindly give ethical advice.

3 Is one obliged to accept the consultation? Occasional advice's very nature suggests that it is voluntary, at least on many occasions. However, there are also many other circumstances in which there may exist a certain obligation to give advice: when the person giving the advice is the advice-seeker's superior on subjects within his field of activity, or when the consulter is also a counselor. If the advisor is an expert in a particular subject, which is also the subject of the consultation, they will be more obliged to accept but not necessarily without charge, if consulting is a professional activity (ethical advisor, lawyer, tax advisor, etc.). There may also be a moral duty to accept the consultation

for reasons of closeness to the advice-giver (a relative, a friend, a colleague) or because of the urgency or need for the consultation.

4 Once the commitment has been accepted, the advisor's professional nature requires that the necessary time, attention and resources are used to give good advice, placing the problem on an objective plane and going down to a detailed level, if required.

5 If, as the consultation process continues, it is seen that extraordinary resources are required (time, knowledge, efforts, etc.), it is not mandatory to provide them, given the consultation's occasional nature (unless this need was detected at the outset and, in spite of this, it was decided to give the advice). However, this should be offset against the degree of commitment accepted, the existence of other alternative methods by which the advice-seeker is able to form an opinion, etc. The manager who is the target for a consultation from a subordinate on an important issue for the company or for its personnel and which lies fully within their range of responsibilities, cannot afford to ignore this request, although, if they are unable to attend to it properly, the subordinate may be referred to another suitable person.

6 The normal procedure is that an occasional consultation not be paid for. Indeed, the advisor should not expect to gain any financial benefit from the advice given, although a gift may accepted, as a sign of the advice-seeker's gratitude, or even formal fees, if the advice-seeker offers to pay them. But neither should it put the advice-giver out of pocket. Consequently, if complications should arise in the case and require additional resources, it may be proposed to convert it into a professional relationship, with the corresponding fees or, at least, with the advice-seeker paying the expenses. Obviously, this is not applicable in some cases (e.g., in the case of a subordinate consulting a manager on subjects related to their work). Furthermore, as the relationship established is voluntary, there is nothing against the advisor considering it a formal consultation right from the start, setting a fee for services (although this would not be acceptable in some cases).

7 The advisor should gain as complete an idea as possible on the case being proposed, depending on the circumstances (urgency, importance, degree of commitment, etc.), as the advice being asked requires the application of ethical rules to this particular situation. Therefore, appropriate questions must be asked, relevant documents requested, conversations with other people, etc.

8 When the case so requires, the advisor should also listen to the reasons or arguments of the other parties involved, for example, when the advice is in fact an arbitration. In such cases, this should be with the consent, even if only implicit, of the advice-seeker.

9 If the nature of the subject so requires, the advisor may – and even should – ask other people for their advice, because of their superior moral or technical knowledge, because of their experience, or simply to get a second opinion. If this means revealing information covered by the secrecy obligation mentioned

below, the advisor should ask the advice-seeker for approval or ask the advice in such terms that it is impossible to identify who the parties concerned are.

10 The consultant should keep reasonably secret the subject of the consultation, the persons involved and what has been learnt as a result of the consultation.[5] The relationship of trust created by accepting the consultation demands this secrecy (and, if it is not accepted, the secrecy obligation also extends to the information given by the advice-seeker when the consultation was proposed, as this information was already given under the above-mentioned relationship of trust). Information that is already available independently from the consultation is not subject to this confidentiality undertaking, although this aspect should be defined more precisely depending on the circumstances of each case. A good rule of thumb for the ethical consultant is to "forget" the case once the matter is settled, unless there are reasons for acting otherwise, for example, to continue helping the advice-seeker, because the latter requests or needs such help. This is particularly important when the advice-seeker is a client or a competitor (existing or potential) or when the information received could be considered insider information, even though it may not be so from the legal standpoint.

11 On occasions, the advisor may reach the conclusion that they must inform a third party of the knowledge received in the course of the consultation, for example, because that person or company may be harmed, etc. However, normally, no such information should be conveyed, not even indirectly, as this would be an infringement of confidentiality undertaken with the advice-seeker. However, the advisor may impose upon the latter the obligation to convey this information, and even discontinue the consultancy if the advice-seeker should not give acceptance. In some cases in which the another person's welfare or the common good so requires, due to the seriousness of the situation, it seems reasonable that the advisor should be exonerated from this confidentiality obligation (if, for example, a crime is going to be committed or severe harm is going to be done), although there may be exceptions to this (for example the secrecy of confession in the Catholic Church).[6]

12 It may be that the advisor has insider information, obtained by other means, that could be useful to the advice-seeker. Obviously, the advisor should follow ethical rules when using this information for such purposes. If the advisor suspects that the reason for the consultation was to gain access to this information, then that is sufficient reason to not accept the consultation, or to discontinue it should it have already begun.

13 On occasions, the advisor discovers a moral problem in a technical consultation – or new moral problems in an ethical consultation. In such cases, it is a duty to state this new situation, because it forms part of the duty as advisor to solve the matter to the best knowledge, in all its aspects. An advisor may even refuse to cooperate in solving a technical problem unless attention is paid to its moral aspects. Thus, strictly speaking, one cannot say that a consultation is

technical or ethical, as there are no purely technical aspects that do not have an ethical side to them.

14 Normally, the consultant should not only give an opinion, but provide the reasons by which this opinion was reached and base it on objective ethical criteria, thereby improving the advice-seeker's moral outlook, although this may vary depending on the nature of the advice sought.

15 The result of the consultation should be advice that is as clear as possible, depending on the circumstances. However, in many cases, this may not be possible as an ethical decision in a particular case requires a prudential opinion by the decision-taker, which the advisor cannot provide in the advice--seeker's place. In such cases, the advisor should clearly state the ethical criteria and help the advice-seeker to form an opinion and take the decision (consideration of the circumstances, assessment of the action's possible effects, etc.), although at all times respecting the advice-seeker's freedom of action. If there is more than one solution for a particular problem and all of these solutions are valid from the ethical viewpoint (perhaps some are valid in some circumstances and others are valid in other circumstances), the advisor should enumerate these solutions, with their respective advantages and disadvantages, and may recommend one but without denying the validity of the others.

16 On some occasions, good advice may require opening up new fields of thought, suggesting actions that are better than those originally considered, for example, if the advice-seeker only wished not to do harm but there are possible decisions that operate on a higher ethical level. It is in this area where the advisor can really excel.

17 The advisor must act with the speed required by the situation, without prolonging more than necessary the collection and examination of information and criteria.

18 As has already been said, the decision must be taken by the advice-seeker, not by the advice-giver. Therefore, the latter must suggest it, but not impose it, for example, by threatening to take reprisals. It should also be made clear that the final responsibility for the decision lies with the advice-seeker, without this meaning any waiver of responsibility as advisor.

19 After giving the advice, it may happen that the advisor changes their mind, because new information has been received or the case has been reconsidered. Depending on the circumstances, the advisor should notify the advice-seeker in case there is still time to reconsider the decision or to be able to react to the possible consequences of the decision.

20 Although the consultation only requires giving advice, the circumstances may be such as to advise that the consultant also take part in implementing the advice, although the advice-seeker continues to bear the major part of the responsibility for the decision. This is a common situation when advising a subordinate in a company.

21 In any case, the advisor must always act with moral rectitude. It is natural to

value one's own opinion but the advisor should not seek to further their personal reputation over the welfare of the advice-seeker. Neither should an advisor direct the consultation so that it will lead to further professional assignments, although this aspect should be considered with discretion. And, of course, the desire to deceive, harm the advice-seeker or a third party, and other immoral motivations should be completely banished.

An Exercise in Prudence

The roles played by the advice-seeker and advice-giver in an occasional ethical consultancy are a true exercise in the virtue of prudence.[7] In fact, asking for advice is a typical act of a prudent person when they do not have the necessary knowledge, or when they are not sure of their opinion or, simply, as one more way of taking good decision – and all the more so when the affair itself or its consequences are important. The advice-giver must also apply the rules of prudent decision-taking when studying and formulating advice.

The key element of ethical advice is not simply to remind about a series of general rules, which the advice-seeker may be familiar with from other sources, but their application to the case in question. Therefore, the consultant should have experience (knowledge of what happens or usually happens in such circumstances), in addition to theoretical and practical knowledge of ethics (and, if appropriate, also of the relevant technical disciplines). Consultants also need to have a sharp mind to detect the key elements of the problem (here the help of other people may be particularly useful); they must be intelligent, sagacious and able to reason (to organize data, interrelate them, form opinions, establish alternatives and choose from among them); they must be foresighted (since they must find the means that will enable the action to be implemented); they must be sensitive to the individual circumstances (which may change the decision's meaning); cautious (in order to avoid the obstacles that may arise, even though he will not implement personally the action); they must even have a certain degree of ingenuity and imagination (when listing the possible consequences of a decision or drawing up alternative actions), etc. The consultant should also be docile, that is, that used to asking advice and considering the guidance received from others, since those who are not prudent in their own affairs are unlikely to be able to give prudent advice to others.

The advice-seeker should also have the same features that define a prudent person. Those that are particularly important are the following: docility, the ability to receive, understand and reflect on the advice received, and, above all, the ability to implement the decision taken, as, unlike the advice-giver, the advice-seeker must act, and it would be a mistake to never go beyond the study phase or delay implementation indefinitely.

Choosing the Consultant

The success or failure of an ethical consultation often lies in the choice of advisor. Thus, the ideal ethical counsellor is a person who is expert, ethical and close to the advice-seeker.[8] Expert means that the person has the necessary theoretical knowledge – about ethics and the technical disciplines with which the consultation is related – and experience in decision-taking. In order to provide the theoretical knowledge, the candidate would be an academician – moralist, philosopher, theologian, etc. In order to provide the experience, the candidate would be a person of action – business owner, manager, consultant, etc. Depending on the nature of the problem, the emphasis should be placed on theoretical knowledge or on experience.

In any case, it may be useful to approach different people, with different backgrounds and interests, who may be able to provide complementary suggestions. The academic consultant may also seek the advice of the person of action – or vice versa -when preparing advice. Technical knowledge may be important, for example, in questions concerning a decision's legality, or in the implementation of tax legislation, but it will often not be decisive in ethical consultancy. In any case, ethical consultations are usually received by experts in technical disciplines – finance, accounting, marketing, economics, personnel management, corporate policy, sociology, etc. – perhaps because the ethical problems come about as a result of technical problems, or because the advice-seeker expects the expert-professor, consultant, etc. – to have the necessary technical and moral knowledge.

As "nobody can give what he does not have," the advisor is required to show proper ethical behavior. Example-setting is an important factor in the request for advice, because it is assumed that a person who leads a faultless moral life should have the necessary qualities to give good advice: theoretical ethical knowledge (sometimes not explicitly stated but always present), a habit of putting it into practice in personal life (experience), a consistent lifestyle (which leads one to think as they live and to live as they think, instead of trying to build up theories that fit in with life), prudence (with the features stated above), etc.

Finally, it may be preferable that there exist a certain closeness – physical, emotional, and mental – between the advice-seeker and the advice-giver. Sometimes, it will be a professional relationship, sometimes it will be a family relationship or a friendship; sometimes, one approaches an old teacher, or an expert one was introduced to some time ago, etc. It is logical that people look for this proximity, because, as we have already said, the relationship established between advice-seeker and advice-giver is one of mutual trust, closer to friendship than mere professionalism. In any case, the advice-giver should be prepared to help the advice-seeker and closeness is one means of guaranteeing cooperation.

These considerations lead us to one final question. When is it better to go to an expert and when is it better to go to a friend? The ideal person would probably be an advisor who meets both conditions. If such a person does not exist, then it seems that the experience and knowledge factor should predominate when the problem is ethically and technically complex. In the case of more personal problems, in which the advice-giver needs to know something about the advice-seeker's individual circumstances, emotional closeness may be more important (and also when personal or family secrets are involved). In any case, it is not possible to give any general rules on this. Furthermore, it is not always easy to contact the right person for each case. (And this suggests that when advice-seekers find themselves at a loss and unsure and has no-one to turn to, the greater the advice-giver's obligation to help, precisely because the advice-seeker has greater need of advice and does not know who to ask).

The Responsibility of the Advice-Giver

Has the advisor any responsibility for the counsel given? Probably not from the legal point of view, but we cannot preclude the existence of a moral responsibility. Obviously, if the advice-seeker remains always the only master of the decision, the responsibility of the advice-giver must be limited. This will vary according to the subject of the consultation, the personal conditions of the advice seeker – if he or she is a person with limited ethical knowledge and training, or very young, or without experience, etc., and the role played by the advisor – if, e.g., they voluntarily offered the advise, etc. The moral responsibility of the advice-giver is related to the obligations stated before – mainly the duty of study and diligence, the secrecy of the information received, the non-disclosure of inside information, etc.

Usually the moral responsibility of the advisor does not include the duty to compensate the advice-seeker for his or her economic losses, but may require other compensations: apologizing for the error, clarifying the issues, suggesting remedies, etc.

Occasional Consultancy Within the Company

Many ethical consultations on professional matters are made to peers or superiors (and sometimes subordinates) in the same organization in which the person works. In such cases, one seeks experience, knowledge of the environment in which the problem arises, and emotional closeness. However, the relationship that exists in such situations has certain unique features.

First of all, it is people involved in the same project who carry out coordinated activities: therefore, both are interested – or at least, should be interested – in everyone's decisions having a successful outcome. Consequently, there exists a community of interests which makes the problem being consulted common to both. This is even more so if the consultation is made to a superior on a matter within his or her sphere of responsibility, because then it takes on the nature of a professional activity, as one of management's obligations is to be aware of everything that is happening around them, on both the ethical and technical levels, which are invariably interlinked. As a result, if ethical advice is suitably requested and given, it enhances internal unity and communication.

Ethical consultancy within the company offers the additional advantage of both parties sharing the same knowledge of their environment and the circumstances. The advice has thus a greater chance of being correct; however, it may also have negative implications, perhaps involuntarily (for example it may make it easier for secrets to be revealed, for unfair opinions to be formed about people, for communications barriers to be raised, etc.). Hence, the need for uprightness in those people who within the company exercise the right and duty to ask for ethical advice.

In general, asking for advice is part of good management. The importance of the affairs involved, the effects they may have on people and organizations, the need to be right, the complexity of the circumstances, the varied interests of the people involved and a thousand and one more reasons recommend that a manager be a person who is used to listening to other people, to laying problems before others – above, at the same level or below in the organization, and to people unrelated with the company, advisors, consultants, etc. They should take these other opinions into account, etc., without shirking from their own responsibility in the final decision. It is true, the manager's "solitude" does exist but this should not be exaggerated as this solitude is often only that of the people who voluntarily isolate themselves from other people's advice (and criticism), because of pride, immaturity, or because they have not been able to find the right people to help them. Asking for advice is also a way of putting problems into an objective perspective, so that the manager's point of view is offset by others and preferences are qualified and not just passively justified. Finally, asking for advice may help to overcome lethargy, or prevent being led by feelings and not by reason.

These remarks assume that regular consulting, whether institutionalized or not, should form part of the manager's way of working. Obviously, this is much more than the occasional consultation considered here but, nevertheless, this too should be present in his or her work, when necessary.

Another of the manager's tasks is to heed consultations from superiors, peers or subordinates. Again, this is for many reasons: facilitate communication, integrate people, find out about their problems, take part in solving problems at other levels, widen perspectives and suggest new opportunities, raise other people's outlook to a higher level and help them to naturally integrate ethical aspects into it, commit oneself in other people's actions (even if it only be as occasional advisors), convey our experience or knowledge to them, etc.

The above remarks about consultation within the company can also be extended to people who, in a more or less regular fashion, work with the company: the board of directors, the management consultant, the legal advisor, the auditor, the tax advisor, etc., and even retired executives. These people satisfy the two-fold requirement of being experts in technical matters and closely involved with the company and are therefore clear candidates for receiving occasional consultancy. Precisely because of their association with the company, they must be able to advise also on ethical matters, or at least be able to indicate who to talk to about these matters.

These considerations also overcome possible criticisms regarding unfair competition to the ethics consultant by occasional consultancy. The ethics consultant has a specific role to play in the company, particularly for long-lasting and important assignments, but there is also a place for brief – amateur or professional – advice, normally free and altruistic, from a relative, colleague, superior or friend.

Notes

1. On ethical consultancy, see Block (1981), van Es (1993), van Luijk (1993), and van Willigenburg (1991).

2. Of course, many of the rights and duties of the occasional consultant are similar to those of the professional consultant; cfr. Block (1981), Brady (1987), Kubr (1980), Sims (1991), White (1989). The literature on professional ethics is also relevant on this subject; see, for example, Bayles (1981), Behrman (1988), Kultgen (1988), Windt et al. (1989).

3. On truth and lying, see Bok (1989a).

4. Pelaez (1989) is a good account of professional virtues; see also Jennings (1991), and Kultgen (1988).

5. See Bok (1989b) for the duty to secrecy.

6. On professionals and consultants as whistleblowers, see Vinten (1992); also Bowman, Elliston and Lockhart (1984).

7. Pieper (1966) gives a complete treatment of prudence.

8. This means that the counsellor must have moral "authority" (Simon, 1980).

References

Bayles, M. D. 1981: *Professional Ethics*. Belmont: Wadsworth.

Behrman, J. N. 1988: *Essays on Ethics in Business and the Professions*. Englewood Cliffs: Prentice Hall.

Block, P. 1981: *Flawless Consulting*. San Diego: University Associates.

Bok, S. 1989a: *Lying. Moral Choice in Public and Private Life*. New York: Vintage Books. 1989b: Secrets. *On the Ethics of Concealment and Reservation*. New York: Vintage Books.

Bowman, J. S., Ellinston, F. and Lockhart, P. 1984: *Professional Dissent. An Annotated Bibliography and Guide*. New York: Garland.

Brady, J. 1987: *How to Select and Use Management Consultants*. New York: Association of Management Consulting Firms.

Jennings, B. 1991: The regulation of virtue: Cross-currents in professional ethics. *Journal of Business Ethics,* 10, 561-568.

Kubr, M. (ed) 1980: *Management Consulting: A Guide to the Profession*. Geneva: International Labour Organization.

Kultgen, J. 1988: *Ethics and Professionalism*. Philadelphia: University of Pennsylvania Press.

Pelaez, M. 1989: *Etica, Professioni, Virtú*. Milano: Ares.

Pieper, J. 1966: *The Four Cardinal Virtues*. Notre Dame: Notre Dame University Press.

Simon, Y. R. 1980: *A General Theory of Authority*. Notre Dame: Notre Dame University Press.

Sims, R. 1991: The institutionalization of organizational ethics. *Journal of Business Ethics,* 10, 493-506.

van Es, R. 1993: On being a consultant in business ethics. *Business Ethics: A European Review,* 2, 228-232.

van Luijk, H. J. L. 1993: Ethical corporate consultancy. *Business Ethics: A European Review,* 2, 149-151.

van Willigenburg, T. 1991: *Inside the Ethical Expert.* Kok: Kampen.

Vinten, G. 1992: Focus: Whistleblowing auditors – the ultimate oxymoron? *Business Ethics: A European Review,* 1, 248-255.

Windt, P. Y., Appleby, P. C., Battin, M. P., Francis, L. P., and Landesman, B. M. 1989: *Ethical Issues in the Professions.* Englewood Cliffs: Prentice Hall.

9

"Advise Us What To Do; Decide For Us" (Isaiah 16,3)

The Impact of Hidden Agendas
in the Consultancy Process

Haavard Koppang and Bente R. Løwendahl

Abstract

Formally, the role of consultants is to advise clients. However, clients may also ask for advice while hoping that the consultant will decide on their behalf in difficult matters, thus – in some cases – implicitly paying the consultant to take on the role of the scapegoat. The consultant who then accepts to give advice, unwittingly also accepts the responsibility for externalized conflicts within the firm or top management team. Conversely, clients who seek independent advice may be coopted into situations where the consultant de facto decides on their behalf through a subtle and informal influence on intra-firm processes.

In order to understand ethical behavior in consulting processes, we need to take such "hidden agendas" into account to a larger extent than what has been common in the business ethics literature to date. An emphasis on interactive processes focusses the attention on three areas which need further investigation: the impact of the interaction, i.e. the fact that there is more than one actor, the impact of evolution over time, and the impact of hidden agendas and non-rational factors on all actors involved.

The purpose of this chapter is to elucidate how a number of such factors may lead to unethical outcomes, despite the best intentions of the actors. When complex process issues substantially influence the interaction, ethical behavior may only be achieved through a high degree of awareness of and competence in the handling of intra- and interpersonal processes. Hence, we propose that the research agenda in business ethics needs to be expanded to include process related issues, including unconscious agendas, dyadic and group interaction, and the dynamic evolution of relationships over time, in addition to the factors related to individual morality and firm codes of ethics emphasized in most research projects to date.

H. von Weltzien Hoivik and A. Føllesdal (eds.), Ethics and Consultancy: European Perspectives, 109-123.

Issues particularly relevant to consulting which are discussed in this paper include the challenges resulting from information asymmetry between consultant and client, the lack of a powerful professional organization policing the consultants, and the "double (or possibly triple) moral hazard" involved as both clients and consultants may behave unethically towards each other or even collude to cheat a third party.

Introduction

Despite the growing interest in the study of conditions enhancing or inhibiting ethical behavior in firms, surprisingly little emphasis has been put on the process perspective. By assuming that actors will follow, e.g. given rules of conduct, our ability to predict behavior may seem to increase. On the other hand, one has to admit that the construction of such a set of ideal conditions, based on an isolation of actors and an over-simplification of the meaning of communication, is possible only at the cost of significant loss of realism. Business ethics needs to encompass not only situations in which the actor knows what is right or wrong, and hence may choose to behave ethically, but also situations in which the actor fails to do the right thing.

An analysis of conditions for ethical behavior in interactive consultancy processes clearly points to the importance of a process perspective for the understanding of ethical behavior. Rules guiding the behavior of clients and consultants are important, but not sufficient, because the actors are involved in social interaction processes, which not only influence but sometimes even impose behaviors that are inconsistent with known and accepted codes of conduct. One illustration of how processes may reveal questions about morality is the situation in which a client asks a consultant for advice, while unknowingly seeking a scapegoat to take the blame for an unpopular decision. Similarly, a consultant may promise a client the best advice, while unconsciously starting a process within the firm leading to employee demands for a solution which requires further involvement by the same consultant. Despite an honest desire to deliver the advice sought, other desires, such as a critical need for further income to pay next month's mortgage, may unconsciously influence the way in which the consultant discusses the issues with people within the firm, such that they come to feel that they really need exactly what the consultant prefers to deliver.

The purpose here is to raise a number of important issues which have, so far, received limited attention in the business ethics literature, namely factors related to interaction processes. These factors are discussed within the context of management consulting processes, where both the client and the consultant may behave unethically, despite the best intentions. A focus on interaction processes highlights the need for further research into three areas which we suggest should be included in an expanded research agenda in business ethics:

- The impact of factors that are largely non-rational and unconscious, e.g. a hidden agenda which is unknown even to the person who has it ("self-deception with sincerity")

- The impact of relationships and interaction, e.g the impact of group processes and the fact that individual, dyadic and group behavior in firms is embedded in a larger intergroup context (Alderfer, 1987; Smith, 1989)
- The impact of time on the evolution of relationships, including the development of trust or distrust, expectations and perceived obligations etc.

We start with a brief discussion of the field of business ethics, the meaning of the "process" and the "consultancy" terms, and a definition of the types of consulting processes covered by this paper. Subsequent sections discuss the consultancy process, and raise a number of ethical issues related to the behavior of the consultant, the client, and their interaction. First, challenges linked to the particular context of management consulting are discussed. Secondly, the three additional aspects of interactive processes mentioned above are discussed in further detail, within the context of management consulting processes. Finally, our suggestions for an expanded research agenda in business ethics are discussed.

Background and Definitions

Business Ethics

The public be damned. I am working for my stockholders.

– Singer, 1986:565

Since ancient times questions about the connection between commerce and moral life have been asked (e.g. Aristotle's, about "chrematisike", which means trade for profit). Business ethics as we know it today, however, is a young (only a couple of decades old) and rather eclectic discipline, and naturally no consensus has been reached as to what should be included in a research agenda for this new discipline.

On the one hand, from an extreme business perspective, business ethics is seen as a means to profit maximization. From this perspective, companies should behave ethically because in the long run it will pay to do so, or at least they should modify their goals so as to maximize profits subject to a minimum ethics constraint. According to Friedman (1970)[1], "the social responsibility of business is to increase its profits". On the other hand, from the perspective of business ethics, a conflict between business and ethics is seen to be unavoidable. From this perspective, the moral imperative is to do the right thing, regardless of worldly business concerns, such as profitability. If a theory of business ethics is to have significant impact on business conduct, it will need to bring together the concerns of both business and ethics simultaneously – business ethics.

Three main streams of research may be identified, similar to those described in the field of ethics in general: descriptive, normative, and meta-ethics. The descriptive category includes studies, e.g. emphasizing individual attitudes, whereas the normative category includes attempts at, e.g. developing codes of conduct in order to achieve ethical behavior in situations where a lack of individual ethical attitudes needs to be compensated. Research on meta-ethics focusses on ethical models and conditions for ethical behavior and includes studies of the impact of contextual factors on individual and organizational behavior, such as industry norms, national culture, internal factors of the firm, and process-related factors. Given its emphasis on the impact of process-related factors on ethical behavior in dyadic or group interaction, this chapter falls into the broad category of research on meta-ethics.

The Terms "Consultancy" and "Process"

The etymological background of the terms "consultancy" and "process" offers some interesting insights, none the least as regards ethical dimensions. The term consultancy may be traced back to a number of latin words, including consulo, consultatio, consulto, and consultor – all of which have a double meaning in most uses. Whether used as verbs or as nouns, these terms often cover both the role of the counsellor/advisor and that of the person who seeks the advice of someone.[2] This mixed and overlapping relation between client and consultant underscores the importance of a process perspective, where the roles may become so intermingled that the client expects the consultant to be the decision maker.

The term "process" may be traced back to the latin words procedo and processus, with the meanings advance/progress both as verbs and as nouns. These terms are used in a number of different contexts, including troops making progress (as opposed to being stuck in one place) and bricklayers' progress when building a house. Both examples are practical and imply an incremental development from one point to another over time. [3]

When the term consultancy is connected to the term process, it becomes clear that we are concerned with giving or taking advice, an incremental and dynamic process involving the interaction of (at least) two parties. In this chapter we discuss a process involving giving and receiving advice, and hence there is an asymmetry of competence involved which leaves ample room for hidden agendas and other types of unethical behavior. A relationship of mutual trust is absolutely critical to the success of a consulting process.

Management Consulting

We limit our focus to a particular type of consultancy process, namely management consulting, whereas consultancy also takes place in a number of other areas in society. Our focus is on management consulting processes involving a high degree of interaction, as we assume that the ethical challenges involved in consulting processes are more extreme in situations where the technical/objective content of the advice is limited. We are primarily interested in the conditions affecting behavior at the individual level, as a client interacts with a consultant, and we will mostly limit our discussion to the dyadic interaction between one consulting firm and one client firm representative. In processes involving more actors as representatives from one or both of the firms, we suggest that the challenges resulting from the nature of interaction processes are likely to become even more complex.

Ethical Challenges Particular to Management Consulting

Consultants: The men who came to dinner. Consulting firms can render a real service to management. But the best service of all is the one they render to themselves.

– Guzzardi, 1965

The Role of Information Asymmetry

When a client seeks advice from a consultant, a high degree of information asymmetry is typically involved. The consultant sells a superior problem-solving ability and is able to charge a price for this service precisely because the clients need know-how they do not already possess. Consultancy involves an asymmetric relationship, where the principle of "caveat emptor" (buyer beware) no longer can apply (Higdon, 1958:140).

"Double (Or Even Triple) Moral Hazard"

The higher the degree of interaction required for a high quality outcome of the consultancy process, the higher the risk of what has been termed in the finance literature as a "double moral hazard" (Baron and Besanko, 1987; Lee and Png, 1990; Mann and Wissink, 1988). Not only is the client dependent on the ethical behavior of the consultant in order to receive a high quality service, but similarly the consultant is dependent on the cooperation of the client in order to be able to deliver the high quality service promised. There is a moral hazard involved for both parties, and the service provider cannot guarantee the service quality without substantial risk involved if the client behaves unethically. Clear examples of such moral hazard are found in auditing, where it is impossible for the auditor to provide a high quality audit if the client succeeds in hiding important information. Similar examples may be found in all areas of highly interactive services.

In addition to the double moral hazard described above, in situations where both the consultant and the client behave unethically two outcomes are possible. In the first case, the client and the consultant cheat each other. In the second case, the client and the consultant collaborate in order to cheat a third party, such as when an auditor and a client together develop a financial statement hiding information from tax authorities. In this case, we suggest there is a triple moral hazard in that there may be three (or more) parties cheated by unethical behavior in a consultancy process.

The Lack of a Profession in Management Consulting

Where consultancy services are based in a profession, a number of professional norms of ethical behavior are presumed to guide the behavior of the consultants, and the professional association serves an important role in policing the activities of their members. If the professional association is effective, membership in such an association may serve as a protection for the client, in terms of enforcing ethical behavior (or exclusion) of members.

Professional norms of ethics include, among others:

- The application of knowledge in an altruistic service to clients, rather than self-seeking motives such as profits or status
- The acceptance of a limited sphere of expertise, and no expert authority outside the scope of that sphere
- Relationships with clients characterized by affective neutrality (objective advice)
- Professional control based on: long training including the internalization of a code of ethics which governs professional conduct, and external surveillance "by peers who, since they have a personal stake in the reputation of their profession, are motivated to exercise the necessary sanctions." (Blau and Scott 1962:61-63)

Despite the efforts to develop a profession of management consultants, it is doubtful whether management consultants may be called members of a profession, judging by the criteria outlined in the literature (e.g. Blau and Scott, 1962; Etzioni, 1964; Hughes, 1958; Schön, 1983; Vollmer and Mills, 1966). There is no established body of knowledge for consultants as such, and there is no licensing of management consultants, nor any professional organization with the right to supervise and potentially exclude consultants from the management consulting ranks. For individual professionals there is no established system of peer reviews beyond the firms, and there is no set of sanctions to enforce ethical behavior. In fact, any individual who manages to sell advice in the broad area of management, may call him/herself a management consultant.

As a result, a number of firms try to signal firm-level codes of ethics and indicate that only consultants with a high degree of personal integrity are allowed to work for the firm. The uncertainty about service quality, the numerous possibilities of being cheated in a consulting process, and the lack of a profession policing the behavior of individual consultants may be one of the main reasons why so many clients prefer to pay the higher costs involved in hiring a large, international consulting firm, even when a small local company could do an equally good job.

When the firm's reputation is at stake, the client may feel assured that the consultants will be "kept in line". One challenge is, however, that the link between the consultant and the employing company is frequently quite weak, as most of the work takes place at the client site. In the extreme case, the consultants run more or less their own independent business under the umbrella name of the firm. When this link is weak, the impact of firm roles, norms and expectations is likely to be limited, and thus, the quality of company codes of conduct may be of minimal importance to the actual behavior of individual consultants. As a result, the buyer still needs to be aware of all the dangers involved, included those concerning the influence of unconscious processes.

Hidden Agendas in Consulting Processes

The Seller of Advice

From the perspective of the consulting firm, there are three critical parts to value creation: selling a credible promise, delivering the promised value, and learning from the client for improved future value creation (Lorange and Løwendahl, 1990). For each of these parts of the value creating process, a number of ethical issues may result.

First, in terms of selling a credible promise, there is a potential conflict of interest between the goal of maximizing the number of "billable hours" and the best interests of the client. The consultant needs to convince the potential client of his/her ability to provide high quality solutions to a not yet diagnosed problem, whereas the client may need a consultant with a different type of expertise altogether. This problem may become particularly acute when the consultant desperately needs new contracts, when the client is perceived as one of high status thus offering a potential increase in the reputation of the consultant, and/or when the consultant perceives a danger of losing a well-established and profitable relationship to a client through the client's hiring of a different consultant for a specific problem.

Secondly, even if the promised value is within the area of expertise of the consultant, delivering the promised value – and only that – may also involve ethical challenges. The first, and most obvious, challenge may be that of diagnosing the actual problem to the best interest of the client, and participating in a process to solve this problem at maximum quality and minimum cost. Temptations for the consultant may include issues such as: adding unnecessary services to the "package", cutting costs by using junior assistants for all parts of the contract not visible to the client, and designing the service such that additional services bought from the same consultant are almost inevitable at the completion of the contract.

The third part of the process, namely that of learning from the client, may also involve difficult ethical challenges. In particular in times where the consultant faces inadequate demand for his/her services, potential opportunities for new contracts and economies of scope may lead to a violation of client confidentiality. An example may be the situation in which a consulting company gives advice to both parties in a negotiation, without informing the clients.

The Buyer of Advice

The consultant may not be the only one subject to challenges resulting from conflicting and incompatible goals. The client who seeks advice from a consulting firm typically asks for technical assistance in issues such as organization design, market analysis, efficiency improvement and cost reductions, etc. However, in many cases there are other and more subtle objectives involved, such as stifling discussions, boosting own image, reducing the power of a middle manager, or relief from a difficult decision ("decide for us", and take the blame if criticism follows). Through the careful selection and timing of entry points into the organization, who is asked to participate in the process, who functions as the key informant(s) for the consultant, etc., the process may be managed such that the results are biased in the direction preferred by the person hiring the consultant. E.g. experts may be drawn in to boost the legitimacy of one of the parties in a conflict. Through both the choice of consultant and the management of the context in which the consultant is allowed to operate, the persons employing the consultant on behalf of the firm may be able to get the advice they personally wanted, as opposed to what would have been the best solution for the firm.

The Impact of Hidden Agendas

When consultants or clients have other objectives than those stated in the contract, there is a hidden agenda involved. Hidden agendas in which the other party to the process is coopted into a role of playing the game of one party to the detriment of others, are examples of unethical challenges involved in interactive processes. One illustration may be the situation in which a middle manager employs a consultant to design and implement a reorganization in order to force out a colleague who might block his own promotion. For the consultant, it is extremely important to be aware of the potential existence of such hidden agendas, in order not to become a hostage in an underlying conflict.

If such a hidden agenda is known to the person manipulating the process, it is an example of unethical manipulation, and as such would clearly be denounced if others came to know about it. It may therefore be in the best interest of the person manipulating not to consider such possibilities, and if successful, (s)he may be engaged in a process of "self-deception with sincerity". In such situations, it is not enough to improve the morality of the individual nor the norms and codes of conduct of the firm. The first step required in order to avoid unethical behavior in such a situation, would be to make the person aware of the hidden agenda.

For the other party, who is subject to manipulation, the awareness of the possibility may increase the probability of detecting early warning signals, with the possibility of making the issue "discussable" (Argyris, e.g. 1985). Once the issue is brought out in the open, the manipulator will no longer be able to manipulate the situation, and the party subject to such manipulation will avoid being used in an unethical process. This is why we suggest that in order to reduce the probability of unethical behavior and manipulation in processes involving vague and non-technical types of advice, both parties need to have the necessary ethical as well as process related competence. Process competence involves both the ability to perceive such ethical challenges at an early stage, the ability to articulate the challenges and to communicate them to the other person involved without risking that the interaction breaks down, and the ability to find creative and ethical solutions to such problems.

There is, however, yet another challenge involved in the process of dealing with hidden agendas, and that is the issue of knowing the underlying objectives of another person. In addition to the competence in seeing, communicating and solving such ethical problems, it is crucial for both parties to respect the other, as even in situations where one person perceives a number of signals indicating a hidden agenda, the signals may be interpreted in the wrong way. This is why it is important to look at consulting processes as dynamic relationships evolving over time, where both parties are likely to try each other out several times before they conclude that mutual trust is merited. Both clients and consultants typically engage in careful selection processes before a contract is signed, involving checks of previous experience in similar processes, friends of friends who may know the key actors involved, smaller pre-projects in order to try out the relationship, etc. The reputation of the firm, as well as the individual, is also of importance, as people with substantial reputation to lose may be perceived as less likely to dare getting involved in a process of manipulation and hidden agendas.

Hidden Agendas and the Need for an Expanded Research Agenda

Research in a number of areas of social psychology has highlighted the impact of unconscious processes on human behavior, and we suggest that these processes also need to be accounted for in a complete model or theory of business ethics. In our view, ethical behavior requires not only moral individuals with a high level of ethical competence working within the context of firm and social norms underscoring the importance of ethics. Ethical behavior in complex interaction processes also requires a high degree of process competence, in order to avoid both "self deception with sincerity", where unethical behavior results from one's own hidden agendas, and being manipulated into unethical behavior by the other party. Is it, then, unethical to be stupid? In our opinion, in some cases a lack of process competence may lead to situations which do constitute ethical problems, and hence belong within a research agenda in business ethics. We do not, however, wish to go into the discussion of guilt and responsibility here –that is another topic in which further research is required.

What about the situation of the person being manipulated? In our opinion, in many cases even the person subject to the hidden agenda of the other party is facing a difficult ethical problem. If the person does things (s)he would not otherwise have done and ends up hurting a third party, the ethical problem is obvious. If the person manipulated is the only person to be hurt in the process, it may be less problematic, but even in such situations the ethical problem exists.

A Need for More Joint Research Between Ethicists and Social Psychologists

Individual Processes. Unconscious processes affect the quality of the judgment provided by a consultant in an interactive consulting process. The consultant is a representative of a firm, and the expectations implicitly put on him/her from superiors may substantially affect both what the consultant perceives, and how (s)he chooses to approach the problems discovered. Studies in social psychology have shown how perceptions are affected both by authority figures (e.g. Milgram, 1963) and group pressures (e.g. Asch, 1956). Consultants may be subject to substantial pressures to succeed, both from superiors, peers, and from the clients themselves. If they are employed as experts, it may be very difficult to express doubts about a proposed solution – in particular if the solution is suggested by a superior. The impact of roles on individual behavior may be substantial, and e.g. where the hired consultant is given "guru" status within the client firm, perhaps also based on the image of the consulting firm, (s)he may have great difficulties in admitting not to have the answer. The more implicit and ill-defined the expectations are for a consulting contract, the more tempting it may be for the consultant not to get involved in areas of conflict or complex dilemmas.

Other researchers (e.g. Smith, 1982; 1989) have shown how perceptions are affected by the group identities we take on. E.g. where a consultant criticizes his/her superior (while talking to peers), while advocating the very same type of sanctions vis a vis a subordinate, without being aware of his/her inconsistent behavior.

In addition, consultants – like all experts – are subject to a number of unconscious processes affecting perception even without interpersonal pressures being present. Russo and Schoemaker (1989:86) describe how recency or vividness of past experience affects judgments, such as when engineers facing a problem were asked to give probabilities for different types of diagnoses, and the probabilities went up substantially in the direction of the previous cause found for a similar problem. The estimated probabilities were too high by 15-50% compared to what would have been estimated based on objective data.

Group Processes. Group processes exert substantial influence on individuals, as indicated above. Based on his research on boards of directors, Alderfer (1986) describes the processes as follows:

> Instead of talking about the issue, the directors chose, as individuals, to live with the problem. In other words, no one person thought that he or she could change the behavior. . . . they couldn't act because, at the same time, they felt subordinate to the group. (p. 38)

Paraphrasing Alderfer, we are tempted to say that:

> . . . no consultant (originally director) – regardless of how strong – can escape group forces. (p. 39)

One well-known example is that of groupthink (Janis, 1971), where the individuals are to such an extent influenced by the group that their ability to think and articulate critical opinions is completely suppressed.

Another challenge to individual behavior in a group context is posed by the occurrence of "parallel processes" (Alderfer, 1987), also called "mirrored dynamics" (Krantz and Gilmore, 1991). An example of such unconscious processes is the case of the three consultants engaged by an information services company to help implement a new strategic plan, which included a reorganization from functional to product-line divisions (Krantz and Gilmore, 1991). The junior consultant worked mostly with the manager of the largest product-line, whereas the two senior consultants worked with the CEO and the COO. Soon, major conflicts erupted between the junior consultant and the two seniors, conflicts which later were diagnosed as the result of each of the consultants being "caught in a perplexing unconscious dynamic" (p. 323) stemming from conflicts within the client firm, in particular between the COO and the product-line manager. Conflicts suppressed within the client system became acted out between the consultants.

When client and consulting firm representatives jointly work in a group designed to solve a problem and/or implement a solution, another danger is represented by processes of "escalating commitment", which are frequent in particular where:

> ... the decision is whether to cease a questionable line of behavior or to commit more effort and resources into making that course of action pay off. (Staw, 1981, p. 577)

In such situations, both the consultants and the client firm representatives may have so much prestige involved in the decisions made earlier, that it may be extremely difficult for them to reconsider their joint decisions and actions, despite objective evidence indicating that a new course of action should be chosen. If the consulting firm is aware of such a danger, the results may be substantially improved if new consultants are brought in at important decision points.

Conclusion

Man darf den Prozeß nie aus den Augen verlieren...
— Kafka (1979:138 – first published 1925)

The purpose of this chapter has been to point out a number of important process-related factors which may fundamentally affect ethical behavior, based on an analysis of ethical challenges resulting from the high degree of interaction in process consulting. Further research on the relationship between these factors and the actual ethical behavior of individuals in organizations is clearly needed. In particular, research and theory building in business ethics may need to expand its interdisciplinary nature to include even more collaboration with researchers based in (social) psychology and other disciplines where the dominance of the rational decision maker perspective is less prevalent than in economics (business) and philosophy (ethics).

The Need for an Expanded Research Agenda

Can business ethics theory and research help consultants and clients manage such complex interaction processes? We think it may, but that the research agenda would need to be expanded, in order for the theory to be relevant for the complex reality of highly interactive processes, such as are common in management consulting. Like Gatewood and Carroll (1991) and Kahn (1990), we suggest that a theory of ethical behavior will need to encompass both the normative ("ought to") and the contextual variables. In addition, a theory or model of business ethics needs to take into account not only the behavior resulting from conscious choices, but also the situations in which the actor is unable to behave ethically despite knowing what would be the right thing to do.

In the figures below, we extend one of the more recent and widely encompassing models presented in the literature (Ferrell, Gresham and Fraedrich, 1989; a model adapted from Hunt and Vitell, 1986), to include factors in addition to those affecting judgment and choice. Figure 1 is a reprint of the original figure from Ferrell et al., whereas figure 2 goes beyond figure 1 by putting more content into the boxes at the far right of figure 1.

FIGURE 1. A Model of Business Ethics

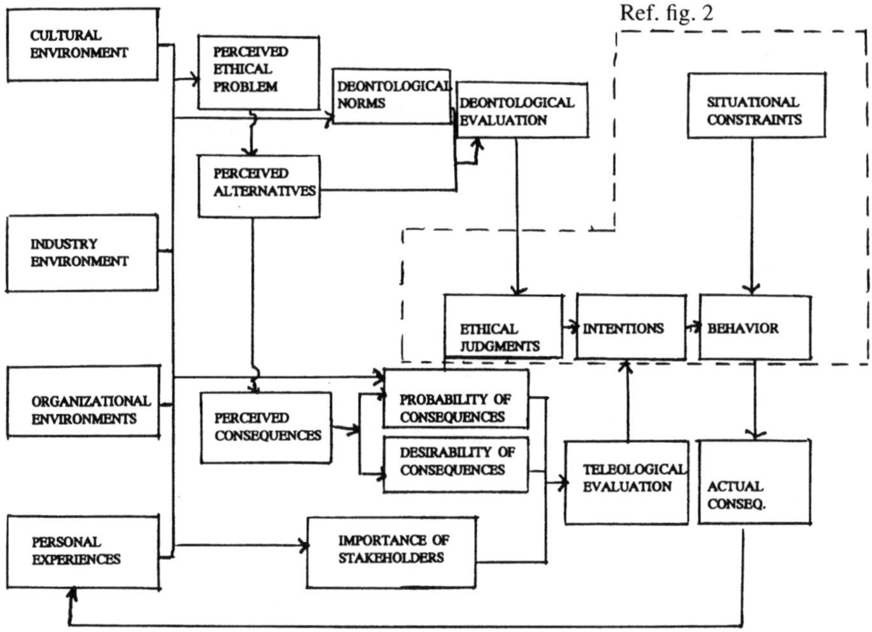

Reproduced from Ferrell, O. C., Gresham, L. G. and Fraedrich, J.: A synthesis of ethical decision models for Marketing. *Journal of Macromarketing,* volume 9. Fall 1989, p. 59.

The Journal of Macromarketing is published by the Business Research Division of the University of Colorado at Boulder.

FIGURE 2.

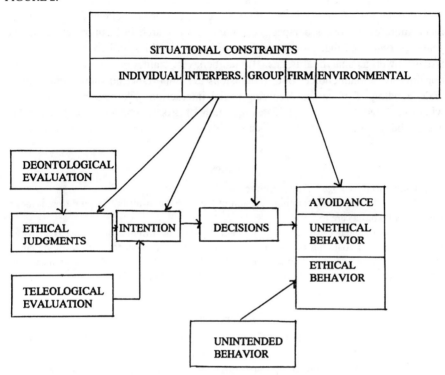

As illustrated in the figures, both individual, interpersonal, group, firm, and broader environmental pressures may influence and even impose behaviors on individual actors, despite their deeply felt desire to behave ethically. One shortcoming of the figures is that they only deal with the perspective of one actor, where the influence of other people only enters in terms of situational constraints. A dynamic figure with an explicitly dyadic perspective would make even clearer our emphasis on interaction processes.

We propose a shift in the traditional ways of looking at the field of business ethics, both in terms of the types of studies encouraged and in terms of the disciplines from which we borrow theories and other insights. We encourage an even more eclectic approach to business ethics, where the present research foci are supplemented by interdisciplinary studies combining researchers from areas such as social psychology, psychotherapy, and organizational diagnosis with researchers specialized in the area of business ethics. In terms of methodologies, we will probably need an emphasis on in depth case studies, anthropological observation methods, etc; i.e. studies of actual-behavior within a complex context. Such studies allow us to focus on both what people really do rather than what they say, and on actual choices and behaviors as opposed to the normative emphasis on what people should do.

Maybe the prevalent emphasis on analytical issues of business ethics is the result of the young age of the discipline. If so, there are reasons to believe that we will see much more of a process perspective influencing research in business ethics in the years to come, and that the mature field of business ethics will encompass process issues as well as analytical issues. Human behavior cannot be seen only as process nor only as rational choice; both dimensions are important and fundamental to the understanding of processes involving social interaction. The statement "advise us what to do, decide for us" elucidates the kinds of process challenges both the seller and the buyer of consulting services are likely to be brought into, sooner or later.

Notes

1. Quote from *New York Times* reprinted in *Nash* (1990).
2. Interestingly, the only feminine version of the term, "consultrix", has a different meaning; "she who has a care for. . . ."
3. In modern science we can find "process" applied in different disciplines, e.g. within decision sciences as data/information process, within psychology as personal development, in law as a process of justice, within sociology as the development of friendships, or in economics as the evolution of competition between different actors in a market.

References

Alderfer, C.P. 1986: The invisible director on corporate boards. *Harvard Business Review,* (Nov-Dec), 38-52.

Alderfer, C.P. 1987: An intergroup perspective on group behavior. In: Lorsch, J.W. (ed). *Handbook of Organizational Behavior,* Englewood Cliffs, NJ: Prentice Hall.

Argyris, C. 1985: *Strategy, Change and Defensive Routines.* Boston, MA: Pitman.

Asch, S. 1956: Studies of independence and submission to group pressure. First published in *Psychological Monograms,* (70). Quoted in Russo, J.E. and Schoemaker, P.J.H. 1989: *Decision Traps.* New York, NY: Simon & Schuster.

Baron, D. P. and D. Besanko 1987: Monitoring, moral hazard, asymmetric information, and risk sharing in procurement contracting. *RAND Journal of Economics,* VOL 18: NO 4: pp. 509-532.

Blau, P. M. and Scott, W. R. 1962: *Formal Organizations: A comparative approach.* San Francisco, CA: Chandler.

Bower, M. 1989: Interview by Meryl Comer, *Entertainment and Sports Programming Network,* November 13-17, 1989. *McKinsey Press Summary,* December, pp. 31-39.

Etzioni, A. 1964: *Modern Organizations.* Englewood Cliffs, NJ: Prentice-Hall.

Etzioni, A. 1988. *The moral dimension: Toward a new economics.* New York, NY: Free Press.

Ferrell, O.C.; Gresham, L.G., and Fraedrich, J. 1989: A synthesis of ethical decision models for marketing. *Journal of Macromarketing,* Vol. 9. Fall 1989, 55-64.

Freeman, R.E. (ed) 1991: *Business Ethics; The state of the art.* Oxford/New York: Oxford University Press.

Gatewood, R.D. and Carroll, A.B. 1991: Assessment of ethical performance of organizational members: A conceptual framework. *Academy of Management Journal,* Vol 16: No. 4, 667-690.

Guzzardi, W. J. 1965: The men who came to dinner. *Fortune:* February: pp. 138-141, 236-238.

Higdon, H. 1969: *The Business Healers.* New York, NY: Random House.

Hughes, E. C. 1958: *Men and Their Work.* Glencoe, IL: Free Press.

Hunt, S.D. and Vitell, S. 1986: A general theory of marketing ethics. *Journal of Macromarketing,* 6 (Spring), 5-16.

Janis, I.L. 1971: Groupthink. *Psychology Today Magazine,* November. Reprinted in: Leavitt, H.J., Pondy, L.R. & Boje, D.M. 1989: *Readings in Managerial Psychology,* 4th ed. Chicago, IL: University of Chicago Press, 439-450.

Kafka, F. 1979 (originally published 1925). *Der Prozess.* Frankfurt am Main: Fischer Taschenbuch Verlag.

Kahn, W.A. 1990: Toward an agenda for business ethics research. *Academy of Management Review,* Vol 15: No. 2, 311-328.

Krantz, T. and Gilmore, T.N. 1986: Understanding the dynamics between consulting teams and client systems. In de Vries, M.F.R. et al. (eds), *Organizations On the Couch; Clinical Perspectives on Organizational Behavior and Change,* San Francisco, CA: Jossey-Bass, 307-330.

Lee, T. K. and I. P. L. Png. 1990: The role of installment payments in contracts for services. *RAND Journal of Economics,* Vol 21: NO 1: pp. 83-99.

Lorange, P. and Løwendahl, B. R. 1990: Global strategies for professional service firms (PSFs). William H. Wurster Center for Multinational Management Studies Working Paper Series, Wharton School, University of Pennsylvania, Philadelphia, PA.

Løwendahl, B.R. 1992: Global strategies for professional business service firms. Unpublished Ph.D. Dissertation, The Wharton School, University of Pennsylvania, PA.

Mann, D. P. and J. P. Wissink 1988: Money-back contracts with double moral hazard. *RAND Journal of Economics,* Vol 19: NO 2: pp. 285-292.

Milgram, S. 1963: Behavioral study of obedience. *Journal of Abnormal and Social Psychology,* Vol: 67, No. 4, pp 371. Reprinted in Bennis, W.G., Schein, E.G., Steelen, F.I. and Berlew, D.E. (eds) 1968: *Interpersonal Dynamics* (revised ed.), Homewood IL: Dorsey, 70-84.

Peck, G.S. 1983: *People of the lie; The hope for healing human evil.* New York, NY: Touchstone/Simon & Schuster.

Russo, J.E. and Schoemaker, P.J.H. 1989: *Decision Traps.* New York, NY: Simon & Schuster.

Schön, D. A. 1983: *The Reflective Practitioner; How professionals think in action.* New York, NY: Basic Books.

Singer, P. 1991: *A Companion to Ethics.* Cambridge, MA: Basil Blackwell.

Smith, K.K. 1982: *Groups in conflict; Prisons in disguise.* Dubuque, Iowa: Kendall/Hunt Publishing Co.

Smith, K.K. 1989: An intergroup perspective on individual behavior. In Leavitt, H.J.; Pondy, L.R. and Boje, D.M., *Readings in Managerial Psychology,* 4th ed. Chicago, IL: University of Chicago Press, 451-468.

Smith, K.K. and Berg, D.N. 1987: A paradoxical conception of group dynamics. *Human Relations,* Vol 40, No. 10, 633-658.

Staw, B.M. 1981: The escalation of commitment: A review and analysis. *Academy of Management Review,* Vol 6, No. 4, 577-587.

Vollmer, H. M. and Mills, D. L. (eds) 1966: *Professionalization.* Englewood Cliffs, NJ: Prentice Hall.

PART III

Special Areas

10

Government Agencies and Consultancy – A Norwegian Perspective

Øystein Blymke

Introduction

The organizational consultant entered Norwegian public administration in a major way in the 1980s. Criticism had mounted against the bureaucracy on several fronts: its work methods, the qualifications of its employees, and its inefficiency and rationality. Free and independent consultants were expected to show their worth, drawing from their experience and qualifications from the private sector to improve on the central government bureaucracy.

This chapter outlines some adjustment problems and value conflicts that emerged in Norway during the expansive 80s, between what we may call the business sector rationality of consultants and the public administration rationality of the bureaucrat.

We must say that the consultant served – and still serves – as a positive catalyst for the common benefits that both parties hoped to gain from the cooperation – the problems aside.

First some background information, to understand the peculiar administrative culture facing the consultant.

Executive Power and the Surrounding Society

The public administration serves as the extended branch of executive power. According to the doctrine of distribution of power, and according to our democratic foundations, public administration shall carry out the policies of Parliament and the Government. The Central administration, with the government ministries as ultimate administrative powers, bases their exercise of power on what we call the Principle of Legality and on the Principles of Equal Treatment and the Rule of Law.

The bureaucratic system includes the ministries, and should be organized such that the public, political bodies and the press can see that power is exercised in a safe and fair way.

H. von Weltzien Hoivik and A. Føllesdal (eds.), Ethics and Consultancy: European Perspectives, 127-133.
© 1995 *Kluwer Academic Publishers. Printed in the Netherlands.*

These ideal requirements of the executive branch are partly embedded in law, and partly based on long traditions – often called "constitutional conventions and customary law."

The Government offices, the employees of the ministry bureaucracies, shall serve as guarantors for these constitutional values. Society takes for granted that an incorruptible, loyal and law-abiding public administration secures the rights of the population. Individuals are to be treated equally and fairly, whatever their condition.

These expectations are hardly unreasonable, considering the power of the government services. The legal rights to enter the legal spheres of individuals are so great that the citizens must control the exercise of this power.

This description of the central administration is perhaps idealized. Nevertheless, from that perspective, much of current business practice must be regarded critically, including the business culture, the "laws" of economics, the use of market mechanisms, modern principles of management and the uses of advanced information technology. Many feared that principles of business life will supplant the old and tested principles of public administration. This fear is warranted if we uncritically mixed the two cultures. Competition and efficiency threatened the central values of public administration, of the rule of law and equal treatment.

There was also a fear that the new requirements of efficiency in the decision procedures would reduce the possibilities of maintaining the integrity of public servants and the independence that have characterized the hierarchical bureaucracy.

New and Unusual Demands of the Central Administration

The demand for reforms of the central administration grew in strength, in spite of internal resistance and wariness of reforms. On the one hand, people expected the traditional values of public administration to remain, but on the other hand, the public was expected to rely more on the procedures of the private sector. The assumption was that the procedures of efficiency and rationality of private business could replace the slow central administration without loss.

"Restructure public administration" thus became an oft-repeated slogan and demand of the 80s. Nevertheless, it was difficult for bureaucrats to adjust to many of the new and untried methods and means proposed by private business for developing a more modern state.

The Entrance of Consultants!

Bureaucratic reservations notwithstanding, the requirements for modernization were complied with, and consultant services were accepted. There were comprehensive offers of consultancy, including offers of assistance for thorough organizational analyses, for new administrative and economic systems, and total solutions for the use of new electronic technologies. Politicians – the bureaucrats' employers – joined the chorus requiring more use of consultants.

The traditional professionals in civil service were lawyers and economists. Now the civil service was faced with consultants with similar, though competing, expert knowledge, complemented by technocrats and social scientists. Traditional bureaucrats found their qualifications at risk and their positions under siege.

The needs for knowledge and for reforms in the civil service were not quite as large as claimed by the consultancy companies. For the companies these needs for change provided a unique chance for new markets and new opportunities for profit. New possibilities opened up for alliances between the politician and the consultant. New slogans appeared in political daily life, such as "Vitalize old fashioned unwieldy bureaucrats."

The new consultancy gurus were to help the bureaucracy find its new shape.

Assistance From Consultants: On Whose Terms?

A wide variety of reforms were started by the government. Consultants could pick and choose projects, in part because of a widespread view that the bureaucracy was unable to adjust and that it lacked flexibility. The buyers of consultancy services were unable to assess the consultants' proposals. Furthermore, there was a lack of counter expertise within the bureaucracy itself.

The consultant was often given too much freedom – not only regarding the nature of the project, but also concerning where consultants were needed, and the extent of services required. The central bureaucracy became a major source of income for consultants.

The central bureaucracy also became a laboratory for consultants, where they could develop further methods and elaborate solutions – naturally, this possibility was not left untried. The lack of written agreements was an additional weakness making such freedom possible. The consultants would take the lead in organizing the project, and they would also include an appropriate setup for evaluating their own projects. The consultant thus had complete control over the projects.

The consultant's plans were often expressed using complicated concepts. Instead of asking for an explanation of these concepts, the buyers were too often afraid to ask. To admit ignorance was unacceptable. To reject offers of consultancy as 'of little interest to the ministry' would show a "lack of renewal spirit" – a criticism the hard pressed bureaucrat could not accept.

The bureaucrat nevertheless remained competent in one field: the procedures for hiring, and the formalities regarding contract negotiations with the consulting companies. Fair and correct bid procedures were complied with – even the tiniest contract was put out for bid. All consulting companies were treated equally and given an equal chance. However, it was difficult to maintain these considerations in practice; the consulting company which got the first job made itself irreplaceable once it got its foot in the door. Their arguments were often both legitimate and rational: it would be "an absurd waste of resources" to change consultants in the middle of a project.

The bureaucracy could not stand criticism regarding its alleged lack of ability to adjust; nor could it accept criticism along the lines of wasting taxpayers' money.

The Market Value of Consultants – The Value of the Work

The bureaucrats' wages are fixed within a state system of wages. This system has traditionally been open, predictable, not too flexible, and with low wages compared to positions with equivalent levels of responsibility within business. The wages in public sector have been regulated by the principle of equality, seniority, and other predictable criteria for wage levels and promotions. The consultant came from a world where market forces determine price, both for consultants and for their services. The central bureaucracy thus reacted strongly when the consultant billed services according to so-called market-adjusted rates.

The paradoxical result was that the civil servant would receive knowledge and training from the consultant – this is presumably the point of consultant services? – and then continue, with more knowledge and renewed effort – but without any improvement in pay or working conditions. Under such circumstances civil servants would easily turn sour. With increased self confidence and increased market value they had become irreplaceable. Lack of pay increases led to frustration for bureaucrats, who were now more aware of their own value – measured by standard market rates. As a result, they would either be bought by the consulting company, or quit to start their own company, and then turn around and offer their expertise to the old state employer.

If the employees were irreplaceable, the state would have to use great creativity to get them back. Conditions of employment could not be subject to the traditional constraints of wage budgets. One possibility would be to "buy services" thus ignoring the traditional wage levels.

When projects were carried out you would thus find consultants and bureaucrats in the same project groups with similar professional modes of participation. Some would ask the question: Are we not faced with contracting operations, and not ordinary consulting? Regardless, the 'irreplaceable' consultants could work full time with ordinary project tasks and maintenance tasks, and bill according to hourly rates which the government-employed colleague next door could only dream of as a daily wage.

Different principles and concerns came into conflict. The government, as employer, needed to consider several issues:

- Wage and employment solidarity within the Norwegian government services as opposed to buying necessary market-priced expertise.
- Dependency on the consultant. Was the job one of contracting or one of consulting? Was the project so enmeshed with the services of consultants that it would be irresponsible to fire them?

The consultant would often have developed a symbiotic relationship with the client. This reciprocal dependency was sometimes so well developed that the bureaucrat and the consultant would become allies against external criticism. Some would say that the reign of consultants had gone too far.

Several disadvantageous side effects had to be considered. The government could become a price leader because of the high consulting fees, the government might hire consultants for tasks which the state employer could manage equally well. One also started to ask whether such consulting actually led to a better central administration.

Consultants in Policy Planning and Research

The government continually needs broad expert advice in boards, councils and committees. These bodies explore and develop suggestions for improving government administration and suggestions about improving the quality of our welfare state generally. Members of these bodies are partly drawn from the central administration, and partly from society at large. Lawyers, doctors, house wives, fishermen and farmers all participate, in the belief that a representative sample of the population contributes to the planning of government activities.

Many professions put a high price on their own abilities and experience. Their knowledge and insights are offered the state, but at a market price. The state remuneration for this kind of social contribution is regarded as laughably low. Representatives of these price-conscious professions are often not motivated by idealism, but ask for payments based on what is provided in "their own environments." There they put a price on one another according to market oriented indicators of contribution.

In discussions, one might carefully suggest that this is an opportunity for them to take on social responsibility, gain influence, and join socially useful planning. But such suggestions do not stand up as arguments against purely pecuniary considerations. Still, the government regards these persons as both necessary and decisive for planning and research. Therefore, sometimes one agrees to special arrangements with very sophisticated systems of remuneration.

If the government wants to utilize the expertise available on the market, it is subjected to market prices. A conflict emerges if, at the same time that the government buys services at that price, it wants to make a case for idealistically motivated low prices. There is a conflict between two different attitudes regarding measures of contribution and the meaning – and price of – knowledge.

The Consultant and Selection of Administrators in the State

The central administration is often accused of inbreeding and nepotism when selecting supervisors and leaders. They care for their own colleagues in the bureaucracy. It is sometimes said that the central administration is unable to go beyond the ranks of the bureaucracy when making appointments, and is unwilling to appoint external applicants with business-oriented managerial skills.

The private consulting companies which deal with selection of managers and directors give valuable contributions when it comes to competent assistance. Their techniques regarding selection provide new and interesting methods and perspectives which the central administration should be able to utilize.

Consultants can often provide a more objective point of assessment than the person responsible for appointments, when that person works closely with the applicant. They also have a useful basis of comparison, drawing on manager selection in private business. The private consultant seeks leadership characteristics which are highly valued in the private sector, and which have been less customary in the central administration; 'results oriented and dynamic'. These characteristics were often absent in the government bureaucracy, which requested a rulebound, solid bureaucrat and didn't pay so much attention to results.

On the other hand, public administration can correctly criticize the generalizations which consultants have a tendency to make regarding manager assessments: "the good manager should be able to manage a car factory as well as a government department" is an example of such a generalization of managerial abilities. Perhaps there is a kernel of truth in this phrase, but there are special aspects of the civil servant as manager and leader which should not be forgotten. On the other hand, special requirements regarding experience and commitment to civil servant values can easily become vicarious motives for appointing one's colleagues in the bureaucracy.

When the public administration bureaucrat has made an appointment, with assistance from the consultant, the bureaucrat must not resort to using the consultant as a scapegoat in order to avoid taking responsibility for the selection. The responsible state employer must be held accountable for the choice, if any blame emerges.

To conclude this point: The use of consulting in recruitment for government administrators provides a new and necessary dimension for personnel management.

Concluding Remarks

I hope that this chapter gives some perspectives for discussion regarding some conflicts in the intersection between the values and motives of public administrators and the values and motives of consultants in the Norwegian society. One might also observe the kernels of some ethical problems and dilemmas regarding the choices one faces – in light of the values one wants to promote.

Used in the right way, the consultant can bridge the two kinds of values which set private and public sectors apart. Public administration must dare to be open for advice from consultants, but at the same time they must maintain the specific values of public administration which society should ensure. The Norwegian government bureaucracy must not copy, uncritically, principles of organization from private business. The consultant must not be allowed to replace good civil servant craftsmanship with principles from market approaches which only appear to offer a more efficient or more user friendly central administration. The definition of the concepts 'efficiency' and 'rationality' are, as we know, dependent on which values we endorse.

11

Ethical Issues
in Executive Search Consultancy

Domènec Melé & Barto Roig

Generally, the work of consulting firms that search for executives implies a direct commitment between the client and the consultant to find a proper candidate for a specific job position. Throughout the process there are various actions that demand a respect for the persons and organizations involved, the firm in search of an executive, the candidate, and the firm where the candidate is currently working.

In this chapter we identify some relevant ethical issues in the search for executives. After discussing these issues, we suggest some ethical criteria for executive search consulting from the basic moral values of justice, veracity, and trustworthiness.

Introduction [1]

Consultants specializing in executive search (headhunters – hereafter referred to as HH) act as information channels helping companies to fill management positions with suitable executives and allowing managers to advance their professional careers. Their activities help the client companies manage better and help ensure, as far as possible, that everyone holds a post that fulfills his or her needs. [2]

Sometimes, there are criticisms of HHs. [3] However, not all are justified. Generally, companies have both praise and criticism for HHs (Perkins, 1991) about technical and ethical issues. [4]

Part of the criticism stems from the fact that the term "headhunter" often covers a wide range of professionals (including all types of personnel selection consultants) irrespective of their qualifications and work methods. In some countries, HHs try to enhance their standing through membership in professional associations that demand certain quality standards and acceptance of the association's code of practice. [5] However, these associations do not exist in many countries and their absence allows entry to the sector people who are not always the best prepared or willing to provide the necessary minimum ethical guarantees.

H. von Weltzien Hoivik and A. Føllesdal (eds.), Ethics and Consultancy: European Perspectives, 135-148.
© 1995 *Kluwer Academic Publishers. Printed in the Netherlands.*

In this chapter, we will refer only to the smaller number of HHs who specialize in executive search for the highest company echelons, such as the posts of managing director, resident, executive vice president and so on.[6]

We begin by analyzing briefly what makes up the work of the HHs and then introduce the ethical values that, we think, are most relevant to them. Later, we attempt to analyze some ethical considerations that we have identified[7] through interviewing many HHs and business people who have used their services, and from our own knowledge.[8] We will illustrate these with minicases where appropriate. Finally, we conclude by proposing some specific ethical criteria that can guide the professional activity of HHs.

The Work of the Headhunters

The work of an executive search consultancy involves a mutual undertaking of a promissory nature by the client company and the consultant to find a suitable candidate for a certain position (Byrne, 1986). This carries with it the fundamental ethical requirement that the undertaking will be fulfilled. But this is not the only ethical requirement. From the initial instructions through the selection of the suitable candidate to a final placement in a position, various stages exist in which certain actions should be taken.[9] The most relevant action points that take up most of the consultant's time are the following:[10]

- To know and analyze the vacant position and the company that has requested the service.
- To establish the requirements of the client and define the ideal profile of the candidate to be recruited.
- To identify the market of potential candidates.
- To seek information about them and possible contacts.
- To interview the candidates personally and in depth.
- To request detailed references for the candidate selected.

Each of these activities has ethical implications for the people and organizations involved; directly regarding the client company and the candidate and indirectly regarding the candidate's present company.

The Ethical Values Involved

Among the ever present and universal ethical values present in any business activity, there are, in our judgement, three that are especially important in executive search consultancy:

1 Justice that demands that everyone receive their due. This involves, first, respecting peoples rights, more specifically, the right to a good name, the right

to a fair deal and the right to be judged fairly. Justice also demands that agreements and pacts be made in good faith and that their terms are strictly followed. Justice further demands that due consideration be given to people; treating them respectfully and sincerely throughout the process of search and selection.

2 Truthfulness, that is, the search for and manifestation of the truth wherever possible. Certainly, in this type of consultancy, as in every other form of human activity, the truth can never be known absolutely. It is not possible to reach a state of absolute and definite knowledge about the intricacies of a person's inner life. This includes people whom we think we know well; it can often happen that even after years of shared experience we are surprised by a friend and remark "And I thought I knew him well!" However, it is possible to reach certain, prudent conclusions (despite the fact that everyone is unique and different), and to compare them with others or to relate them to previously defined profiles.

Truthfulness demands always i) not lying when supplying information (this applies equally to both the client company and the candidate), and describing what is really relevant in everyday easily understandable language, and ii) ensuring that the client company and the candidate know everything about each other necessary for them to make an informed decision about accepting or rejecting the candidate or position.

3 Trustworthiness demands that parties do what they say they are going to do not only regarding what has been explicitly agreed but also regarding those implicit elements that are part of any agreement. It is particularly important that the degree of trust established by one party matches the trust given by the other, whether it is the client company or the candidate. Much confidential information is revealed in the selection process only to provide the knowledge necessary to properly fill the position. Trustworthiness demands discretion in the use of this information that is frequently obtained by people confiding in the consultant and relying on him to keeping professional secrets.

Search Options and Contracting in Good Faith

The first ethical issue concerns the client company's need for the consultant and the undertakings assumed by both. Let us consider the following minicase:

Minicase 1: Company ER requires a candidate to fill the position of personnel director at the site of an important factory that is a considerable distance from the city. The client insists that the candidate be experienced and comes from the area. These are difficult conditions to meet. In fact, ER has been looking unsuccessfully for a candidate for an entire year. To resolve this problem, ER instructs a firm of HHs who undertake to find three suitable candidates from which ER could make a final selection all within the space of three months. They seek payment of a third of their fees at the time of signing the contract.

The HHs begin the search. After three months, the HHs can only find one poten-tially good candidate but he has little experience. ER insists that he has to have experience and requests that a short list be sent as agreed. The HHs insist that the candidate they have sent is suitable but ER does not wish to take the risk of recruit-ing someone without experience.

This firm of HHs has promised too much and now it can't deliver. It has acted badly; it should have been aware of the difficulty at the outset. Also, the HHs should have understood the client's needs and not tried to impose the only candidate that they can find. Situations like this, in which a reputable firm of HHs would not be involved, seem to occur with some regularity. According to Adshead (1990), there are many companies who are dissatisfied with the results obtained from execu-tive search consultancies when compared with the promises initially made, and many positions end up not being filled as a result.[11]

Consultants should only accept those contracts where they really have sufficient capacity in terms of both qualified staff and available time to fulfill them. Obvious-ly, instructions given in bad faith are also unacceptable, for example, going through the process only to find out information about a competitor.

To avoid misunderstandings a clear and detailed contract should be drawn up in writing setting out the HHs undertakings. The contract must be based on good faith, result from a profound systematic analysis of what is being attempted (including the analysis of conflicting factors in the work and the difficulty of finding candidates), and take a prudent approach on how best to solve the client's problem. As in all commercial relationships, fairness demands that ethically correct contracts are rigor-ously observed and their conditions are fulfilled.

Something which limits the search option is the existence of avenues that are often described as "off limits", that is, places or organizations where one is not allowed to search for candidates. The HHs generally undertake not to attempt to recruit any person working in their client company for a certain period, normally one or two years, after the completion of their services. The ethical question here is whether this obligation requires a firm of HHs to tell a new client which companies are "off limits" to it. It seems to us that if such information about the extent of the "hunting ground" appears relevant for a client in making his decision to contract a particular firm of HHs, then the consultant must tell the client before formalizing the search contract. This is especially the case where the "hunting ground" for potential candidates is relatively small. However, we are of the view that this infor-mation does not have to be disclosed if special difficulties in obtaining candidates are not foreseen and where it is reasonable to assume that the client does not place too much importance on it.

Prior Knowledge and the Vacant Position

Before starting the search and selection process, the HHs fully have to under-stand the problem that has to be solved. This involves knowing a lot about the client company and the vacant position including such matters as labor relations, the company's values and even it's financial standing. Moreover, the HHs usually have a series of meetings before agreeing to carry out the search with the person to whom the successful candidate will report, all with the end of establishing the job requirements better and obtaining a good idea about how the candidate fits into the position.

Minicase 2: The managing director (MD) of ABC company needs a product manager (PM) to expand the MD's team. The PM must improve his product's penetration.

Now, ABC company has a difficult structure when it comes to incorporating a PM. Everyone on the sales team is a salesman with various products to place. They believe that it is not necessary to have a PM. His work would interfere with the work of the sales staff in the area as their interests lie not only in one product but in the entire range.

The HHs select three candidates. The client recruits one of them but a short while later this candidate is spurned by the organization and has to leave the company.

This case shows a clear lack of professionalism by the HHs that translates into an ethical problem causing serious prejudice to the candidate and, in some measure, to the organization. The HHs had deficient information about the job concerning not only its technical requirements and professional challenge but also the potential pitfalls, including the personalities of those sharing the work environment, which require special qualities and disposition to successfully avoid. When such situations arise they are usually due to a lack of adequate analysis of the job requirements and working environment from both the human and professional viewpoints. If the initial description is full and profound and the consultant is a good professional he will usually come up with a good candidate. But if it can be foreseen that the search is not feasible, it is better to refuse the work and explain why.

In assessing the candidate's suitability remember that people always form a culture (or microculture) in their respective organizations, effecting their values, ways of doing things, preferences, fears and so on. A new person in an organization must overcome a certain barrier of resistance and will not be part of the culture until he aligns or changes himself accordingly. Therefore, to define a position properly, one must specify its technical and professional content including the company culture and, above all, what we can call "the micro climate of hostility and rejection".

In other circumstances, if the consultant has information and uses it unwisely or without sufficient foresight the result can be the same. Often, what the company needs is not to fill a position, but to reorganize the distribution of responsibilities and authority within the company by moving its existing staff about. The consultant should detect this problem and explore it frankly and openly. The easiest thing for a consultant to do is not involve himself in these matters and to assure the client that he will find them an ideal candidate. But this would not be ethical and would lead to the selection of a candidate who would not fit in. To properly explore the job requirements can mean that the consultant has to say to the client that, in reality, they do not need a new executive so that he loses this assignment. In the worst case, he will lose the contract. He will avoid giving unethical and useless service while winning confidence and trust for the future.

Knowing and Evaluating the Candidate

Detailed knowledge and sound evaluation of the candidate is fundamental to the task entrusted to the executive search consultant. Moreover, it is a clear expression of the quality of his work. It will be apparent in the analysis, the insight displayed in the proposed solution and the suitability of the people proposed. A failure in this respect denotes, then, a lack of professional competence and, as far as this deficiency is negligent and avoidable, an ethically blameworthy omission. Let us consider the following situation:

Minicase 3: The managing director, who is also an owner of TXC a company specializing in machine equipment, needs to recruit an engineer to manage a parts assembly plant which the company has brought under it's wing as a specialist supplier. He instructs a firm of HHs to carry out the search for and evaluation of candidates. The HHs select an engineer who works for a public sector production company with a very deeply rooted culture. The record and references of the candidate are excellent.

However, after only a short while, it can be seen that the culture of the public company has completely imposed itself upon the candidate and that he is incapable of adapting himself to a new way of working. Moreover, he has a reclusive jealous character that disinclines him to cooperate. It appears that he is only interested in status and position with in the hierarchy.

The consultant has failed to discover one essential aspect of the candidate. Something like "professionalism" can be self evident in the curriculum vitae or it can be deduced with relative ease from knowledge of the candidates prior experience. However, more personal aspects are difficult to unearth. Therefore, it is necessary: i) to figure out what information is relevant in making an adequate selection, ii) to use methods that are both adequate and rigorous to obtain it, and iii) to evaluate the suitability of the candidate to fill the position in question. It is necessary to carry out, in depth, interviews exploring the professional, psychological, social and moral values of the candidate. Also, personal references help in knowing the candidate better. These are generally obtained after having agreed in principle between the prospective successful candidate and the client.

Ethical behavior requires professional competence and diligent and honest conduct. A good definition of consultants and their modus operandi is the following: "A consultant is a well-trained professional with moral integrity and relevant experience who discharges his duties conforming to his profession's code of practice. He is concerned about updating his knowledge through ongoing training . . . and acquiring as much experience as possible."[12]

The candidate evaluation process requires the consultant to evaluate each candidate honestly and fairly, in light of the job requirements, without forming dogmatic views about him.

On the other hand, it is necessary to balance the right to know a candidate well (as required by the nature of the contractual relationship between the client and the consultant) and the candidate's right to privacy, in short, to know the candidate well without obtaining information irrelevant to the post.

Introduction of Candidates and Guarantees

Normally, three candidates are presented. The consultant should give his client a detailed biography of the candidates. This requires an in depth interview to ensure that all of them have the requisites to properly adapt to the job. It would be dishonorable, and show a lack of trustworthiness, to present candidates who do not meet the stipulated conditions; someone who, colloquially, is called "a make do" candidate.

The consultant should be faithful in his role as an adviser, although the final decision of accepting the candidate will be taken by the client. Before reaching this point, the consultant can and must help to facilitate honest communication between the potential candidates and the eventual employer to establish a climate of reciprocal trust.

In every case, easy adaptation to the job and good performance in it are the final objectives of the executive search consultant's work. Difficulties in evaluation and in seeing the potential fit should not be an obstacle to the consultancy offering a guarantee of good service.

The guarantee is a key factor that, to a degree, sets the tone and decides the quality of all the work. It is advisable to have the guarantee set out in the contract (Batstone & Clark 1990) and, indeed, it is usually to be found there. In this way the moral obligation to correctly serve the client is made manifest.

The service guarantee usually takes one of two forms. First, it can guarantee that the search for a candidate is carried out in a way that minimizes possible difficulties that may arise at the commencement of his employment. The HHs, by virtue of knowing both parties, can facilitate a correct understanding. Secondly, it can take the form of a commitment to find a replacement candidate if, at the end of the day and despite one's best efforts, the candidate originally proposed does not suit the position. Varying periods of guarantee are provided according to the level of responsibility assumed by the successful candidate; for example, one year for a managing director, six months for a division or department director and three months for a section head.

Fees

Fees have to be fair and not outrageous. Ordinarily, they can be considered fair if they are agreed to by both parties in advance and at arms length. However, given the special characteristics of this service, situations can arise that require revision of previously agreed upon fees. The best thing to do is to outline, as far as possible, all foreseeable contingencies to avoid misunderstandings and surprises. Many HHs work with fixed fees paid by the client independent of the success of the search. These HHs usually cooperate closely with the client in a climate of confidence to find a suitable candidate. Others, by contrast, operate on a contingency fee basis where the fee is conditioned on the success of the search, in short, "no satisfaction, no fee". In the following minicase we present an HH firm's fee policy that, to us, appears very reasonable.

Minicase 4: The fees for services rendered by this firm are determined as follows:

i *The fees are fixed and communicated in advance to the client in writing. They are dependent on the difficulty of the work carried out and the responsibilities of the vacant position, and not on the salary of the successful candidate.*

ii *During the work, unforeseen circumstances can result in the client withdrawing instructions. When this occurs we will only charge fees in respect of work carried out before receipt of the notice of cancellation.*

iii *During the search phase it may be necessary to change the job's specifications. Such a change normally implies additional work. In such cases, we will agree on a new budget with the client with respect to the additional costs, which we will use our best efforts to minimize.*

iv *If more than one presented candidate is employed by the client, we reserve the right to charge additional fees.*

Candidate Details

The candidate confides in the consultant, giving information about a considerable part of his life. In exchange, he has the right to receive information about the job for which he is being interviewed and about the company that is offering it. He can obtain some information about the post and the company from the presentation of the company's outline curriculum. Later, as his possibility of being selected increases, he can legitimately seek and be granted access to more information. When the candidate is a real prospect, it is necessary to give him the name of the company. In general terms, given that the client information requires some protection, we would say that it is best to give information in stages and in exchange for information received.

An important and often difficult matter is the following. How much is it necessary to tell the candidate about the company? The best response here is also a prudent one. The company information that a candidate has the right to know is that which he needs to make his decision and avoid frustration.

Minicase 5: A nationally well known businessman is looking for a vice president. The offer is very attractive. The firm of HHs knows that it is a difficult position because the businessman has a unique and difficult personality. However, as they want the attractive fees, they find him a candidate with some prospects of success. The HHs persuade the candidate to accept the challenge without giving too much away about the difficulties that he will encounter. A short while later, the candidate is fired.

Here, not enough information has been given to the candidate. He was tricked into going to the company. Honest HHs would not only encourage the candidate to accept the post but also would explain clearly to him the challenge that he is taking on, and the risks involved, providing him with sufficient information about the position and the businessman to make a fully informed decision.

Now, the candidate should also receive information on the financial position of the company so that he can take necessary precautions to protect himself against the consequences of financial collapse.

It is necessary to take special care when providing information about family businesses where the company culture, and the way of operating, can be very peculiar. These situations and consequences should be foreseen and considered from the outset of a search for suitable candidates.

It is reprehensible for a firm of HHs to allow a candidate to wear rose colored glasses when contemplating a job move; they should disabuse him of any notions he may have that are far removed from reality. HHs know that potential candidates are, generally, well placed and that they can only be attracted by something that appears to them to be better than what they have now. This can lead to the HHs being tempted to avoid highlighting all the cons, along with the pros. Instead, they can offer the prospective candidate more than they are going to get, as illustrated in the following case that requires no explanation:

Minicase 6: KHF is a company producing and distributing industrial chemical products. It employs very competent professionals. Almost all of them are chemical engineers specializing in a rarefied area.

Company KHF does not pay as high of salaries as other companies in the sector, although they distribute a share of the profits at the end of the year. There is a good atmosphere in this company because there is much freedom, creative spirit and personal appreciation for the people who work there. The owner and president are very well liked.

However, the managing director is very angry about what the HHs are doing; he feels that they are persecuting him by luring away his best managers with promises of higher salaries and better professional opportunities. Some managers allow themselves to be seduced. Afterwards, they confess that they were wrong and that what they had been offered by the HHs was far removed from reality. Some of them, in the fullness of time, return to their old company with their tails between their legs.

Other information that a candidate should receive includes the progress of his candidacy and his suitability for the position. It is no secret that every human being possesses his share of good points, positive qualities and virtues, but also weaknesses, faults and vices, which should be detected and "fed back" to the candidate so he can assess for himself his suitability for the post. Eventually his limitations are going to appear, and they would be an obstacle to his fitting into the position. Another beneficial outcome could be that, having received this feedback, the prospective candidate could clarify some point for the consultant and change his view to some extent. It should always be remembered that before giving this type of feedback, it is necessary to consider what to say and how to say it. It is necessary to deal with people respectfully and sensitively when giving them feedback to avoid injuring their feelings.

Confidentiality

The information obtained from the candidate and the client company is confidential. This is the basis of the trust placed in the consultant so he can achieve the objective of finding the most suitable candidate for the vacant job. Revealing company data to the outside world would be prejudicial to it. Also, the candidate, who by the mere fact of it being known that he was in a selection process, would be left in a difficult situation vis a vis his present company. Therefore, HHs have to keep all this information strictly confidential respecting the sensibilities of those involved, whether they are client company or candidate.

There is, then, a requirement in this area for confidential candidate information, that:

> the dossiers managed by the search company in the exercise of its functions be strictly protected by professional discretion ... and that no element of information contained in the dossiers be conveyed to third parties except with the agreement of the candidate in question (always excepting the potential employer)... Even when they have been asked expressly, the search company is never obliged to reveal the identity of the candidates not selected for a post to it's clients.[13]

The consultant must not use information on candidates for other, or different, ends to those originally intended, at least not without consulting them.

Minicase 7: A consultancy receives instructions from a client company to find a certain type of manager. Recently, the consultancy carried out a search for this type of manager and possesses many curriculum vitae of potential candidates. However, before passing the curriculum vitae to the client company, they ask permission from the candidates. They have established a rule that they will not pass candidate details obtained through a search for one company to another company without the consent of the candidates.

This is a perfectly correct course of action resulting from the implicit or explicit undertaking between the consultancy and the candidate not to use the information supplied except to achieve placement in a specific position.

Avoiding Conflicts of Interest

A good way to avoid being considered untrustworthy is to not be in situations where there is a conflict of interest. These can take many forms. One of them would involve presenting fresh offers to candidates who have already been placed in a client company. It is best for the HHs to promise not to go back and try to attract away, either directly or indirectly, any person previously placed by them with one client when undertaking a search for another client as long as that person occupies that position.

Another potential source of conflict is with their pool of client companies. One extensive practice is for the HHs to undertake not to search for candidates among their client companies, at least during a reasonable period after their last assignment. This should apply to all types and forms of companies or organizations whether they are small, medium or large (including different divisions of large companies). In reality it does not appear that this practice has a strictly ethical foundation unless it has been established in the contract or by undertaking to comply with the code of practice of the sector. However, it would be a good idea to always follow this approach to achieve a climate of trust and confidence between the consultant and the client. This practice is closely allied to the "off limits" concept whose revelation to new clients presupposes this moral obligation, as already mentioned.

Another area where a conflict of interest can arise is in trying to find a company for a candidate. It is not really practical for the HHs to accept this type of undertaking. In some codes of practice it is explicitly prohibited.[14] This does not mean that the HHs cannot approach or help managers especially if they have been discarded during selection. This can be a form of compensation for submitting themselves to the process, unsuccessfully as it turned out, in the first place but no payment should ever be involved. One good solution is to recommend such managers contact out lacement consultancies.

Indirect Damage to the Candidate's Present Company

Lastly, it is necessary to consider the possible damage that can be done to the company in which the candidate is currently working. If the process culminates in the candidate accepting a post in the client company, his former company will lose a director, with all that that implies. This is an indirect but very real result of looking for a better manager to improve the direction of the client company.

Clearly every person is free to work wherever he likes. But before leaving his present company a manager should try to find out what he owes the company for whom he has worked. There he has learned a good deal of what he knows through accumulated experience. Probably, his present company has invested time and money to train him.

The consultant must correctly weigh what the change really means, considering how it will benefit the candidate and the damage that could befall his present company. In certain circumstances, for a director "to quit" a company can prejudice them in a way completely disproportionate to the combined benefits for the candidate and the client company. This is a very difficult matter to judge but a prudent evaluation, in our judgement, is essential in reaching a morally correct decision.[15] In any event it is necessary to minimize the negative effects to the candidate's present company as far as possible. One way is to prevent the candidate from leaving his company too quickly. It is best for the HHs to advise the candidate to give his company proper, or required, notice (often one month but it can be longer depending on the contractual terms). This allows his company to begin a search for an internal or external substitute who can be brought up to speed on the most important matters with which the candidate is dealing.

Conclusions: Some Ethical Criteria

In the light of the above discussion and by way of conclusion, some ethical criteria for the executive search consultancy suggest themselves. They certainly give food for thought and could also act as guidelines in drawing up a code of practice for the sector:

i   The consultant should be professionally competent, and force himself to continually improve his knowledge, acting diligently and honestly at all times.

ii   The consultant should avoid undertaking more than what is reasonable for him to do given his skills and available time.

iii   The consultant must not accept immoral contracts or those that contain unjust clauses.

iv   There must be good faith in the interpretation of the contract and in its renegotiation when necessary.

v   The consultant should advise the prospective client companies of his "offlimits" areas when it is relevant to the proposed recruitment.

vi   The consultant should know the most relevant characteristics of both the client company and the vacant position, in both professional and human terms, to correctly evaluate the candidates and prevent possible disasters and frustrations. He should be prepared in the latter event to forgo recommending a new manager, although this may result in his losing the work and fees.

vii   In the search process, the consultant must safeguard the confidentiality of information obtained from the client company and from the candidates, and keep faith with the undertakings made to them.

viii   Conflicts of interest should be avoided. One should not consider a candidate whom one has already placed with a client company except with the permission of both parties. Also, it is advisable not to look for any candidates within the client company during a certain period after the last placement (generally two years).

ix   Interviewing candidates, obtaining references and final evaluations should all be done fairly, rigorous methods and keeping in mind the job requirements, while trying to foresee, as far as possible, how the candidate will fit into his new position.

x   To get sufficient information on the vacant position and the company, the consultant must be straightforward and honest. When dealing with the candidate, he should outline the company's position and job description without raising false expectations or exaggerating the advantages of the post offered. He should also make the potential difficulties involved clear.

xi   The consultant should maintain confidentiality about candidates' details, and not distribute their curriculum vitae and personal details indiscriminately without the appropriate permission of those interested.

xii   When introducing the selected candidate, the consultant should facilitate reciprocal sincerity and an atmosphere of trust between the candidate and the client.

xiii   The consultant should guarantee the adequacy of the candidate for the position and, in the case of failure, look freely, or with reduced tariffs, for a replacement.

xiv   Concerning the candidate's present company, it is necessary to avoid collaborating with the candidate to violate legitimate commitments he has to his firm. Moreover, it is necessary to weigh prudently the indirect damage against the present company against the need for change.

These criteria are not exhaustive. They form a model that can be used as a point of reference for subsequent development and which can, above all, be an aid to ensuring the ethical conduct of executive search consultants.

Notes

1. The authors wish to express their gratitude to D. Miguel de Gomis, Director of "Robert Allen," an executive search consultancy in Barcelona, Spain, for his comments and suggestions regarding the first draft of this work. However, they wish to point out that responsibility for this final version is theirs alone.

2. HHs are necessary for several reasons (Roig 1992, p.284): i) the best executives do not look for new companies for themselves because they are already well-placed, ii) increasing competition demands that companies find the best managers, iii) many managers have more potential than they are actually using and iv) information on the best managers, while not readily available, is essential to have.

3. See "Survey Criticizes European Headhunters," *Financial Times,* 1 Feb. 1990.

4. According to a survey carried out in 1990 among Catalunian companies 68% thought HHs efficient and 57% that it was profitable to use them. Among the positive characteristics highlighted were: their confidentiality (76%), their analytical capacity (71%), their understanding of problems (70%), their ability to find suitable candidates (65%) and a rigorous methodology (60%). See *La Actualidad Económica,* 24 Dec. 1990, p. 84.

5. For example, the French association APROCERD (Association Professionnelle des Conseils d'Entreprise pour la Recherche de Dirigeants) and the American AERC (Association of Executive Recruiting Consultants).

6. The following are therefore excluded: a) personnel selection firms, b) those professionals who have mastered in-depth the complex techniques of executive search, and c) professionals who focus on middle and lower management levels of companies.

7. We have tried to concentrate on those considerations which are most specific to HHs, although, obviously, a number of ethical problems dealt with here are common to all consultancies. (see White 1989).

8. All these minicases correspond to real events which happened in Spain in the last few years. However, some details have been changed, such as proper names, in order to prevent identification.

9. For an analysis of the various stages in the HHs process from the perspective of efficiency, see Rauch (1991).

10. Reference, in part, with Belda (1992 p.50).

11. In Great Britain the figure is one-third, according to Hester (1991).

12. *Code d"Ethique Professionnelle des Conseils en Recruitement,* nn. 3 y 6.

13. *Code d'Ethique Professionnelle des Conseils en Recruitement,* nn. 10 y 11.

14. For example, the *Code d'Ethique Professionnelle des Conseils en Recruitement,* n.4, establishes that "the selection company can only accept remuneration from companies that are his clients, and never from individuals."

15. When this weighty matter is not taken into consideration a bad image results for headhunters; more than as "hunters", they are seen as "predators". This complaint can be observed, for example, in places where local industry can come to a virtual halt in the face of competition from multinational companies (ref. "Look out for the headhunters!" *Business Corea,* vol. 9. no 2, agos., pp. 51-52, 1991).

References

Adshead, J. 1990: Headhunters without tears. *Personnel Management,* vol. 22, October, pp. 56 -57.

Batstone, S. and Clark, T. 1990: Trust and the headhunter. *Multinational Business,* no 1, pp. 1-8.

Byrne, J.A. 1986: *The Headhunters.* London: McMillan.

Belda, J. 1992: *Revelacions d'un caçatalens.* Ed. Gestio 2000, Barcelona.

Hester, T. 1991: Headhunters: Offers you should sometimes refuse. *Accountancy (UK),* vol. 107, June, pp. 88-89.

Perkins, G. 1991: *Snakes or Ladders?.* London: Pitman Publishing.

Rauch, H. 1991: Job hunting? Take it step by step. *Professional Development,* En. pp. 48-49.

Roig, B. 1992: *La empresa ante las realidades de fin de siglo.* Pamplona: Eunsa.

White, W. 1989: The ethical challenges of consulting. *Business Forum,* Fall Winter.

12

Organizational Ethics Consulting in the Health Care Environment: A Look at a US Children's Medical Center

Joseph A. Petrick and John F. Quinn

Abstract

Through a detailed treatment of an ethics consulting case study, the authors identify the need to enhance the ethical culture in the health care environment of Children's Medical Center in Dayton, Ohio, U.S.A. Their models and methods of managerial ethics consulting demonstrate the value added to the client health care culture by professionally addressing stages in the consulting process. The benefits to domestic and international children's medical centers, other health care organizations in a European context, purchasing agents of managerial ethics consultancy services and other managerial ethics consultants are highlighted.

Introduction

Children's Medical Center in Dayton, Ohio is one of fifty-six full-service children's medical centers in the United States (Brockman, 1992). Children's medical centers, however, exist globally and have established international networks to address common health care concerns of children (Association for the Care of Children's Health, 1992). European children's medical centers share the challenges and dilemmas of their U.S. counterparts in providing the highest quality care for patients and their families.

The origins of children's medical centers spring from secular and religious philanthropic foundations. However, the free market system and the growing global privatization trends have exerted pressures for financial accountability and organizational effectiveness along with the traditional tradeoffs among quality, access and cost for children's health care services (Knafl and Cavalleri, 1988).

In order to manage the conflicts from these competing influences, children's medical centers have begun to turn to managerial ethics consultants to assist them

H. von Weltzien Hoivik and A. Føllesdal (eds.), Ethics and Consultancy: European Perspectives, 149-161.
© 1995 *Kluwer Academic Publishers. Printed in the Netherlands.*

with institutionalizing ethics development systems. These systems diagnose organizational ethical climates, promote strategic values, facilitate the formation of ethics committees and/or ethics officers to settle ethical disputes and coordinate ethics policies, clarify ethical guidelines for employee conduct, enact horizontal voice systems to counterbalance traditional hierarchial medical structures, empower employees to resolve ethical dilemmas at the lowest possible level, create fair and swift enforcement procedures to ensure compliance with regulatory standards, link quality service and ethical culture development for continuous long-term improvement and apply ethics audit instruments to measure and benchmark ethical progress on a pre-determined basis.

This chapter highlights the ethical demands faced by the U.S. managerial ethics consulting firm, Organizational Ethics Associates, in its intervention at Children's Medical Center in Ohio. The demands encountered by the firm are representative of many ethics consulting challenges and will be discussed in terms of the consulting process and products provided by Organizational Ethics Associates to meet client needs. Finally, the benefits to domestic and international children's medical centers, other health care organizations in the European context, purchasing agents of managerial ethics consulting services and other managerial ethics consultants will be discussed.

Children's Medical Center (CMC)

From its origins in 1918 as a location for therapeutic treatment of handicapped children to its current status as a major regional service and referral center for a twenty-nine county region in Ohio and Indiana, Children's Medical Center (CMC) of Dayton has kept pace with a myriad of changes in health care technology, patient demands, hospital management and funding sources (Brockman, 1992). The development from early philanthropic roots to a more professional, full service children's medical center was marked by an array of contributing agents. Early social philanthropic and community leaders, such as Annae Barney Gorman, Elsie Talbott Mead, Miriam Rosenthal, and the Arthur Beerman family, combined with early medical professional staff, such as Dr. Alan Shafer, Dr. Wallace B. Taggart, Dr. George Sperry and Dr. Emanuel Kauder, to provide the foundations for a children's medical center in Dayton (Brockman, 1992).

In the 1970s CMC affiliated with Wright State University's School of Medicine and grew together with the medical school as professional partners in caring. The university medical school link ensured that CMC would remain in contact with state-of-the-art research and technology and provide a teaching environment for the medical staff.

In the 1980s, CMC emphasized professional hospital administration, community relations and the business aspects of running a medical institution by bringing in Laurence P. Harkness as its chief administrator. Over his ten-year tenure, Harkness applied his human resource background to provide leadership in staff stability, community relations, pediatric subspecialty development, fiscal soundness and superior patient care.

In the 1990s and beyond, outpatient services for children and families have become major health delivery trends, as well as, sources of ethical challenges. Sixty-five percent of surgeries at CMC are now performed on children as outpatients, demanding a balanced concern for patient health needs and recuperative resources along with respect for the constraints of fiscal soundness (Brockman, 1992). In order to face these diverse demands for technical sophistication and flexible delivery, the progressive senior leadership at CMC solicited a reputable ethics consulting firm to strengthen its caring culture to meet the children's health care needs for the twenty-first century.

Organizational Ethics Associates (OEA)

Organizational Ethics Associates is a U.S.-based managerial ethics consulting firm started in 1991. The core partners, Dr. Joseph A. Petrick and Dr. John F. Quinn, are leading national and international ethics authors, researchers, educators, trainers and consultants who combine legal, managerial, organizational, human resource, philosophical and ethical resources to improve the quality of work and work life domestically and globally (Petrick, Claunch and Scherer, 1991; Quinn and Crawford, 1991). OEA offers a full range of ethics products and services designed to equip clients with the practical resources to meet or exceed international, government, industry, legal and professional standards for a certified comprehensive ethics development program and to improve the quality, congruence and effectiveness of individual, group and organizational ethical decision making through separate programs.

The core partners' doctoral qualifications, consulting experience and university affiliations demonstrate sustained adherence to the highest professional consulting standards. They are Senior Professional Human Resource (SPHR) and Professional Human Resource (PHR) certified and ascribe to the code of ethics of U.S. Human Resource Professionals; they are also Registered Organizational Development Professional (RODP) certified and ascribe to the code of ethics of Organizational Development Professionals.

Along with their contracted associates, the core partners provide the following specific services and products: ethical climate diagnostic surveys; senior management assistance in formulating an ethics mission, vision and set of values; design and formulation of codes of ethical conduct and ethics handbooks; design and formulation of ethical instruments for recruitment processes, performance appraisals and reward programs; creation of ethical voice systems and communication channels; delivery of ethics training for all organizational levels; ethics officer specialized training; delivery of train-the-trainers service for greater client self-sufficiency; ethics training evaluation services; ethical conflict resolution services; organizational justice procedures; ethics audits; ethics compliance and enforcement subsystems;

link between quality management and organizational ethical culture development and a variety of ancillary related services.

The major client benefits provided by OEA include: more integrated and committed ethical cultures; more responsible, empowered ethical decision making at all levels in the organization; a proactive, cost-effective conflict management subsystem that reduces litigation expenses; enhanced team leadership development through shared ethical values; and a diagnostic assessment of current organizational ethical climate with models and methods to continually improve the ethical climate for world-class integrity and excellence (Petrick and Manning, 1990).

OEA normally operates under a four-phase consulting process (Greiner and Metzger, 1983). These phases are: assessment of current client needs, interactive prognosis of desired organizational future, implementation of endorsed developmental change, and evaluation of interventional impact and organizational change. In concrete terms, OEA asks client representatives to address the following four prioritized questions: "Where are we now?", "Where do we want to be?", "How do we get there?" and "How do we stay on track and move forward?" A range of models, methods and products are used for enhancing client benefits while engaging in these consulting phases.

Assessing Client Needs

On January 15, 1992, OEA was contacted by Ms. Gerri Dalrymple, Assistant for Special Projects to the CMC President, Mr. Laurence Harkness. She requested information on the firm and told Dr. Petrick that she would contact him if OEA resources met CMC organizational needs. Approximately two weeks later, Drs. Petrick and Quinn were invited to a meeting with both Ms. Gerri Dalrymple and Mr. James K. Pruitt, the Executive Vice President and Chief Operating Officer at CMC.

At the meeting the OEA partners provided more details about their services. The CMC officers indicated that they had contacted other ethics consultant vendors and were prepared to open a bidding process with approved vendors. Mr. Pruitt discussed a range of CMC strategic initiatives started by Mr. Harkness and he focused on the sixth strategic initiative -organizational culture development. The thrust of the organizational culture development initiative was to nurture a work environment that promoted high levels of quality, customer service, productivity and innovation.

After discussion with the OEA partners, it was agreed that the sixth strategic initiative could best be achieved by consistently demonstrated value-based service to patients, families, employees and other key stakeholders. Next, six items were determined after considerable discussion and mutual agreement. First, to ensure appropriate understanding and application of CMC's shared values a clearer articulation and interpretation of them in an easily accessible format would be required. Second, although CMC had a medical ethics committee to resolve technical medical problems, there was a need for an organizational ethics committee to address broader cross-specialization work value conflicts. Third, the process for arriving at the explicit formulation of CMC's values should be representatively participatory rather than autocratically imposed upon others by senior management or by an external consultant firm (Hoffman and Petry, 1989). Fourth, legal and ethical training would be necessary to provide uniform interpretation of shared value applications and ethical dilemma resolutions so the culture would be empowered to develop on its own even if senior management changed or downsizing occurred. Fifth, whatever organizational ethics interventions occurred, they had to be compatible with other ongoing CMC organizational development programs. Sixth, the ethics consulting service provided must be sensitive to CMC's culture, have top quality intervention skills and have a fee structure within CMC's budgetary guidelines.

At the close of the meeting, Mr. Pruitt apologized about Mr. Harkness' unavoidable absence, but that he had Mr. Harkness' full support and encouragement of the ethical culture development effort. He then requested a formal bid from OEA within a ten day period.

The OEA partners agreed to submit an ethics consulting/training proposal within the time frame and requested any non-proprietary information relating to recent organizational development efforts pursued by CMC. The OEA partners wanted to avoid duplication of prior services and have access to valid organizational diagnosis data that would either confirm or disconfirm the client's self-diagnosis of ethical needs. The ethical issue faced here was the professional consulting obligation to listen carefully to a client's expressed need but also to suspend judgment about the deeper, multiple causes for bringing in an external consultant firm, until other diagnostic data could be examined.

Fortunately, CMC had recently contracted with Numerof and Associates in St. Louis to conduct an Organizational Practices Survey. The CMC representatives provided OEA with a copy of the survey results, as they had other vendors. The survey results were statistically reliable and the validated instruments categorized results into eleven dimensions of managerial practice: clarity, autonomy, performance emphasis, participation, feedback, reinforcement, team building, work facilitation, time emphasis, interpersonal relations and innovation. With the survey report in hand, the OEA partners left the client premises and began the proposal writing process.

Ten days later, OEA submitted a competitive proposal. In preparing the proposal, they had analyzed the Organizational Practices Survey Report, historical CMC documents and CMC human resource department policies and procedures. Learning the culture, after all, is part of the professional ethical commitment that a responsible external consultant firm must do, so that the submitted proposal is not superimposed on but integrated into the client culture. The OEA partners were satisfied that the survey report, once fully analyzed from an ethical rather than solely a managerial perspective, provided an adequate recent diagnosis of the value climate of CMC, given the client budgetary constraints.

The stated goals in the OEA proposal, therefore, focused on three tasks: (1) to provide CMC management and employees with a CMC Ethics Handbook that provides a clear statement of the policies and practices that should govern moral conduct and decision-making at CMC; (2) to provide legal and ethical training in responsible ethical conflict resolution and compliance enforcement procedures; and (3) to facilitate participatory involvement of the CMC stakeholders in the creation and implementation of an ethics development system that supports and complements the existing caring, value-driven CMC culture. Part of the proposal was to dovetail the ethical dimension of the proposed ethics intervention with another organizational development effort focused on commitment to caring. The latter effort used the following mnemonic device to emphasize the managerial dimensions of caring: C=Customer-Focused; A=Accountable; R=Responsive + Simple Systems; I=Innovative; N=Necessity For Change and G=Goal of Continuous Quality Improvement. The OEA partners supplemented this mnemonic device with one of their own which emphasized the ethical dimension of caring: C=Concern for Multiple Stakeholder Needs; A=Accountable At All Levels; R=Responsive to Patient/-Staff Feedback; I=Incentives and Rewards for Excellence; N=Networking for Communication and Cooperation, and G=Goal of Ongoing Development of CMC's Caring Culture.

The managerial perspective tends to emphasize the instrumental use of resources to achieve organizational objectives whereas the ethical perspective also emphasizes the intrinsic value of people that develop organizational integrity while adding value to multiple stakeholders.

Desired Organizational Future

Three weeks after the proposal submission deadline, OEA was notified that it had the winning bid. A meeting was arranged within two days between the OEA partners and an expanded group of the CMC senior management team – James Pruitt, Gerri Dalrymple, Dennis Dietz, Director of Human Resources, and Karen Borgert, Employee Relations Director. The approach adopted by OEA was a two-tiered group involvement process; the first input on the desired organizational future would be from the four-member senior management team and the second input would be from a 23-member Ethics Advisory Committee. The latter team would be composed of medical staff, employees and volunteer representatives from each major department, all members of the existing CMC Grievance Committee and all members of the CMC Human Resources Advisory Committee. By using a mix of representatives from existing committees and at-large volunteers, OEA wanted to ensure widespread involvement while keeping the actual advisory committee to a manageable size.

At the first senior management meeting, the human resource professionals were briefed on the progress to date. The OEA partners reassured the human resource professionals that the ethics initiatives would mesh with their past, current and future human resource policies and organizational development initiatives. On the other hand, the OEA partners indicated that if the ethics development system were to be implemented at CMC, the human resource functional responsibilities would likely have to be enlarged to handle the duties of an Organizational Ethics Officer, including additional training in the collection of reported ethics violations, preliminary screening of ethics grievances, establishing communication channels to facilitate employee preventive and remedial voice systems, and specialized training in ethical conflict resolution. The burden of additional human resource responsibilities would be balanced by the opportunity for the human resource department to have a strategic role in organizational development.

Next, OEA negotiated a proposed timeline for all services and completion deadlines for specific consultancy tasks. The original proposed timeline to fulfill the contract terms was six months; the actual time turned out to be nearly one year. The rate of implementation of the designed interventions was ultimately determined by the participative process and the accustomed scheduling pace of the client culture. Respecting the pace of the CMC culture while sustaining the momentum for ethical culture enhancement demanded patience, perseverance, vigilance to capitalize on breakthroughs, honesty in confronting resistance, logical rigor to dispel confusion, sensitivity to employee apprehensions and good humor to relieve tensions during heated exchanges (Murphy, 1993; Solomon, 1992).

After the timeline was established, the OEA partners requested the following: (1) a memorandum from Mr. Pruitt to all senior management team members, all managers and all supervisors announcing that the sixth strategic initiative of organizational culture development was being met in part by the development of a CMC Ethics Handbook and requesting their referral support for names of employees who would constructively contribute to the newly-forming Ethics Advisory Committee; (2) a public announcement in the CMC newsletter, The Centerline, soliciting volunteer participation in the Ethics Advisory Committee with a clear indication that a minimum commitment of 18 hours over a three month period would be required to complete the Ethics Handbook; and (3) a CMC representative close to the CEO, such as Gerri Dalrymple, collect all committee nominations and coordinate the formation of the Ethics Advisory Committee with the consultation of the senior management team.

The first two meetings of the Ethics Advisory Committee took place on May 19 and June 2; each meeting lasted 3 hours and was characterized by energetic concern and active dialogue even though there was an underlying apprehension about the efficacy of their efforts. It was clear to the OEA partners that this forum for expressing concern about the CMC work environment produced a fundamental change in the attitude of the participants. The dynamics of the Ethics Advisory Committee shifted form the articulation of work value frustrations into a concrete, positive desired vision of their organizational future.

At the first meeting, James Pruitt announced the purpose and importance of the committee's work, as well as, senior management's willingness to endorse the outcome of the committee's deliberations in the form of an Ethics Handbook. Shortly after this announcement, he left the meeting to preclude any perceived manipulation from senior management and to encourage uninhibited openness in the committee's deliberations.

The chief ethical issue addressed during this phase of the intervention by the OEA partners was their professional commitment to design an interactive structure for the ethical development and empowerment of the CMC culture from the bottom up rather than from the top down. The vision of the desired organizational ethical future required multiple stakeholder inputs to insure effective implementation at a later date (Petrick and Wagley, 1992).

The inputs from the two-tiered system generated consensus on two important dimensions of the desired CMC organizational culture: the prioritization of key stakeholders in the CMC mission and the commitment to four prioritized ethical principles as foundational for the development and justification of all CMC policies. The CMC stakeholders were prioritized in the following manner: the primary stakeholders were patients and their families; the secondary stakeholders were staff, volunteers, medical school officials and health foundation institutions; and the tertiary stakeholders were government, third-party payers, community support groups, competitors, suppliers and the broader social/national environment. The four prioritized ethical principles for CMC were: (1) Principle of Justice/Fairness, in which CMC promises to make every attempt to reward individuals/groups on the basis of their contributions, distributing benefits and costs fairly; (2) Principle of Dignity, in which CMC promises to make every attempt to respect the uniqueness, interests and rights of each person/group; (3) Principle of Liberty, in which CMC promises to make every attempt to help all individuals/group make responsible choices that are free and informed; and (4) Principle of Fiscal Responsibility, in which CMC makes every attempt to economically balance the benefits and costs of quality service and professional performance within the limits of its financial resources.

Implementation of Change

With client needs assessed and desired organizational futures outlined, the implementation of endorsed developmental change was the next order of business for the OEA partners. The major tasks contractually agreed to by OEA was the participatory design and implementation of an ethics development system with two prominent outcomes – the CMC Ethics Handbook and the CMC Ethics Advisory Committee Ethics Training.

The OEA partners decided to utilize the CMC Ethics Advisory Committee as the organizational fulcrum for completing its tasks. Their intervention style included emotional inputs to relieve tension and encourage commitment, directional inputs to coherently probe and guide committee deliberations in uncharted moral waters and knowledge inputs to theoretically explain, experientially compare and insightfully resolve ethical dilemmas.

As the deliberations of the committee ensued over the months, a noticeable shift occurred. The shift was from a centralized, static vision of the current hierarchic CMC culture to a decentralized, emerging set of voices committed to the dynamic perpetuation of the genuine CMC caring culture. The predominantly female workforce at CMC began to "speak up for" the network of relationships and processes that would protect, transmit and perpetuate CMC's caring culture for all its employees. Just as the historical success of CMC was rooted in the combined efforts and dialogue between female philanthropists and male medical staff and administrators, so also in the 1990's the intra-organizational exchange of expectations between a predominantly female workforce and a predominantly male administration provided the symbiosis for organizational renewal.

The committee eventually arrived at ten components of an ethics development system that would enhance CMC's trusting, mutually supportive caring culture. First, senior management and board of trustees' endorsements of the commitment to organizational ethical development in word and deed were crucial (Goodpaster, 1991). Second, the use of the CMC Ethics Handbook to provide practical guidelines for appropriate conduct by CMC employees and volunteers was essential. Third, the creation of the CMC Ethics Coordinator position to accept reports of unethical conduct and authorized to investigate, analyze and resolve ethical conflicts would operationally anchor the system. Fourth, the continuation of the Ethics Advisory Committee to provide centralization, oversight and policy update services was necessary to sustain coherent and continuous ethical culture improvement at CMC. Fifth, widespread ethics training to empower all CMC employees and volunteers, supervisors and non-supervisors, is necessary to handle value conflicts in a non-punitive, non-retaliatory, professional manner. Sixth, the development of an ethics voice system at CMC is desirable to expand communication channels to raise ethical issues, reinforce the importance and legitimacy of ethical discourse, and provide constructive moral feedback that ensured accountability at all organizational levels for relying on principled justifications of decisions in line with prioritized stakeholder commitments. Seventh, the CMC Ethics Coordinator Office needed to design and distribute appropriate procedures for confidential or anonymous reporting of ethics violations after the fact and soliciting advice before the fact. Eighth, provisions for swift and fair resolution of ethical conflicts and enforcement of behavioral compliance through due process procedures are necessary to ensure that everyone at CMC is aware that organizational justice standards are uniformly upheld. Ninth, ethical factors are to be considered in recruitment procedures, performance appraisals, and reward systems to identify and commend those who have a constructive ethical impact on the CMC caring culture. Tenth, the use of an ethics audit is advisable to monitor congruence of organizational ethical practices with the CMC developmental goals, and if necessary, to bring organizational ethical conduct in line with acceptable CMC standards.

The CMC Ethics Handbook supplemented the CMC Employee Handbook by clarifying the day-to-day relationship between general policy standards and specific employee practices. The guidelines for specific practices were placed in a question-and-answer format to guarantee easy accessibility for everyone. In addition, the Ethics Handbook outlined the ethics development system for all current employees and new recruits, "spelled out" ethics reporting procedures, provided a compact, structured checklist of ten questions that empowered all CMC stakeholders to assume more responsibility in professionally analyzing and resolving ethical disputes and included a glossary of easy-to-understand definitions of ethical terms.

The CMC ethics training by the OEA partners provided the analytic tools to professionally resolve ethical dilemmas along with experiential practice sessions requiring the application of reasoning skills to work conflicts frequently encountered at CMC (Petrick, Wagley and Von der Embse, 1991). The CMC Ethics Advisory Committee was exposed to developmental models of individual and organizational moral development along with practical transition steps from one stage to another (Petrick and Wagley, 1992). The ethical problems they analyzed dealt with both internal and external stakeholder concerns. The ethics training approach de-emphasized control through compliance enforcement and instead focused on culture development through competence, commendation, accountability and commitment. By providing a train-the-trainers session, the OEA partners were fostering greater CMC ethics self-sufficiency. OEA further offered Certificates of Ethics Training Completion to symbolically recognize those who had invested so much of their time and so much of themselves in building a better work environment.

Evaluation of Intervention Impact and Organizational Change

In evaluating the OEA intervention impact and the resultant CMC organizational change, it is necessary to focus on the contracted outcomes and the intervention processes utilized. The tasks of designing and implementing an ethics development system, with an Ethics Handbook and Ethics Training as key ingredients, were completed through the ongoing, interactive exchange in the CMC Ethics Advisory Committee. The result was that after one year CMC had evolved a 10 point ethics development system, created an Ethics Handbook and had key representatives go through a systematic ethics training workshop. The specific terms of the original consulting contract had been met. In the process, ethical concerns were voiced, divisional barriers were overcome, employees developed more competence and confidence in resolving ethical disputes, employees shouldered more responsibility for shaping their work culture, and there was a widespread organizational momentum to sustain the short term benefits of daily contributions to the ethics development system.

The long range impact of the intervention will be an ongoing one and will be determined over time by the degree of sustained enactment and refinement of the ethics development system.

The reported and witnessed outcomes attest to the promise of sustainable future development built on a strong organizational ethics foundation provided by OEA.

The quantitative measurement instruments to detect and document improvement in the ethical climate at CMC include the Ethics Audit, which was provided by the OEA partners, and the readministration of the Organizational Practices Survey to compare the benchmark results obtained in 1990 with those to be achieved in 1993. The proposed quantitative measurement instruments are scheduled for use in 1993.

Until they are administered, there are no quantitative measures of macrochange in the CMC culture. However, measurement systems for microchange after the ethics training indicated both high client satisfaction with ethics training sessions and demonstrated increase in content learned through pre- and post-test measures. Actual on-the-job behavioral changes or scientific control group comparisons were not employed due to client budgetary constraints.

Qualitative measurement of the Ethics Handbook development indicates extensive pride of community authorship, support for its integration with other CMC initiatives and anticipation of its widespread use at CMC in the near future. Qualitative feedback on the effectiveness of the emotional, directional and knowledge inputs from the intervention style of OEA partners has been uniformly positive. Having competent external ethics consultants validate work feelings, constructively channel energies and bring insight and structure to unspoken, amorphous moral sensitivities in the workplace adds value to the quality of the work life for CMC employees and volunteers and adds value to the quality of work for CMC administrators and external customers.

Implications

There are at least four implications that flow from this study. First, the lessons learned by the OEA intervention in the CMC culture can benefit domestic and international children's medical centers. The unique caring culture of a children's medical center can be enhanced by an ethics development system that includes an ethics handbook and ethics training. The staff and volunteers at a domestic or international children's medical center often exhibit exceptional caregiving behavior to patients and their families and they need a commensurate level of institutionalized organizational justice and mutual, respectful regard among themselves to avoid emotional burnout and moral exhaustion (Sheppard, Lewicki and Minton, 1992).

Second, health care organizations and consultancy providers in the European context need to be sensitive to the expanding and escalating quality standards for products and services under the ISO 9000 series. The European Union (EU) has adopted the ISO 9000 series as their preferred quality standards. The current 12-member European Union consists of: Belgium, Denmark, France, Germany, Greece, Ireland, Italy, Luxembourg, the Netherlands, Portugal, Spain and the United Kingdom. In addition, the ISO 9000 series has been adopted by the European Free Trade Association (EFTA) countries, which are seeking to ally themselves economically with the EU. These countries include Austria, Finland, Iceland, Liechtenstein, Norway, Sweden and Switzerland. The development of quality work cultures to meet European ISO 9000 standards in health care products and services will ultimately require organizational ethical cultures that drive fear out of the workplace and institutionalize support for collaborative teamwork based on mutual trust and respect – not fear of medical autocracy.

Third, purchasers of ethics consulting services need to be aware of the benefits of comprehensive, systemic organizational ethics services and to be wary of "quick-fix artists," who want to cut costs by getting rid of the "bad apples" in the workplace. Quite frequently "good apples" can become "bad apples" because they are in a "bad barrel," so apples and barrels both need to be examined. A competent managerial ethics consulting service needs to address both individual and organizational ethical concerns using something akin to the four-phase consulting model employed by OEA.

Fourth, other managerial ethics consultants can realize that even though children's medical centers are a fertile ground for moral sensibilities for patients and families, there is a strong need for voice and/or ethics development systems that treat caregivers with justice and dignity. Voice and/or ethics development systems enhance the sense of organizational community, assure employees of fair treatment, provide a context in which unfair treatment can be appealed, channel informal organizational dissent into acceptable forms, sustain employee loyalty and commitment, improve organizational performance effectiveness and reinforce individual dignity at work (Ewing, 1989).

Summary

The authors have used their detailed treatment of an organizational ethics consulting case dealing with a children's medical center in a developed country to illustrate generic phases of professional ethics consulting interventions and to demonstrate the benefits of sound ethics consulting to a wide range of stakeholders.

References

Association for the Care of Children's Health 1992: *Caring for Children-Families: Guidelines for Hospitals*. Bethesda, MD: Association for the Care of Children's Health.

Block, Peter 1981: *A Guide To Flawless Consulting*. LaJolla, CA: University Associates.

Brockman, Susan A. (ed) 1992: *The History of The Children's Medical Center*. Dayton, OH: Central Printing.

Ewing, D.J. 1989: *Justice On The Job*. Cambridge, MA: Harvard University Press.

Goodpaster, K.E. 1991: Ethical imperatives and corporate leadership. In R. Edward Freeman (ed), *Business Ethics: The State of the Art*, NY: Oxford University Press.

Greiner, L. and R. Metzger 1983: *Consulting To Management*. Englewood Cliffs, NJ: Prentice-Hall.

Hoffman, W. Michael and Ed Petry, Jr. 1989: *The Ethics of Organizational Transformation*. NY: Quorum Publications.

Knafl, K. A. and K. Cavalleri 1988: *Pediatric Hospitalization: Family and Nurse Perspectives*. Philadelphia, PA: Lippincott Press.

Murphy, Kevin R. 1993: *Honesty in the Workplace*. Belmont, CA: Wadsworth Publishers.

Petrick, Joseph A. and Robert A. Wagley 1992: Enhancing responsible strategic management in organizations. *Journal of Management Development*, 11, 57-72.

Petrick, J., W. Claunch and R. Scherer 1991: *Institutionalizing Organizational Ethics Programs: Contemporary Perspectives.* Dayton, OH: Wright State University College of Business.

Petrick, J., R. Wagley and T. Von der Embse 1991: Structured ethical decision making and the prospect of managerial success. *SAM Advanced Management Journal,* 56, 72-78.

Petrick, Joseph A. and George E. Manning 1990: Developing an ethical climate for excellence. *The Journal for Quality and Participation,* 14, 84-90.

Quinn, John F. and J.M.B. Crawford 1991: *The Foundations of Criminal Responsibility.* NY: Mellon Press.

Sheppard, B., R. Lewicki and J. Minton 1992: *Organizational Justice.* NY: Lexington Books.

Solomon, Robert C. 1992: *Ethics and Excellence.* NY: Oxford University Press.

13

Consultants' Roles and Responsibilities: Lessons From Public Relations in Germany

Horst Steinmann, Ansgar Zerfaß and Rupert Ahrens

Introduction

Throughout the industrialized world, media exposure, grassroots activism and consumerism bring about new challenges for corporate communications. Managers and researchers have to realize that "reasoning will from now on belong to the basic requirements of self-assertion on the market, too" (Beck, 1986: 356). As a consequence, the demand for professional consultancy is growing faster than ever. In Germany, the gross income earned by consulting firms specializing in public relations almost doubled from 109.5 Million DM in 1988 up to 190.5 Million DM in 1992.

In this contribution, we take a close look at the two-fold relationship between ethics and public relations consultancy. We will start with a few reflections on corporate ethics, outlining how dialogic approaches to public relations contribute to the social performance of business. Dialogic communication, as it is understood here, is as opposed to the traditional concept of asymmetrical one-way communication. It relies on symmetrical concepts to foster an open dialogue between corporations and their publics. This new approach obviously brings about new ethical demands for public relations consultants. We will draw on role theory and a short case study to discuss the most important roles in communication consultancy and try to identify the ethical dilemmas associated with these roles. Later we indicate some implications for the practice of consultancy. Following the philosophy of the European Business Ethics Network, the whole article brings together professional experiences with recent developments in public relations theory.

A General Concept of Corporate Ethics

The framework depicted in figure 1 tries to summarize the "republican approach" to corporate behavior. This concept has been explained elsewhere in more detail (Löhr, 1991; Steinmann/Löhr, 1994). Our framework incorporates what one may call a republican view of the entrepreneurial role in a market economy as opposed

163

H. von Weltzien Hoivik and A. Føllesdal (eds.), Ethics and Consultancy: European Perspectives, 163-177.
© 1995 *Kluwer Academic Publishers. Printed in the Netherlands.*

to the traditional liberal view. In the republican view the modern corporation – though organized by law as a private economic actor – is understood as nevertheless remaining responsible for the public interest (Steinmann/Zerfaß, 1993b). This responsibility is a specific one which holds the corporation being responsible for the corporate strategy not to cause severe social conflicts. Positively spoken: The corporation is responsible for its strategy contributing to social peace. Peace is regarded here as the highest social value, meaning not merely "absentia belli" – but the free consensus based on rational reasoning, as opposed to the use of power in resolving conflicts (Lorenzen, 1987: 228).

Peace in this sense incorporates, of course, by definition the freedom of speech. Obviously this view owes much to the German tradition of communicative ethics as worked out by Habermas (1990), Apel (1988) and Lorenzen (1982). It is our assertion that by starting from this philosophical basis, from the regulative idea of peace, it is possible to gain a new understanding of the role of the corporation. Moreover, this epistemological approach offers a sound foundation to the theory and practice of public relations (Pearson, 1989) and business ethics (Löhr, 1991). As a consequence, the republican concept of corporate ethics draws on communicative ethics in contrast to utilitarian, rights or justice approaches.

FIGURE 1. Two Levels of Legitimation in a Market Economy

Objectives / Legitimation level	Peace as free consensus	
	Peaceful coordination of economic action via	
	Economic efficiency	Social acceptability
(1) Politics (Law)	I. Rules to constitute freedom to act in a market economy	II. Rules to settle structural conflicts of the market economy (e.g.. co-determination)
	System Ethics	
(2) Corporation	III. Develop successful strategies (product-market strategies)	IV. Ensure the legitimacy of chosen strategies with stakeholders via a) corporate dialogue b) stimulating collective or political action
	Corporate Strategy	*Corporate Ethics*

Along these lines, our framework is able to show how dialogic communication makes sense within the notion of corporate strategy and a market economy. The corporation is held responsible for contributions to social peace by seeking legitimacy of its strategies in two ways (figure 1, box IV):

1 First by initiating "corporate dialogues" (Steinmann/Zerfaß, 1993a) in case of severe (potential or actual) conflicts, meaning a lack of trust in its corporate strategy. Following this approach, corporations try to solve problems on the spot by submitting themselves to moral rules defined in an open dialogue with relevant stakeholders. Public relations experts are called in to facilitate those dialogues using the symmetrical approaches mentioned above.

2 Second, corporations may stimulate collective or legal action on a higher (industrial or political) level. This strategy has been named "ethical displacement" (DeGeorge, 1990). It is required if the corporation's problem-solving potential is insufficient and public interest requires action on a broader scale, e.g. for a whole branch of business.

These two aspects constitute the core of what one may call "corporate ethics", in contrast to system ethics and individual ethics (Enderle, 1993).

Our argument basically rests on two central points, which at the same time constitute the difference between the republican and the liberal view of the corporation. The first point relates to the corporation's freedom to act (box I). If peace is regarded as the ultimate goal of any society, then freedom "to" act in a market economy is established as an institution to stimulate efficient allocation of resources. From this perspective, freedom to act and efficiency are means to achieve social peace. As we know from the empirical evidence of the former communist states, a decentralized market economy is able to master resource allocation far more efficiently than a planned economy. This understanding of freedom is different from the prevailing liberal understanding of freedom, regarded as the ultimate end of the state, meaning freedom "from" political suppression. In contrast to this negative notion, our concept is compatible with the idea that the republican state establishes both free competition and all the laws which are necessary to handle structural conflicts. Those conflicts are due to the limitations of the market mechanism and well known in advance. For instance, co-determination law in Germany tries to settle conflicts between capital and labor in a peaceful way (box II). System ethics thus deals with all rules constituting the freedom to act and provisions for solving structural conflicts in a market economy.

The second point is that not only the legislator but all economic actors, including the corporation – though they are principally free to act according to the rules of the law – remain responsible for the ultimate end of society, for peace. The reason is, of course, that neither market nor law, nor both of those institutions established at the political level, can guarantee a peaceful coordination of economic action for themselves. In this respect, many lessons can be learned from the theory of market failures. Moreover, we all know about the limited capacity of law. There always will come up new conflicts which are not yet covered by law (Stone, 1975)

It is here that corporate ethics as an "ethics of peace" is required to support state and society in its goal of creating a peaceful life. Corporations themselves must try to find rules which are adequate to solve conflicts caused by their strategy and the profit motive. The well-known case of Nestlé is a good example for this idea of corporate ethics (Löhr, 1991). Of course, this way of resolving conflicts on the corporate level may be jeopardized by the need to survive in a competitive environment. In this case, joint actions by industrial associations or legislative efforts are required to overcome the situation of a prisoner's dilemma.

It is in this conceptual context of corporate ethics, in which we integrate our understanding of the twofold role of the corporation and hence of public relations consultancy:

1 The economic role of the corporation is to develop successful strategies in order to make profits.
2 But, at the same time, the corporation must take on the responsibility to contribute to social peace, if those strategies or the means of getting things done are questioned with good reasons by one ore more stakeholders. In this case, the corporation is asked to set up moral rules in an open dialogue with everybody who is affected by corporate strategies or to stimulate collective or legal action on a higher level.

In the following, we will try to link this conceptual framework of an efficient and responsible entrepreneur to the various roles of consultants working in the field of public relations.

The Context of Public Relations Consultancy

What are the specific aspects of communication consultancy? A public relations expert tries to manage the process of communication between a client (corporation) and various publics (stakeholders). In doing so, any consultant takes on completely different roles.

Role theory defines "role" as a bundle of general behavior expectations. These expectations are communicated to a certain social position or its occupant (Katz/ Kahn, 1987: 185, Culbertson, 1991). The interactive process depicted in figure 2 shows how these expectations are communicated to the role receiver and how they are modified by actual role behavior.

Of course, role expectations are communicated by various senders. These persons or groups may have contradicting expectations, and their expectations may change during the course of a consulting process. Along these lines, a communication consultant has to comply with different behavior expectations, too. We may draw on the theoretical considerations of Broom and Smith (1979) and a corresponding stream of empirical research in the United States to explain different roles in public relations (Dozier, 1992). Moreover, we will refer to an actual case from the last-named authors' experience in communication consultancy.

In fact, we are talking about the development and implementation of a communi-

FIGURE 2. Model of a Role Episode. (Katz/Kahn 1978;196)

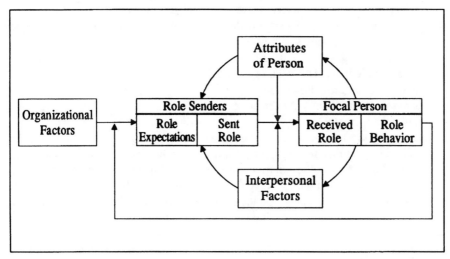

Reproduced from Katz, D. and Kahn, R. L., *The Social Psychology of Organizations*, 2nd edition, Copyright © 1978 Wiley.

cation campaign for an energy supplier in the Southwest of Germany (Ahrens/Hütt, 1993; Steinmann/Zerfaß, 1993a). The Energie-Versorgung Schwaben was faced with the problem that public acceptance had been decreasing constantly for years. A general trend towards a stronger awareness for ecological questions and the increasing popularization of alternative power supply concepts established this trend. The declining acceptance was even verified in several surveys. As far as the citizens of the supply district were concerned, the burdens caused by the production and distribution of electricity shaped the company's image. The benefits and particularly the underlying connection between these burdens and individual consumption were not seen. For some years, the energy supplier had promoted energy thrift campaigns in order to show that it was prepared to work on these problems. Nevertheless, the predominant opinion among its publics was that the company was only interested in selling electricity and not in environmental protection. Consequently, the basis for long-term investments was in serious danger and a peacefully realization of corporate strategies put in jeopardy.

Under these circumstances, a communication counseling firm was asked for advice. Its consultants took on completely different roles in the course of the following cooperation with this major client:

1 Consultants enacting the role of a *communication technician* were expected to place communicative and journalistic capabilities at the client's disposal. They should put public relations campaigns into practice and convey messages to various publics. In the case at hand, it was necessary to develop and realize a

touring exhibition and a computer-controlled information system. Moreover, technical experts were asked to produce a video film about the new campaign.

2 A communication manager, on the other hand, is expected to provide the client with comprehensive advice for planning, realization and control of public relations policies. Furthermore, this should entail the use of scientific research methods. This role, of course, was of predominant importance in the campaign we are talking about. It was even possible to identify every single sub-role delineated by American research (Broom/Dozier, 1986; Grunig/Hunt 1984; Dozier, 1992):

2a Enacting the role of an *expert prescriber*, the consultant should take on the sole responsibility for problem definition as well as for the development and implementation of the solution. In the case at hand, the consultants were initially confronted with this type of role expectation often found in crisis situations. Joint discussions with the client, however, soon led to the result that a communication expert working alone would not be able to solve the conflicts in the long run. Of course, this role may be gratifying to the consultant and reassuring to the client, but the main drawback, from the client's point of view, is the danger of dependent relationships. In addition to this, a communication campaign will not be credible if the client's organization did not participate in its development.

2b A second sub-role has been named *problem-solving process facilitator*. Here the consultant is expected to ensure that all members of the client organization participate in tackling communicative weak points and problems. Therefore, this important role may be characterized as a kind of "communication coaching." This kind of coaching was done in the case at hand, too. First, the consultants tried to support the client in order to identify the roots of his communication problem. They were forced to realize that press releases until then had been particularly dominated by an overly technocratic corporate culture. In doing this kind of public relations, the energy supplier was not able to influence its critics, whose argumentation based on completely different categories. Furthermore, the client could not succeed in public debate and provide a clear impression of the various interests and their factual and moral dimensions. In other words, the company and its critics simply weren't communicating with each other. How did the consultants facilitate a solution to this problem? The declared goal of the new communication campaign, which had been designed in joint discussions with the client's staff, was to establish a mutual communication with the critics. This was to enable real discussions to be carried out, instead of pseudo-battles in the media. The consultants were eager to ensure a long-term acceptance for the strategic decisions which had been made in the past and, of course, which possibly required modification in the future. In other words: The consultants tried to help the energy supplier leading corporate dialogues with its critics – the primary way to take responsibility at the corporate level.

2c During the realization of this campaign, some consultants took on the role of *communication facilitators*. Above all, they were concerned with creating a platform for communication between the energy supplier and its stakeholders. In the simplest case, consultants acting as *liaisons* tried to create opportunities for such a communication to take place. They had to identify potential, but not yet active claimants and set up contact with the leaders of opinion in already known stakeholder groups. In other phases of the consulting process, consultants were active as *interpreters*. This, for instance, involved backing up top management by analyzing the topic of "energy consumption" within the public agenda. Furthermore, corporate statements full of managerial and technical terminology had to be translated into the language of the media and citizen groups. Finally, some consultants would even take on the most sophisticated role of a *moderator* or *mediator* in some situations. In the role of a mainly neutral third party, they were in a position to set up direct communication between company representatives and critics. A number of meetings with citizens and representatives of local stakeholders in various towns of the supply district were arranged. At these meetings, the consultants tried to push towards a joint solution of the questions at hand through an appropriate arrangement of procedures.[1] Consequently, it was necessary to use appropriate moderation techniques in order to remove emotions from the discussion and ensure the clearest possible explanation of involvement.

The variety of roles described above is one of the most important aspects of public relations practice. Nevertheless, not all of these roles come into play in the course of each consulting process. Role enactment may be restricted by contingent environmental constellations and alternative assumptions about the purpose and effects of public relations (Grunig/White, 1992). These presuppositions are part of public relations paradigms which can be identified at the roots of any communication campaign. Traditionally, public relations has been thought of as a pure social technology for the creation of images in the media. A broader paradigm, on the other hand, will also cast a glance at processes of direct communication, aiming at true understanding with relevant stakeholders.

According to the traditional paradigm, a company uses persuasive messages in order to make the attitudes and behavior of target publics compatible with organizational goals. The epistemologic roots of this conceptual framework, which has only recently been elaborated by prominent German communication researchers, may be found within autopoietic systems theory (Ronneberger/Rühl, 1992; Merten, 1993).[2] In practice, this approach results in neglecting one of the most promising ways of conceptualizing and practicing communication management (Zerfaß/Scherer, 1993). Following the persuasive paradigm, practitioners will only take into account the first three of four situative models depicted in figure 3, which Grunig et al. have identified and empirically verified as relevant guidelines for the practice of public relations (Grunig/Hunt, 1984; Grunig/Grunig, 1992).

FIGURE 3. Roles and Models of Public Relations

PR - Client				
Underlying PR - Paradigm	Persuasive Public Relations oriented to success			+ Public Relations oriented to reaching understanding
Applied PR - Models	Press Agentry Model	Public Information Model	Two-Way Asym- metrical Model	Two-Way Sym- metrical Model
Purpose	Influencing publics	Influencing publics	Gaining compliance	Solving mutual problems
Means	Media publicity	Dissemination of information	Scientific persuasion	Non-persuasive communication
Potential Consultant's Roles	Communication technician			
	Expert prescriber			
	Problem-solving process facilitator			
			Liasion	
			Interpreter	
				Mediator
PR - Consultant				

The predominant model in practice, the press agentry model, is concerned primarily with obtaining a good press in the mass media. This may be attained, for instance, by staging high-publicity "pseudo-events". Supporters of the public information model, on the other hand, are used to "disseminate relatively objective information through the mass media and controlled media such as newsletters, brochures and direct mail" (Grunig, 1992: 18). In the foreground, there remains a one-sided flow of communications from the organization to its publics. This changes with the two-way asymmetrical model. In this case, an organization tries to compete in the "market of opinions" with messages developed to persuade strategic publics. The coordination of diverging interests should be achieved, therefore, through the interlacing of egocentric attempts to persuade each other.

Following a broader paradigm, the organization acts on the assumption that, under certain circumstances, a direct dialogue with internal and external publics will be necessary. This seems to be especially true for the communications with (ecological) activist groups, which may have their own specialized communications networks and newsletters (Anderson, 1992). Conducting a direct dialogue was also the rational procedure in the case at hand, which aimed at a consent about actual corporate strategies and those to come. This calls for public relations oriented towards mutual understanding, which goes beyond a mere exchange of information. It should, for instance, enable a critical questioning of self-representation and interpersonal or interorganizational relationships, too. The theoretical foundation of this paradigm draws upon the "Theory of Communicative Action" by Habermas (1984) (Burkart/Probst, 1991; Zerfaß/Scherer, 1993). All in all, this corresponds with the two-way symmetrical model by Grunig et al., which is concerned about achieving true understanding (in the sense of a cooperative process of interpretation). This in turn allows for a "coordination among the goal-directed actions of different parties" (Habermas, 1984: 101). Public relations following this model will often neglect mass media activities and turn towards interpersonal communication; the latter may be promoted by mediators.

Figure 3 shows the analytical correlation [3], which originates from coupling the predominant paradigms and the appropriate models with the roles described above. The skilled services of the communication technician are mainly required for the press agentry and public information models. As was shown by our case study, rhetoric and journalistic know-how are also required in the course of managing a two-way campaign and communicating its results to a wider range of publics through the media. Another look at the sub-roles will help us to analyze the potential activities of a communications manager: A problem-solving process facilitator can support both the choice of an appropriate model and the development of actual policies based on one of the models, irrespective of the underlying paradigm. The prescribing expert can be commissioned with the planning and realization of one-way and asymmetrical campaigns. On the other hand, the "expert" is not able to carry out a substantial dialogue with critical publics for the client. However, there is no need to create such a platform for bilateral communications in the one-way models. Accordingly, a consultant will then above all take on the role of a communication facilitator to stimulate two-way communications between the client and stakeholders as liaison or interpreter. Furthermore, acting as a credible mediator or neutral third party requires a symmetrical communications campaign, which aims at agreements based on rationally motivated consent.

Ethical Dilemmas in Public Relations Consultancy

In a next step, we look at the most important ethical dilemmas in the daily work of communications consultants. Our key argument is that the particular ethical challenge for public relations consultants results from their ambiguity of roles. The consultant has to enact completely different roles and comply with differing ethical demands arising from each of these roles. Therefore, predominant ethical problems in public relations consultancy may be identified by a more detailed analysis of role theory.

Role theory conceptualizes conflicting interests as role conflicts (Katz/Kahn 1978: 204). Different interests of various parties may result in contradictory expectations of what the role occupant should do or should not do. We can make a difference between three types of role conflicts:

1   *Inter-role conflicts* are caused because one person always has to take on several roles in various fields of life. To name but one example: A communications expert who works for a consulting firm and who is an active member of the anti-smoking movement, may be asked to carry out a campaign for the tobacco industry. Under these circumstances, corporate ethics demand that the counseling firm's top management first of all should try to foster ethical reasoning within its own organization. For this purpose, structural efforts such as ethics officers or corporate ethics committees are dysfunctional from a practical point of view. They imply a delegation of responsibility which would not be appropriate to the consultant's far-reaching autonomy of action. A better step, however, would be to establish a participative corporate culture which is responsive to criticism. Such a kind of culture could, at the same time, also promote the creativity which is indispensable within public relations consultancy. In order to make those organizational efforts effective on the individual level, personnel management should try to develop moral judgement and argumentative competence. These steps should provide an identification with the client's goals (Bartholomew, 1992) and, as a consequence, enable the consultant to act in a credible and successful manner outwardly, too.

2   *Intra-sender conflicts* are caused because the expectations communicated by one sender, usually the client, are unclear and contradictory. [4] The communication consultant is, of course, supposed to avoid conflicts with the client's interests in carrying out activities. This means, first of all, that performance must be reconcilable with the negotiated roles. The practitioner should also be prepared to refuse unsuitable role expectations. If, for example, experience shows that asymmetrical public relations are not suitable to set up sound contact with local activist groups, a reformulation of the commission can be claimed or the commission even refused. This would prevent a social conflict from escalating and, in the end, not only serve the client's interests but also contribute to social peace as discussed above.

3   An *inter-sender conflict*, on the other hand, can be attributed to the incompatibility of expectations expressed by different parties. This kind of conflict depicts the fact that consultants or counseling firms are very often faced with differing perceptions from their clients and those affected by the recommended campaigns (figure 4). For example, a corporation may ask a consultant to facilitate an open flow of information with regional newspapers. Journalist counterparts, however, may draw on past experiences and assume that communications experts only distribute propaganda in favor of their clients. Therefore, they may turn down any offer of a dialogue without further consideration.

In the case of inter-sender conflicts, to whom should consultants be obliged? On

FIGURE 4. Inter-Sender Role Conflicts in Public Relations Consultancy

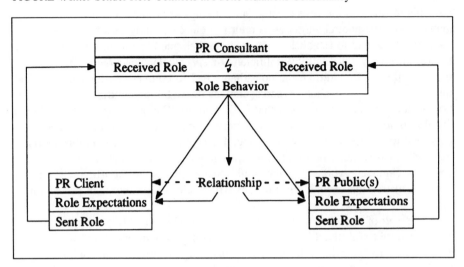

one hand, they could remain loyal to the expectations of their client. On the other hand, one could argue that they should take into account the interests of the various publics as well.

Law pleads quite clearly in favor of a unilateral representation of the client's interests, because there is only a contractual relationship with the client. However, both the theoretical framework and our case study showed that this may be insufficient to reconcile diverging interests and expectations. At this point, additional ethical efforts are necessary to ensure the peaceful implementation of consulting activities.

In a first step, the practitioner should try to resolve the inter-sender conflict by explaining his individual roles and functions to everybody who is concerned. Some practical implications of this request can be learned from our case study: An important matter of concern for the consultants acting as mediators was to emphasize the dialogic character of the whole communications campaign to the client's staff and external publics. In doing so, they ensured a uniform comprehension of their own roles, which in turn allowed them to act successfully as communications facilitators and mediators.

Once a common definition of the communication situation has been established, the consultant is obliged to meet the particular role expectations (Bivins, 1989). Acting as communications technician or expert prescriber, a consultant would be obliged to serve only the client's interests. Once it has been established that the publics share this role perception, and do not see the consultant as something like a neutral information broker, such activity should not cause conflicts anymore. However, the communications consultant may also enact the role of a liaison, interpreter or even mediator as part of a symmetrical campaign. In this case, the practitioner is still obliged to observe the concurring role expectations of client and publics. But now this means that the consultant should attempt to promote the process of communications in a neutral way. Let us return to our case study: Acting as mediators, the consultants had to establish a constructive dialogue. To do so, it was necessary to prevent empty sales talk by politicians or spectacular appearances by environmental activists. In addition, the consultants had to compensate for the rhetorical inferiority of some stakeholder representatives through a thoughtful use of moderation techniques and personal assistance. To sum up: The overall goal of enabling a fair discussion between the energy supplier and its critics was achieved. The campaign led to a significant increase of social acceptance for the client. On the other hand, these discussions also led to some promising bilateral initiatives. For instance, company engineers worked together with local activists to establish new standards for the construction of high tension lines which allow for a thorough protection of birds.

As a result of our discussion of role conflicts, we have to stress the point that the public relations consultant is confronted with completely different ethical challenges according to his or her roles during a consulting process. To succeed, they must be able to establish open dialogues with both the client and those affected by the recommended communications campaigns.

Epilogue

What are the practical consequences of our suggestions? First of all, we must have a look at the various codes of ethical conduct passed by professional and industrial associations. There are a number of national and international codes in the field of public relations and communication consultancy, but none of them makes any difference between the various roles and their ethical demands (Bivins 1989). Therefore, professional and business associations are asked to work on a suitable, realistic, and problem-related rephrasing of the appropriate codes. A participation of clients, journalists, employees and other stakeholders affected by professional consulting may improve these activities. Moreover, any effort on an European or international level would require a thorough examination of the diverging cultural and socioeconomic factors that could impede the acceptance of professional codes of conduct (Cohen/Pant/Sharp, 1992).

Irrespective of this, public relations consultants as well as communication counseling firms are called upon to evaluate their activities and the consequences thereof on the expectations of those concerned. In this respect, public relations may benefit from many concepts developed in the field of business ethics.

We would like to thank Dr. Albert Löhr, University of Erlangen-Nürnberg, for his suggestions and comments that contributed to the development of this paper.

Notes

1. Acting as moderators, communications consultants may refer to the vast body of literature about alternative dispute resolution (ADR) and especially mediation processes (Wall/Lynn, 1993). Of course, in the context at hand the role of a mediator can only be enacted if the expert (paid by the client) is regarded as sufficiently neutral by the publics. If this is not the case, the communication consultant should recommend an outside mediator (Grunig/Grunig, 1992:316).

2. Miller (1989) calls on a similar paradigm when he equates public relations and persuasion because "both are primarily concerned with exerting symbolic control over relevant aspects of the environment" (p. 45).

3. The correlation depicted in figure 3 is compatible with several empirical surveys from the USA. These studies were able to prove a dominance of the technician role in the press agentry and the public information model as well as a more frequent enactment of manager roles in the two-way models; crf. Dozier (1992), p. 345 ff.

4. See Johnson (1989) and Pincus/Acharya/Trotter/St. Michel (1991) for a discussion of consultant-client-relationships within public relations.

References

Ahrens, R. and Hütt, H. 1993: *Dialogorientierte Öffentlichkeitsarbeit*. In Kalt, G. (ed), *Öffentlichkeitsarbeit und Werbung*, 4th edition. Frankfurt a.M.: Institut für Medienentwicklung und Kommunikation, pp. 101-113.

Anderson, D.S. 1992: Identifying and responding to activist publics: A case study. *Journal of Public Relations Research*, vol. 4, no. 3, pp. 151-165.

Apel, K.-O. 1988: *Diskurs und Verantwortung*. Frankfurt a.M.: Suhrkamp.

Bartholomew, M. 1992: Corporate communications in a New Europe. In Mahoney, J. and Vallance, E. (eds), *Business Ethics in a New Europe*, Dordrecht et al.: Kluwer, pp. 75-83.

Beck, U. 1986: *Risikogesellschaft*. Frankfurt a.M.: Suhrkamp.

Bivins, Th.H. 1989: Ethical implications of the relationship of purpose to role and function in public relations. *Journal of Business Ethics*, vol. 8, pp. 65-73.

Broom, G.M. and Dozier, D.M. 1986: Advancement for public relations role models. *Public Relations Review*, vol. 12, no. 1, pp. 37-56.

Broom, G.M. and Smith, G.D. 1979: Testing the practitioner's impact on clients. *Public Relations Review*, vol. 5, no. 3, pp. 47-59.

Burkart, R. and Probst, S. 1991: Verständigungsorientierte Öffentlichkeitsarbeit – eine kommunikationstheoretisch begründete Perspektive. *Publizistik*, vol. 30, pp. 56-76.

Cohen, J.R., Pant, L.W. and Sharp, D.J. 1992: Cultural and socioeconomic constraints in international codes of ethics: Lessons from accounting. *Journal of Business Ethics*, vol. 11, p. 687-700.

Culbertson, H.M. 1991: Role taking and sensitivity: Keys to playing and making public relations roles. In Grunig, L.A. and Grunig, J.E. (eds), *Public Relations Research Annual*, vol. 3, Hillsdale, NJ: Lawrence Erlbaum, pp. 37-65

DeGeorge, R.T. 1990: Using the techniques of ethical analysis in corporate practice. In Enderle, G., Almond, B.and Argandona, A. (eds), *People in Corporations: Ethical Responsibilities and Corporate Effectiveness*, Dordrecht: Kluwer, pp. 25-33.

Dozier, D.M. 1992: The organizational roles of communication and public relations practitioners. In Grunig, J.E. (ed), *Excellence in Communication and Public Relations Management,* Hillsdale, NJ: Lawrence Erlbaum, pp. 327-355.

Enderle, G. 1993: Zum Zusammenhang von Wirtschaftsethik, Unternehmensethik und Führungsethik. In Enderle, G., *Handlungsorientierte Wirtschaftsethik,* Bern and Stuttgart: Haupt, pp. 54-72.

Grunig, J.E. 1992: Communication, public relations, and effective organizations. In Grunig, J.E. (ed), *Excellence in Communication and Public Relations Management,* Hillsdale, NJ: Lawrence Erlbaum, pp. 1-28.

Grunig, J.E.and Grunig, L.A. 1992: Models of public relations and communication. In Grunig, J.E. (ed), *Excellence in Communication and Public Relations Management,* Hillsdale, NJ: Lawrence Erlbaum, pp. 285-325.

Grunig, J.E. and Hunt, T. 1984: *Managing Public Relations.* Fort Worth: Holt, Rinehart and Winston.

Grunig, J.E. and White, J. 1992: The effect of worldviews on public relations theory and practice. In Grunig, J.E. (ed), *Excellence in Communication and Public Relations Management,* Hillsdale, NJ: Lawrence Erlbaum, pp. 31-64.

Habermas, J. (1984) *The theory of communicative action. Volume 1: Reason and the rationalization of society.* Boston: Beacon Press.

Habermas, J. 1990: Discourse ethics: notes on a program of justification. In Benhabib, S. and Dallmayr, F. (eds), *The Communicative Ethics Controversy,* Cambridge, Mass.: MIT Press, pp. 60-110.

Johnson, D.J. 1989: The coorientation model and consultant roles. In Botan, C.H. and Hazleton, V. Jr. (eds), *Public Relations Theory,* Hillsdale, NJ: Lawrence Erlbaum, pp. 243-263.

Katz, D. and Kahn, R.L. 1978: *The Social Psychology of Organizations,* 2nd edition. New York: Wiley.

Löhr, A. 1991: *Unternehmensethik und Betriebswirtschaftslehre.* Stuttgart: M & P Verlag für Wissenschaft und Forschung.

Lorenzen, P. 1982: Ethics and the philosophy of science. In Christensen, D.E., Riedel, M., Spaemann, R., Wiehl, R. and Wieland, W. (eds), *Contemporary German Philosophy, vol. 1,* University Park and London: The Pennsylvania State University Press, pp. 1-14.

Lorenzen, P. 1987: *Lehrbuch der konstruktiven Wissenschaftstheorie.* Mannheim: BI-Wissenschaftsverlag.

Merten, K. 1992: Begriff und Funktionen von Public Relations. *PR-Magazin,* vol. 23, no. 11, pp. 35-46.

Miller, G.R. 1989: Persuasion and Public Relations: Two "Ps" in a Pod. In Botan, C.H. and Hazleton, V. Jr. (eds), *Public Relations Theory,* Hillsdale, NJ: Lawrence Erlbaum, pp. 45-66.

Pearson, R.A. 1989: *A theory of public relations ethics.* Dissertation, College of Communication, Ohio University, USA.

Pincus, J.D., Acharya, L., Trotter, E.P. and St. Michel, C. 1991: Conflict between public relations agencies and their clients: A game theory analysis. In Grunig, L.A. and Grunig, J.E. (eds), *Public Relations Research Annual, vol. 3,* Hillsdale, NJ: Lawrence Erlbaum, pp. 151-163.

Ronneberger, F. and Rühl, M. 1992: *Theorie der Public Relations.* Opladen: Westdeutscher Verlag.

Steinmann, H. and Löhr, A. 1994: *Grundlagen der Unternehmensethik,* 2nd edition. Stuttgart: Schäffer-Poeschel.

Steinmann, H. and Zerfaß, A. 1993a: Corporate dialogue – a new perspective for public relations. *Business Ethics – A European Review,* vol. 2, no. 2, pp. 58-63.

1993b: Privates Unternehmertum und öffentliches Interesse. In G.R. Wagner (ed), *Betriebswirtschaft und Umweltschutz,* Stuttgart: Schäffer-Poeschel, pp. 3-26.

Stone, Ch.D. 1975: *Where the Law Ends.* New York: Harper & Row.

Wall, J.A. and Lynn, A. 1993: Mediation – A current review. *Journal of Conflict Resolution,* vol. 37, pp. 160-194.

Zerfaß, A. and Scherer, A.G. 1993: *Die Irrtümer der Imagekonstrukteure – Ein Plädoyer gegen die sozialtechnologische Verkürzung der Public Relations-Forschung.* Diskussionsbeitrag Nr. 77 des Lehrstuhls für Allgemeine Betriebswirtschaftslehre und Unternehmensführung. Nürnberg: Universität Erlangen-Nürnberg.

PART IV

Actual Ethical Issues of Consulting Services in Post-Communist Countries

14

Actual Ethical Issues of Consulting Services in Post-Communist Countries

Lidmila Nemcová

Introduction

In the course of the last several years significant changes in political systems over a large territory of Central and Eastern Europe and Northern Asia have taken place. They have been gradually succeeded by radical changes in the economic and social life in these territories. The return of the private sector is one of the most prominent features characterizing the new development. Also, consulting services have begun with a renewed activity on an appropriate level.

Economic activities in various countries of given territory are a little different when it comes to speed of changes and reprivatization. They are also not very coordinated. Nevertheless, practically all the phenomena described here, which are based on my experiences in my home country, are being observed by various colleagues also in other post-communist countries. Therefore some more general validity can be associated with this article.

Previous Situation

For over 40 years (and in several countries of the former USSR at least 25–30 years can be added) the economic life in the given territory was based on a bureaucratic central planning system. Consulting services were mainly concentrated in various state and co-operative organizations described as a socialist sector of economy. Various firms were ensured such services, either by means of their proper employees or by means of some specialized organizations (belonging also to the socialist sector). Consulting services of that time were focussed mainly on the needs of the socialist sector.

The socialist sector substantially neglected various services needed for the personal ownership of citizens. This gradually caused an illegal development of various private services (e.g. some artisans and repairmen). This was the so-called "grey" economy which grew into a large but officially unidentified dimension. The

H. von Weltzien Hoivik and A. Føllesdal (eds.), Ethics and Consultancy: European Perspectives, 181-189.
© 1995 *Kluwer Academic Publishers. Printed in the Netherlands.*

increase of this economy has brought serious damages to the people's ethical way of thinking. The repairmen illegally took needed material from their employers and used other equipment of their employers as well. Some levelling of salaries was typical for a socialist economic system (especially in the then-Czechoslovakia) and moreover manual work was relatively preferred to any intellectual activity. In the same way the "grey" economy also preferred a higher financial appreciation of manual workers whereas intellectual activities were systematically undervalued. Ownership of ideas and intellectual capacities were losing their importance among the population. In many situations free-of-charge private consultations were considered as a normal phenomenon.

Come-Back of Private Consultants

The changes after 1989 have made it possible to be open for the broader and intensively increasing role of the private sector, including special consultant activities. This fact represents a come-back of the middle class on the economic scene with numerous new and renewed small and medium size businesses.

Numerous private consultant agencies have been founded consisting of individuals or of groups of persons. These agencies focus their activities on highly diversified technical fields (including the introduction of new computers and of various other previously hardly accessible or even completely inaccessible technologies), but an extraordinary increase in their activities is connected with consulting services in the economy and in the law. New systems of taxes, accounting for new private entrepreneurs, marketing, management, restitution of private properties and business, transformation of the former socialist sector, etc. all need some help from specialists (at first for those private entrepreneurs who are just beginning with their business activity). In some situations such specialized help is incredibly difficult because, very often, numerous new legislative instructions are being revised and changed in relatively short periods.

Therefore, sometimes the consultants have to work under extremely difficult circumstances. Let us emphasize also the fact that some real effects of various transforming operations have not yet been fully verified in practice.

A new position, a new style of work and new needs are also typical for various unions, associations and chambers (as co-operative unions, associations of entrepreneurs, chambers of commerce etc.). Some of them also existed in the previous period but their activities were strongly dependent on the political and economic system of that time. Usually they did not resemble any function or activity in analogous organizations in countries with a highly developed market economy. Therefore if some of them continue to exist they need a complete reorientation of their work. This should be emphasized in connection with the fact that for all mentioned organizations consulting services represent a considerable part of their activities.

Ethical Codes

Both Czech and Slovak associations for consulting services issued their members an ethical code (which should be used also by non-members of these associations). The following text is presented in the code's first paragraph: "The consultant prefers the interest of his clients to his own interest. He is obliged to extend his service in such a way that it is his client to whom a primary benefit is accorded. All specialized knowledge and experiences of the consultant are to be used to ensure objectivity and competence of given consultations." Significant attention is paid to problems of how to ensure the confidential nature of consulting activities, what to do to avoid parallel consulting service for controversial clients competing with one another, how to achieve maximum objectivity, and how to individualize any case. Consultants have to present to their clients a written proposal or contract including some estimation of fees or at least some principles of how this fee will be calculated. Also the case of possible simultaneous activities of several independent consultants or consulting agencies for one client has been solved in this ethical code.

At first sight the ethical code seems to give all conditions needed for any ethically pure consulting service. When effectuating their service, consultants anywhere in the world have to solve various ethical problems and dilemmas. If we look more carefully and in detail at actual situations in consulting activities in the post-communist countries, some specific ethical problems arise, especially when other views are taken into consideration. Some of these specific problems are of extraordinary importance or they appear in such a dimension that they are completely unusual in countries with a highly developed market economy. These phenomena are connected with a lack of morality as well as with an "ethical" feeling caused by the old political system.

Evidently any ethical code itself cannot be considered as completely satisfactory for consulting services when the whole ethical climate of the country needs to be purified from long-term contamination and brought to some higher level of individual thinking.

Ethical Problems

Professionalism

Basic ethical problems concern a needed high level of the professional knowledge and of the know how of consultants. In practice many consultants often are just beginning with their own consulting activities. They are able to present documents about their professional education which makes it possible to get needed official registrations. Usually there is not any demand to prove a real professional skill. Until now, no limiting conditions exist which demand, for some consulting services, either some needed minimum period of an appropriate practical activity or some special examination of an appropriate ability. A low level of professionalism and especially a lack of practical experience cannot be compensated by anything. In fact, a consultant-beginner is just learning how to work when starting up a consultant practice.

It happens sometimes that a fresh consultant does not want to plan some long-term consulting activity in the given fields and tries to use just a temporarily high demand for consulting services to get a high income very rapidly. On the other hand, it is very difficult for a beginning private entrepreneur to identify which consultant really is highly qualified and serious and who is a not-too-serious one, with low quality services, with a poor knowledge and with poor experiences. Some consultants in the fields of economy and law take advantage of the relatively low level of knowledge and lack of experience of their clients.

Access to Information

In some cases consultants try to misuse their priority access to some important information. E.g. as members of legislative teams they possess some instructions prior to their official publication. In a period of some information vacuum they are able to get an advantage on the market by publishing their private books on various subjects. Sometimes this activity is not done by members of legislation teams, but analogous expensive textbooks are published or special courses and workshops are organized thanks to information leaks.

Various examples can be given concerning very expensive textbooks or courses on newly introduced taxes, health and social insurance etc., effective in the Czech Republic since January 1, 1993. All of these problems were highly important (especially for new entrepreneurs) and any information was really urgently needed. One paid high prices for any information. However, official information was, for some time, completely inaccessible by the public media or other official public channels. This official way – also with a guaranty of completeness and authenticity – has caused delays (maybe initiated by somebody from the entrepreneurs?) By causing delays various courses have been organized under low-cost conditions by official training centers, etc. How "ethical" is then a question of "What shall we do now?", presented by a manager of a consulting and publishing agency when new, officially published documents hindered him from continuing in easy profit-making.

Price of Services

Consultants enter a purely market environment. Their services can be considered a merchandise. The prices of consulting services are influenced by supply and demand. If their service is really needed and if it is of a high quality then their clients are ready to pay for it. For example, the actual need for commercial lawyers is far higher than their supply. Very often, there is a criticism of the high prices of consultants. But, according to respective instructions, a commercial lawyer cannot ask less than 200 Czech crowns (about 7 USD) for one hour of consultation. Evidently the number of consultants will increase and their services will then be at lower prices.

One of the interesting incidental effects of a high need for commercial lawyers and of high profits coming from their consultations has been the considerable defection of lawyers in justice institutions. Presently only about two-thirds of regularly planned posts in the Czech justice are occupied, in some regions vacancies are even higher. And this is all taking place now, when our tribunals are overloaded with numerous specific cases typical for this period: increased criminality in all branches of social and economic life, complicated restitutions of property rights, reparation of various wrongdoing of the previous political system to some citizens, etc.

The effort of some consultants and other entrepreneurs to get easy profits through minimum work already has been mentioned. Let us go back to an opposite problem of public underestimation of consulting services. Some remnants of previous periods can be seen in this phenomenon. On the other hand, it should be emphasized that even highly honest consultants need to take care, not only of their proper consulting activity, but also when establishing an appropriate background and conditions for it. They need to get an office (often in a non-standard room after an expensive adaptation), to purchase appropriate equipment (telephone, fax, literature, PC), to ensure a needed system of work (secretarial service, accounting). New laws and official instructions need to be studied constantly. In some situations consultants need to know foreign languages. Their looks have to correspond to some high standard as well. Working and studying need a very intensive concentration of 12-14 hours per day. Therefore a high financial appreciation of their work – especially when in perfect accordance with official price lists – cannot be criticized at all.

Commercial lawyers and other consultants wanting to establish their consulting services permanently need to have not only a market behavior but also an ethical behavior. Legal instructions are based on legal norms. These ensure at least some minimum ethics. Consultants have to follow and keep at least this minimum of ethics in their work.

Location of Consulting Services

The consulting activity takes place in various ways and at various places. If consultants decide to establish their own office then their prices will also be influenced by prices of purchased or rented rooms as well as by various state and communal taxes. The market for real estate, rooms, etc. has not yet been established and stabilized in the Czech Republic at the same level as in other post-communist countries. The prices for office space, especially in centers of cities, are relatively high and they are put into the calculation of consulting services.

Some consultants are satisfied with some minimum space in their own apartments. They prefer to visit their clients (if necessary), often they also focus their attention and activity on specific segments of clients. Increased expenses for transport, for long-term stays at long distances from their homes, etc. are also put into the calculation of prices. Increased advertizing is perhaps common for all groups of consultants.

Ethical problems can arise when consultants realize their service as a lateral second profession. In some situations they use the same offices, telephones, computers and various other technical equipment and services which are put at their disposal by their employers to ensure their basic profession. Non-ethical behavior is directed mainly against their employers. In many organizations this way of realizing private consulting services has already been strongly forbidden.

Another specific ethical case is represented by those consultants who are employed by the government (on any level). This is not necessarily a problem of misusing technical equipments. On the contrary, these consultants usually have their own private offices. As already mentioned, the special advantage of these consultants consists in their specific know-how, in various otherwise inaccessible information (e.g. reprivatization projects, preference in getting new legislative documents, etc.). It causes delays when the government organs begin to hinder any escape of information and to forbid their employees to consult in their field of business which is at the same time an object of their main profession.

Relations With Clients

Some ethical problems concerning various interrelationships among consultants and their clients already have been discussed in other circumstances. As a matter of fact these relations are to be cultivated in both directions. An effort of clients to get some needed information as cheap as possible (if not for free) by using apparently simple and independently given questions is as far from an ethical attitude as any effort of consultants to choose only those clients guaranteeing a possible high profit. Also, some free-of-charge consultations can be re-estimated from an ethical point of view as it can be only a camouflage covering a real disinterest of the consultant.

Evidently there is some long-term lack of professional ethics and tradition in the reintroduced consulting services in post-communist countries. Consultants have their freedom in deciding whether to act in an ethically indisputable way, including cases where apparently their service will not be fully paid. A lot of education is still needed for any consultant, as well as for any entrepreneur in order for them to cultivate some classic feeling of professional honor, dignity and pride, i.e. all of those virtues which in the old times adorned their ancient precursors.

Risk Measuring

Consultants very often meet classical dilemmas which may cause the end of some lucrative co-operation with their clients. The decision frontier sometimes is not too sharp. However in specific situations some symptoms of increased risk for clients can be observed (for instance when they continue in some already existing activity). The consultant has to present these problems and risks to the client, who has to decide whether, in spite of an increased risk, they are really interested in continuing contacts with this consultant. The interest of the client should be principally superior to the purely egoistic interest of the consultant. This is the basic ethical demand. In an opposite case the consultant is able to get some further financial profit but a real danger exists that trust will be lost. Any inappropriate behavior by any individual consultant may have some influence on the public opinion and could cause real damage to a broader circle of other consultants as well.

Higher Interest Priorities

Should the interests of clients always be considered as absolute priority for any consulting activity? Let us omit any consulting activity for criminal clients looking for some crevice in a given legal status (fraudulent reduction of taxes, etc.). But even the most honest intentions of entrepreneurs can be contradictory to some higher interest of human society at various levels (community, region etc.). We can mention as an example the exploitation of mineral reserves, which – especially if oversized – may be in a serious discrepancy with ecological aspects, with a reasonable long-term strategy of using natural resources, etc. This is an area for which, in many countries, no legislative prescriptions for admissible limits are given. An experienced consultant has to express to the client a warning concerning actual and future risks as well as the possible antisocial character of some intentions.

Foreign Consultants

Rapid changes in political, economic and social situations in post-communist countries, as well as the conscious return of market mechanisms and a full use of technical and scientific progress naturally have caused an increased interest concerning activities of foreign consultants. They have begun to visit these post-communist countries either using official invitations given by local government authorities or special local agencies, or by using special missions organized by their own governments or non-governmental organs (in a framework of various projects etc.). Numerous individual consultants tried to penetrate into post-communist countries very rapidly on their own and exactly in this group many attempts to misuse the new markets have been realized in a purely non-ethical way. Also the lack of experience in new possible business partners have allowed a disproportional, and often only a single, profit without any guaranty for the given services. These individuals were practically on the same level as various local would-be entrepreneurs to whom they were also serving as very unfortunate "examples" and models.

But let us examine activities of those foreign consultants who enter the post-communist territories backed by serious recommendations and undoubtedly with highly serious intentions to help in overcoming local economic troubles.

It is necessary to not forget that even consultants who have proven their ability in their own countries or in some other regions where they were completely familiar with local conditions, developments, mentality of population and mentality of clients may completely collapse when starting to work under conditions which have been completely unknown and where it is possible to get only gradually and with great difficulties some basic knowledge of all possible circumstances. Naturally, experts from abroad ask to be paid for their consultations on a level which is equivalent to their income in their own country. Differences in levels of income and living expenses and of their stratification and distribution in various countries of the world seem to be very often neglected even by prominent consultants. And some comparison of situations in various post-communist countries with that of economically highly-developed countries is needed to get at least some minimum idea about the absurdity of the actual situation in the world. For instance, the monthly salary of the Russian President, if expressed in any hard currency, is equal to the monthly income of a better retired specialist in the Czech Republic but also to the monthly pocket money of a middle class student in the USA.

Further, a foreign consultant very often needs local staff as translators, local consultants, and other people who are able to ensure needed services. Ethical problems consist primarily in the fact that, in many situations, a top foreign consultant arrives in a new and unknown country where they need to learn very much about local conditions as well as to get a further service from local advisers.

In order to revive international cooperation and to help post-communist countries in their rapid transition to a free market economy, various foundations and international projects have been established. Sometimes rich partners try to use these projects and foundations to become familiar with local conditions in unknown countries. Some foreign experts and consultants use these projects only to organize rather than to bind visits to their potential new foreign partners. They continue to keep their own habits, they use air connections only, they prefer a top level accommodation in thoroughly comfortable hotels, they try to study local conditions and existing experiences. But sometimes this is all what they want to do. Their mission is the end product and nobody tries to continue in some cooperation. Often, one forgets that specialists and consultants from post-communist countries would prefer to realize some reciprocal visits to highly developed countries to study local conditions, local situations, or local high level technology. They would enjoy a modest accommodation in student hostels, less expensive means of transport, etc. However, it should also be honestly admitted that a low ethical thinking of some of these experts from post-communist countries serves as the background for misusing such visits abroad for egoistic purposes (e.g. instead of buying some specialized and otherwise inaccessible literature they prefer to buy some private use objects for themselves or for members of their families).

It should be emphasized that the aforementioned negative features in the activity of some foreign consultants fortunately cannot be generalized. The activity of many top consultants coming from abroad to help with developing new economic and other systems in post-communist countries is really very important and successful, and it is also highly appreciated by the top authorities as well as by the new partners.

Conclusions

It can be concluded that in the ethics of consultants – whatever part of the world they come from – some defects continue to exist. Ethical principles for consultancy service are of high importance, and the personality of any consultant has to play a decisive role in this service. The consultant is also able to influence some ethical way of thinking as well as the activity of the client. Therefore the consultants are to be considered as possible agents for increasing the level of business ethics (including also respect for the interest of the whole of human society).

15

Cases Studies on Consultancy Issues in the Age of Economic Transition in Hungary

László Fekete

The general role of consultancy in the transition process of the Hungarian economy cannot yet be assessed. Although almost one hundred domestic and international consulting companies are commissioned by the government agency for state property to arrange the privatization processes in firms, factories, state farms, institutions, and even whole branches of industry, their business activities are regarded as confidential and their obligation is to keep it officially secret. Therefore there is no reliable and comprehensive information about their business activities, especially in the privatization process. Almost the only place to get some information about their business activities are the parliamentary debates, and economic and political newspapers. Needless to say, these information sources are rather politically loaded. As a consequence of confronting economic policies the different economic interest groups (domestic and international) frequently try to discredit each other by using politicians, political and economic newspapers, or even diplomatic channels. (The GSM 900 phone tender case discussed later is such an example.)

Besides the huge mass of distorted information, a few reliable sources can be found to learn something about the role of the consultant, especially in privatization. For example, the State Audit Office released its official statement about the privatization process at the beginning of September 1993. According to this official statement, there was no single case found wherein the legality to a certain extent would not have been broken. The State Audit Office investigated hundreds of different cases only from the formal-legal point of view without specifying the responsibility of the consultancy agents or giving reasons why their works did not meet the legal requirements. There is no answer, for example, for why the payments for the consultancy firms doubled while the returns of the government agency for state property on privatization declined to zero in the same year. (It must be added that according to the director of Ernst & Young there is a very serious competition among the largest international consultant companies in Hungary which significantly reduces their earnings.)

H. von Weltzien Hoivik and A. Føllesdal (eds.), Ethics and Consultancy: European Perspectives, 191-196.
© 1995 *Kluwer Academic Publishers. Printed in the Netherlands.*

The debates about consultancy especially focus on three particular fields: breaking with the rules of the tendering process, incorrect appraisal, and inside trading by the consultancy agents. These debates appear to show the very typical cases when the consultancy agent breaks with his or her own professional ethical principles. However, it is not easy to distinguish between their ethics and the economic aspects of the different cases. In doing his or her business the consultancy agent does not simply follow his or her professional ethical principles but acts willy-nilly under the political and economic pressures. (Pressure, of course, can be named with some empathy as necessity, too.) Not to make excuses for consultancy agents for breaking with their professional ethical principles, but it must be emphasized that every single case shows the lack of the moral community in society as well. If their business activities are regarded as confidential and their obligation is to keep the official secret, especially in privatization, those requirements and prescriptions also manifest the fact that social confidence toward each other is not sound. (Because the other side of the meaning of confidential is withdrawing confidence from others.)

I would like to survey briefly three different cases in which the business activities and the economic advice of the consulting agents and firms (domestic and international) can be critically discussed, especially, from the ethical point of view.

Case 1 – The Privatization of the Economics and Jurisprudence Publishing Co

After the significant reduction of the state subsidy, the Economics and Jurisprudence Publishing Co. went through a deep financial (especially liquidity) crisis from the end of the 1980's. As a consequence of the new business policy of the management, the Economics and Jurisprudence Publishing Co. today is a solid economic enterprise in a solvent market. It must be emphasized that few publishing houses are managed to survive the reduction of the state subsidy in the last few years. The majority of the publishing houses is in a very fragile economic situation. Books in the fields of theoretical and applied economics, finance, marketing, economic history, statistics, law (civil, criminal, public, economic, international, and etc.), reference books, special dictionaries, university textbooks for the Law Schools and Economic Departments are published there. Because of the expertise of the editors, its publications are characterized by a high professional standard. In recent years, the Government Agency for State Property wanted to privatize the publishing houses. The Kossuth Consulting Co. was commissioned by the Government Agency for State Property to arrange the privatization process of the mentioned publishing company. As mentioned, it is a solid economic enterprise and, in addition, its office building is located in downtown Budapest in a frequented place. Therefore there was some risk during the privatization process that the new owner would allow, or even drive, the publishing company into a financial crisis in order to be able to sell its office building. This could result in an up to a 6-700 percent return on its investment. It seemed that the Kossuth Consulting Co. liked the group of editors and the employees of the Economics and Jurisprudence Publishing Co. Therefore it set the rules of the tender such that they could be met by the financial capacity of the group. Needless to say, this group could offer only a lot of skills but certainly not significant amount of money, especially not in cash. They offered in payment laid on loan. Finally, the consulting company accepted the offer of the group of the editors and the employees which was 20 percent less in terms of money than the second best company's offer.

After announcing the result of the tender, the Kossuth Consulting Co. was publicly charged with dishonest business activity by the state secretary of the Ministry of Culture and Public Education because he rather supported the second best company whose offer was really more impressive, at least in terms of money. It turned out later that the second best company was a "Strohmann" company backed by the business circle of the politicians of the recent governing party. This business circle tried to establish a great media emporium including daily and weekly newspapers, reviews, a record company, television, video studio, etc. (Generally speaking, the fate of such publishing houses is that they are besieged and fall. The new management usually is not able to run them even with modest profitability because of lack of support from employees.)

The Economics and Jurisprudence Publishing Co. was besieged but did not fall. As a consequence, the Kossuth Consulting Co. set the rules of the tender on behalf of the editors and the employees. It seemed that in this case the private vice of the Kossuth Consulting Co. is certainly public benefit.

Case 2 – The Administrative Autonomy of Csepel Island

Csepel Island is the largest industrial district of Budapest and is populated by about one hundred thousand people. This district was an administratively independent urban settlement until 1950. Since then it has been the 21st district of the capital. Csepel Island was one of the birth places of the Hungarian industry in the nineteenth century. Engineering industry, paper mills, steel works, textile industry, track factories are the most significant businesses. In addition, a harbor is located on the island. Many of these industries are in a difficult economic situation because none of them represents the leading edge of the economic activities at the end of the 20th century.

The inhabitants of Csepel Island did not protest against their administrative status. The newly-elected parliament has issued a new law concerning local administration two years ago which frequently creates hard times for the mayor of Budapest as well as the local administration of the districts. (The reason is mainly that the candidates supported by the opposition parties gained in a landslide victory in the local election in 1990. The governing parties did not want to make their life too easy, especially for the administration of the capital, using sometimes their legislative power.)

The local administration of Csepel Island decided to secede from the capital in order to get rid of this difficult situation. The local mayor asked City Consult Co. to investigate the possibility of independent administrative status and to present a cost-benefit analysis. The consultancy agents did their job and quickly submitted their findings. The final result of their findings was that Csepel Island would benefit a lot from independent administrative status. The administration of the capital city also wanted to get the clear picture about the consequences of the independent administrative status of its largest district. Therefore, the mayor of Budapest happened to ask the same consulting firm, City Consult Co., to investigate the possibility of independent administrative status and to present a cost-benefit analysis. The consultancy agents did their job and submitted their findings to the mayor at the same time as the Csepel Island report. The final result of their findings is that Csepel island would lose a lot from independent administrative status.

It would be quite easy to put the blame on the mentioned consulting firm because of its dishonest business activity. But let us return to the original question. According to the request of the local administration, as well as the capital, the consultancy agents were expected to investigate whether independent administrative status would be beneficial for the island or not. Needless to say, especially in this circle, this original question is enormously sophisticated from the scientific point of view. The size of Csepel Island, its complicated economic and institutional structures, and its embeddedness in the everyday life of the capital, means that finding a sound answer to this question needs time, money, and expertise. The consultancy agents lacked almost all of these. Neither the local administration nor the capital furnished them with time and money. And they did not have at their disposal all of the economic, financial, administrative, cultural, sociological, educational skills. Everybody was aware of the immensity of such an investigation, which simply could not be carried out within a couple of months. But the politicians of the local administration and the capital simply wanted to get arguments for supporting their own political conviction and prejudice and they were ready to pay for it. Both of them get it because they managed to find a very cooperative partner, the City Consult Co. for fulfilling their expectations.[1]

Case 3 – The Case of the GSM 900 Mobile Telephone Tender.

For two years the Ministry of Transportation and Telecommunications in Hungary worked on a concession tender for constructing the network of the GSM 900 mobile phone system. According to the rules of the tender, only two groups, the best and the second best offers, could be accepted in order to avoid a monopoly situation and because of the modest size of the Hungarian market. A lot of international and domestic telecommunications companies, well provided with capital, experience and skills, were interested in taking part in the mobile phone tender. But only three groups managed to work out very competitive offers for this fifteen-year-long concession. The three most significant companies were as follows: the DBFH-Group, the US West-Matáv, and the Pannon GSM.[2] The tendering process took an unexpected turn when the minimal offer in payment was quadrupled up to 48 million

USD by the minister of Transportation and Telecommunication in the pre-bid conference. The idea of the increase in payment originally came from the Credit Suisse First Boston Consulting Co. which was commissioned by the Ministry of Transportation and Telecommunications to arrange the GSM 900 mobile phone tender. But the Credit Suisse First Boston Consulting Co. is also the representative for US West in Eastern Europe. The Boston Consulting Co. tried to drive the DBFH-Group out of the phone business by means of the increase in payment. The DBFH-Group, however, happened to give the best offer in payment in the bid conference and of course its offer, from the technical point of view, was at least as competitive as US West-Matáv and Pannon GSM's. To sum up, the DBFH-Group had the best chance to be the winner of this tender. But very soon after the bid conference the committee gave US West-Matáv a second chance to outbid the offer of the DBFH-Group in terms of money, without informing the DBFH-Group about this new development. Finally, US West-Matáv and Pannon GSM were announced as the co-winners of the GSM 900 mobile phone tender in Hungary.

Because the DBFH-Group protested against the decision of the committee by using diplomatic channels, I am sure this story will be continued.

Conclusions

As far as the above-mentioned cases and conflicts are concerned, the ethical responsibilities of the consultancy companies can be verified quite well. However, I want to avoid judging the measure and the dimensions of their non-ethical business practices because they acted in a social environment and under such economic conditions that do not appear to highlight honest business practices and their own professional ethical principles. Therefore their business activities should be investigated in the context of the logic of the existing market system in general and that of the Central and Eastern European economic transition towards the market system in particular. In my view, to discuss the individual accountability of consultancy agents is not particularly productive but rather we should look at the co-responsibility of the consultancy agents and the domestic and international economic communities in regard to this transition.

My first and not very convincing proposal is that the consultancy agents should keep to their own professional ethical principles. I do not think there is any uncertainty about what those ethical principles are. But can one follow any ethical principles in a post-modern society where individual accountability loses its previous domination (which was, of course, rather imaginary in the positive sense of the word originated from the European philosophical and Christian traditions)? Therefore only the ethical co-responsibility of all of the economic agents and other social members in society can contribute to the formation of the moral community. The dilemma is that we know exactly how to act in the moral community but we do not know how to act until we create the moral community.

Notes

1. Since this chapter was written, the local referendum at Csepel Island has taken place. More than 90 percent of the citizens of the island turned down the independent administrative status. So Csepel Island will remain a district of the capital.

2. DBFH-Group (German, British, French, and Hungarian Telecommunication Companies); US West-Matáv (American and Hungarian Telecommunication Companies); and the Pannon GSM (Scandinavian, Holland, and Hungarian Telecommunication Companies.)

16

Situational Ethics in Consulting: The Case of Slovenia

Mitja I. Tavcar

Introduction

Slovenia with 20,000 km^2, 2 million inhabitants and a GNP of 4000 ECU per capita is not an important factor in the global economy. It is somewhat more significant in international politics as the only state in Eastern Europe where the previous "socialist" regime abdicated quietly and voluntarily. It is additionally significant for its role as a buffer zone between the unruly Balkans and Central Europe.

In the last decades Slovenia underwent overwhelming changes in its culture and economy. Being small and yielding, it may be a miniature model of forthcoming processes in Eastern Europe, the largest cluster of markets worldwide to be opened in the next decade – but only to entrants knowledgeable enough of its specifics. Even more, small Slovenia may be an important gate to the uncommon market in Eastern Europe, where so many successful and powerful companies from the West have burned their fingers.

This chapter is based on the author's extensive experience in management and managerial education, primarily in MBA programs. It shall help to evaluate several propositions:

- that Slovenia, by its static and dynamic attributes, may be a convenient model of major social and economic processes in Eastern Europe;
- that huge changes in cultures, values and ethics are occurring in the background of the visible transition from "socialism" to a normal democracy and market economy in a country;
- that changes and disparities in social values within a country or among countries are necessarily reflected in consulting strategies, conduct and ethics;
- that a situational approach both to business and consulting strategies is an indispensable prerequisite to achievement;
- that the consulting ethics shall be appraised both in relation to the culture and

H. von Weltzien Hoivik and A. Føllesdal (eds.), Ethics and Consultancy: European Perspectives, 197-213.
© 1995 *Kluwer Academic Publishers. Printed in the Netherlands.*

development trends in the client's environment as well as in relation to client's abilities, willingness and resources;

- that consultants, for their own benefit, have to determine limits in situational ethics, which they will never transgress, even at the loss of consulting projects and clients.

Due to space limitations this chapter is necessarily fragmental; situations as well as trends are subject to gross oversimplifications. The Slovenian situation never was as black-and-white as reported here; many a lighter shade has been omitted. Only a minimum of material was used to allow for a reasonably credible outline of the situation and of trends observed.

Changing Ethics in Slovenia

The Past

For nearly a thousand years Slovenia belonged to the Austro-Hungarian Empire and received a strong Germanic influence from the north and Italian on the west. After World War I, Slovenia became a part of Yugoslavia with a very limited national autonomy; romantic pan-Slavic emotions soon became forgotten due to the predominance of an alien Byzantine-Balkan culture spreading from the south-east provinces. However, this was – except for the times of the Big Crisis – a period of emancipation. Several industries were set up and flourished, the first independent Slovenian cultural institutions were established – a full-sized university, theaters, art galleries, publishing houses.

During World War II, Slovenes fought for sovereignty, but achieved little. The Slovenian federal republic in the post-war Yugoslavia had limited ethnic autonomy, and was made an integral part of the much less developed and enterprising economy. This meant levies and subsidies to the less developed south-east, but a large and protected market as well; this enabled extensive industrialization and full employment in Slovenia. Politically the "socialist" Titoistic regime enforced the nationalization of all, except very personal property, and the abolishment of the capital and labor market; the workers self-management was introduced, a grandiose humanistic concept, but premature and economically inviable. As time went by, several liberal movements were dealt with and suppressed, initiative started to vanish, and in the course of the 1970s the Yugoslav economy was nearing bankruptcy. Slovenia was slightly better off due to business involvement with developed countries.

The Leaden Years

The damage done, however, on the human side, was more important than that on the economic side. The visionary socialist and unaligned Yugoslavia was overcome by a Byzantine-Balkan culture, a degenerative one by European standards – a culture of dirty tricks and faithlessness and meanness in business and unrestrained political abuse; the recent tragedy in the Balkans offers proof enough of that.

In an environment with distorted basic social structure, immoral behavior remains unpunished and even carries substantial comparative advantages; long-term disadvantages become apparent only later. In this atmosphere "worker self-management" neared manipulation: management had to prepare "expert" proposals and it was up to "workers' councils" to evaluate alternatives and make (unqualified) decisions – for which, if they were legal, the management could be held responsible. Consequently, managers got used to managing by manipulation and workers avoided apparent self-management. Socialism, deplorably, became a term of disrespect, standing for little equality, justice and personal development.

Slovenia, in general, was better off than other parts of Yugoslavia, it was more developed and nearer to the West and due to circumstances it never experienced a truly Stalinist regime. There was more freedom and suppression was subdued, yet whole generations became used to the degraded Yugoslav culture, undergoing an extensive adaptation process, constraining initiative and free thought and creativity. These were the "leaden years" of the late sixties and even more so in the 70s.

The so-much-extolled "socialist ethics" degraded incrementally into relative un-ethics. Too many of the privileged stood for undeserved material values gained ruthlessly, under servile obedience to those above them. Even these values were vanishing: the Yugoslav system of futile discussions and little work inevitably led to economic disintegration and bankruptcy. When there was not enough left even for the privileged, the system gradually collapsed in itself. The so noble experiment to establish a different, less egoistic democracy, ended ingloriously, and will certainly not be repeated in times to come.

The Liberalization Period

Throughout the leaden years Slovenia retained a reserved stance. It was the republic with the oldest industrial tradition. Even if not favored by the central planning in the fifties and sixties, Slovenia has built technologically advanced enough chemical, metalworking, transportation, electronics and telecommunication industries. Slovenia had the best educational system in Yugoslavia with an established network of research institutes, two full-sized universities and other institutions.

Slovenia, soon enough, became too small a market for its own production and the less developed Yugoslav republics were a promising and protected market. Very soon, the domestic market became too small as well and Slovenia turned to exports; in the mid-seventies 1/4 of the industrial output was exported. Even under the restrictions of the Belgrade bureaucracy Slovenian companies established a fairly spread-out network of trading and manufacturing companies in Europe, in developing countries and throughout Eastern Europe.

Thousands of Slovenes were in business contact with foreign business partners – much more than with businesses from the Yugoslav South. Most Slovenian cities are less than a hundred kilometers from the Austrian and Italian borders; even under administrative restrictions, Slovenes had many contacts abroad.

Slovenia attained a higher GNP level, was more industrially developed and more internationally minded than the rest of Yugoslavia. With the partial exception of Croatia in business, Slovenia was considered, with some envy, to be the "Yugoslav Switzerland."

In addition, Slovenia started increasingly to mediate in business projects among the Yugoslav south and developed countries. In the Slavic countries of the Soviet block, Slovenia was emotionally still accepted as a member of the Slavic family. Slovenes were able to understand the "socialist" and Slavic culture of these countries, which, combined with Slovenian business ties to the West, opened many opportunities across the East-West border. These transactions were very profitable; business volumes were extensive and prices attained a multiple of normal market price levels in Europe.

All these strategic factors should have brought about a golden period for Slovenia – but did not. The consequences of the all-embracing degenerative process spread over a majority of important companies. Even though the technological gap was not extremely wide, the competitive position in developed markets waned due to indifference and lack of creativity. Cash-flow from overpriced sales to Eastern Europe and to the Yugoslavian South went down the drain of low productivity.

The economy in southern Yugoslavia was in an even more deplorable state and payments for Slovenian deliveries of goods and services were late or none. The federal state, however, took its share generously. Large individual hard-currency savings were confiscated from Slovenian commercial banks, subsidies for underdeveloped republics in the South were increased etc. In the course of several years even the Slovenian economy slowly collapsed in on itself.

The roots of the collapse were much less in economics than in the decay of the culture, its values and ethics.

The Attainment of Independence

Then a younger and more liberal generation prevailed in the upper layers of the power structure in Slovenia. It rose against the governance from Belgrade and started the disintegration of the already weakened monolithic Yugoslav communist party. In the meantime, however, a nationalistic regime gained control in Serbia and suppressed the autonomy of the two administrative regions, Kosovo and Vojvodina. Pressures on Slovenia increased and a Slovenian initiative to transform Yugoslavia into a confederation was refused.

Slovenia then decided on the formidable step and unilaterally declared independence; Croatia followed this move. The risks were huge and hard to predict. The decision was made in the upper echelons of Slovenian power structures, but the support of the population was immediate and unanimous. When, only several hours later, the Yugoslav army – allegedly the fourth largest in Europe – tried to block with

tanks the border crossings to Italy and Austria, the people on the street gave immediate support to the scarce Slovenian police and militia units. The army intervention
was fortunately limited and badly prepared. It was easily blocked, then diplomacy
went to work and the army decided to leave Slovenia. The "War for Slovenia"
appears now to be an episodic skirmish compared with events following only weeks
and months later in Croatia and in Bosnia.

Six months later, Slovenia was admitted to the United Nations and an
all-embracing restructuring process was started in the Slovenian economy. It was
not a neatly planned and managed process; the small new state had to be established, international relations taken up, the first multi-party parliament went through
initial difficulties. But, for Slovenia, it was a miracle, the beginning of a new age: so
deep-rooted was the repulsion against the alien culture, its mores and values, and its
objectionable moral and ethics.

Slowly, however, the pressures of reality became to be felt. The Serbian market
was blocked, the republics of Macedonia and Montenegro were practically bank-
rupt, without direct communications with Slovenia, Croatia continued its traditional
role of rivalry with Slovenia and Bosnia went under in fighting and destruction. The
average Slovenian company found itself overnight deprived of one half of its markets, left with the tiny domestic market and with exports to the demanding Western
markets experiencing depressed price levels for not-very-modern Slovenian products. Even the once lucrative Eastern European markets changed due to economic
difficulties and Western competition. Even the existing bilateral trading and payment agreements impeded the continuity of Slovenian exports to Eastern Europe.

Yet the flow of taxes, subsidies and other levies to the ex-Yugoslavia was
stopped too. This partially compensated the rising cost of the newly established
Slovenian state.

But another set of problems started to ascend. Slovenes left the corrupt Balkans
to become European, but discovered they had taken with them a surprisingly thick
layer of the Balkan decay. The roots grown in Yugoslavia during 70 years were
much deeper than expected and the symptoms of the underlying ethical degradation
could hardly be disregarded. The image of Slovenia in developed countries was far
from excellent. The once so popular slogan "Europe Now!" had to be reluctantly
reworded to "Europe after-tomorrow."

Many Slovenian companies ran into difficulties, losing money, fighting low
liquidity, wondering where their markets had gone. Retaining the payment of taxes,
modifying loss-and-profit statements to "positive-zero" results (no profit – no taxes!), late payments to suppliers, delayed repayment of bank loans and many more –
all this continued to be the usual practice in business. At the same time,
over-employment and low productivity continued, but wages were still pretty regularly paid and salaries to management were on the rise. Financial auditing and control was still in an embryonic stage, and enforcement of taxation remained weak.

The democratically elected parliament was lost in disputes and struggles. The
law reestablishing private property was unanimously agreed to in principle, but was

delayed, and the fundamental property and denationalization laws were passed only after nearly two-years of parliamentary debates. In the legal vacuum, speculative activities spread widely. Many medium and large companies were not restructured and turned around to profitability, but only broken up in very small companies to facilitate ownership transfers to speculators. The government, after a while, stepped in to stop the mainstream of these speculations, but a lot of irreversible damage to business and to the image of Slovenian companies was already done.

In many medium and large companies which passed the official procedure of ownership definition, boards of directors were established, mostly with a minority of non-executive, external directors. With legislation being fragmental, these boards of directors became effective only in companies with efficient and honest management. Many boards, however, were blocked at the very start; management obstructed any form of control to retain freedom in running the company according to their interests and intentions (Tavcar, 1992).

Thousands of very small companies were registered overnight under provisional regulations; many of them started to fill up the void below the level of the "self-managed" public enterprises, performing very necessary functions, mostly in retail trade and services. Many, however, tried their best to operate in the gaps of the legal system, and many speculated and entered clearly illegal activities. With the old-fashioned administration and overburdened courts of justice the public control over these companies was deplorably inefficient. Several big and internationally respectable Slovenian corporations became involved in scandalous affairs, including criminal actions, which led to bankruptcies, extensive damage to creditors and deterioration of corporate and Slovenian image in general.

On the other hand, with labor unions only beginning to gain influence in direction, tens of thousand of workers were dismissed. Many were deprived of social subsidies, indemnities and early retirement schemes. The social differentiation was accelerated, the living standards of lower income categories deteriorated considerably. On the other hand, the "grey" economy, evading taxes, social security and regulation in general, still remains important; accounting, by some estimates, for as much as one-third of the GNP.

The Slovenian situation is by no means unique; it is typical for an economy and society in a turbulent environment. Slovenia is certainly still much better off materially and morally than the majority of ex-Soviet and Eastern European states today. The initial crisis period is over, a very considerable number of inefficient, large public ("self-managed") companies have been restructured already, exports are on the rise, the balance of payments is positive in spite of a very liberal import policy, the conversion of extensive bad bank loans into public debt is under way, and, after recent elections, a much more effective and efficient parliament and government were instituted. The general decline of industrial production has also been brought under control as well as inflation, which, by a very restrictive monetary policy has been kept in the two-digit range.

But the most important issue in the background and the most difficult to cope with is the restitution of values and ethics and general behavior to a level which would seem acceptable by European standards. This is, evidently, an extremely complex and subtle undertaking.

The teaching of the Slovenia case is apparent: the values of yesterday become unethical tomorrow, but it would be unethical to judge yesterday's ethics by present standards knowing that, in the evolutionary process, the present standards may not persevere as time goes by.

Management Consulting in a Changing Environment

The societal ethics in Slovenia, as already shown, underwent dramatic changes during the last decades. Consulting had to follow these changes, to be useful to clients; a consulting process not adding value for the client is professionally unethical. Therefore consulting ethics have to change in time.

The "Leaden Years"

The consulting process in Slovenia then was mostly limited to straightforward consulting services – in market research, productivity improvement, cost management, logistics and organizational structures and systems in general. An association of consulting organizations was established, not so much for professional purposes, but to serve as an umbrella for consulting organizations, which would otherwise be administratively merged in a single large bureaucratic organization – for easier administrative and political control.

In most cases, a proper analysis of organizational strategies and goals and of strategic management was not performed: this would not be in line with ideological postulates. At this time management was considered to be only a staff function carrying out the decisions of the workers' council. Consultants were hired to build and improve predetermined structures and systems. A lot of hard and honest work was spent for inevitably meager results.

By orthodox professional standards this was unethical; the economic benefits to the customer were much less than the cost of consulting. But then the concept of utility was subordinated to ideological values and "unethical" consulting was quite worthwhile for the management. The consultants, of course, had to stay in the ideological framework to be in business instead of becoming outcasts. Ideology set values – and the majority of managers, honest men and women, sincerely believed in them. This, certainly, was not unethical!

The economics of consulting organizations in those times did not matter. And even if the benefits to clients were necessarily moderate, the prices of consultations were favorable enough. The clients more often than not, were not even able to introduce the recommendations agreed upon due to limited managerial authority. There was no international competition; a foreign consultant would not be allowed to gain an insight into the business affairs of a domestic company.

The Liberalization Period

In the 1980s the dogmatism receded gradually. The concepts of management and strategic planning were accepted incrementally; management consulting became acceptable. Regular organizational audits became a normal part of consulting activities, management training was introduced (first as "marketing – orientation" and only then under the proper name!), the first code of professional consulting ethics was accepted and training of consultants became more widespread. There was much more freedom of thought and expression, the suppressed creativity started to sprout and taboos started to vanish.

But in the period of moral and administrative decay in Yugoslavia and in the making of a new, strictly different legislation, new dimensions of unethical consulting emerged. Some consultants advised on dubious speculations in securities and bonds, in international transactions and foreign-exchange transactions. Many activities were not just using the opportunities of high inflation, low liquidity and limited imports, but were semi-legal at best. In the anarchic environment of the disintegrating Yugoslavia these activities were only sporadically prosecuted and became highly profitable to the clients as well as to some consultants. The overall climate was strictly day-to-day. Unethical conduct became ethical and easily accepted in an unethical society.

Isolated consulting ventures of international consulting firms were accepted with some hesitation, but could mostly not bring change in large bureaucratic corporations, disintegrating internally without real management, lost in disputes and quarrels among cliques and factions. In addition, the local culture was too alien even to experienced consultants to make meaningful advice possible.

Yet the first foreign professional consulting reports with fewer words than impressive graphics had a profound impact on consultants, who, in the semi-past, had to produce impressive if unreadable volumes of verbal analysis and recommendations. Clarity and logical simplicity started to invade consulting.

The Independence Period

The change was sudden, and breathtaking freedom was nearly complete; the Balkans were far away and Europe nearby. Real strategic management consulting based on financial analysis, public auditing, and valuing of companies became the big consulting opportunity. Large self-managed enterprises split into countless small companies, struggling for survival. After restructuring the first groups of companies started to emerge, generating many consulting assignments. A new association for management consulting was founded, and a new code of professional ethics was introduced ("Kodeks", 1992).

However, many consultants still advised management on extremely dubious procedures to appropriate large shares of their companies for next to nothing, or on restructuring projects consisting mostly of ruthless employee dismissals, and manipulations with badly managed government funds for social subsidies.

All medium to large consulting firms in Slovenia then disintegrated, with the exception of the largest, ITEO in Ljubljana, with some 40 consultants and a total staff of seventy; in the past thirty years, ITEO completed more than 2,600 consulting projects. In this consulting firm an extensive strategic reorientation process was introduced, including sixteen week-end workshops led by the author. A new vision was forged, strong cooperation among partners was achieved, consulting programmes, concepts and tools were reconstructed, a modern incentive system introduced, and the ties with a large international consulting firm enriched with mutual benefits. During the three-year process the internal culture changed remarkably.

In the meantime, tens if not hundreds of small, mostly one-person consulting operations were established and tried to survive, using all available tactics. Initially, many enjoyed short-term success; prices were high and consulting standards inconsistent. Companies, on their side, often used these consultants only to get limited advice, but denied to them any insight into the real intents and strategies; it would be unwise to disclose any real inside information to an outsider. Consulting and client ethics were rather inferior in many relationships.

For the first time real international competition in consulting is taking place on a larger scale. It is limited due to costs, which are extremely high by Slovenian standards. The average quality is standard, if not very good by European standards. Straightforward analytic approaches and simple-worded diagnoses have beneficial effects to generations of managers used to eloquence but not to quantifications, to grandiose ideas but not to costs and profits. Yet more projects fail than succeed in implementation, some due to incapable client management, some due to inadequate consultant understanding of the local culture.

Concurrently, however, a healthy differentiation process is in progress between local consultants. The most short-sighted ones are out of business already: expensive, low value consulting is coming to an end. Honest professionals either try to specialize in narrow disciplines or try to work together in informal partnerships. Consulting ethics are beginning to become a substantial competitive advantage.

Situational Consulting Ethics and Environment

Absolute and Relative Consulting Ethics

Uniform ethical standards are meaningless in a turbulently changing society – as seen in the case of Slovenia. Unethical behavior from two decades ago was then permanently under scrutiny for the very reason of being ideologically alien; it would be inconceivable then to introduce consulting in line with present ethical standards. The judgment of "right" and "wrong", of "good" and "bad" is based on prevailing values in the environment. Changing values give rise to new ethics.

Absolute ethics, inflexible and dogmatic may be an intriguing subject for philosophical discussion (Craig and George, 1982) but are utterly inadequate in consulting. The client has to be successful in a real environment and has to adapt largely to the prevailing ethics in it; the same is an imperative for consultants.

Absolute unethics, in which all means are allowed to reach a goal, are also unacceptable as a strategic concept. In all imperfect markets unethical behavior leads to a short-term competitive advantage, but short-term gains are mostly punished by long-term losses. A client may decide on unethical behavior for short-term gains, while consultants will be mostly unwilling to participate in such behavior, knowing that later on they will most likely be found guilty for the consequences. The Slovenia case is proof of that: many small consulting firms, involved in semi-legal counselling, are out of business already, mostly due to loss of credibility.

Consulting ethics have to depend on the situation. Both extremes are excluded, of course: to advise the client along the concept of absolute ethics would be unpractical or applicable too far in the future to be of any use; the concept of absolute unethics, on the extreme, may involve the consultant and/or client in legal prosecution or, at best, bring short-term gains, paid for with ample interest later on.

Environmental influences

There are, obviously, diverse determinants (Kaufmann, 1986) influencing ethics in real situations. It is most likely not unethical for the consultant to give advice leading to short-term gains (nearer to absolute unethic than absolute ethic!) to a client who can't possibly survive long enough for a more long-term (and possibly more ethical) strategy to take effect. The client will, conceivably, be able to use short-term gains for survival and turn-around and be able to endure the inevitable pay-back later on.

It would be unethical not to influence a client by all means available to pursue a long-term strategy (more on the absolute ethic side), if he has sufficient resources to endure a less profitable short-term period. A mediocre client's management could hardly execute a highly ethical, but demanding strategy; a more down-to-earth approach, even if slightly less ethical would be more appropriate.

Consultants will, of course, set limits in the span of ethics in which they are willing to participate. They have to refuse a project which is too unethical by personal standards and by the code of ethics of the professional organization they belong to [1] – but even here the decision is not easy.

The environment, as shown in the Slovenia case, is not stable by any means. If the consulting process shall render long-term benefits possible for the client, it shall consider the trends in the environment as well.[2] To discern causes from effects, driving forces in the background of the trends have to be uncovered.

In the case of Slovenia the following driving forces are being observed in the present and near past:

Structures Preceding Strategy. The so-called inverse Chandler's axiom is certainly valid in Slovenia on a national scale. Fundamental legislation – the denationalization and privatization laws, the new company law, the new accounting and auditing law and several others, as well as the secondary legislative acts needed to implement the fundamental laws – is badly needed. Paradoxically, Slovenia has lost nearly two years in unproductive parliamentary debates – a tribute to the emerging democracy – to approve the most important laws.

Exposure to International Competition. To survive, Slovenian companies have to adapt their business ethics to standards acceptable to their customers. The existing exposure to competition, in foreign as well as in the domestic market, is probably the most forceful agent of change. It is conditioned, however, on a positive payment balance and free imports to Slovenia. Any limitation imposed upon imports would bring back the protectionist environment in which the business ethics can only deteriorate.

Managerial Education and Training. The change of business ethics shall be internalized by an influential majority of Slovenian managers. These, however, have their roots in the past; their managerial education is imperfect. In a protectionist economy only those prevalently dependent on exports were forced to prove themselves in an international managerial competition. The problem in managerial education is mainly the teachers available. The majority of faculties are composed of professors from the semi-past; few among them have insights and personal experiences from business and consulting. Andragogic teaching methods, appropriate for effective managerial training, are practiced by very few professors. The salaries of faculty are still unattractive and many professors seek additional sources of income instead of developing work needed for managerial programs. The interest for managerial training is increasing, but the present extent of studies is still limited. With very few exceptions the managerial graduate education still follows the traditional academic way to the Master of Science and Ph.D. degrees, with little relationship to the needs of business practitioners.

Political Institution as a Model. The behavior in political life and parliamentary activity certainly sets standards for business ethics as well. The initial period of independence was marked by a noticeable lack of tradition in parliamentary democracy. The methods used by political parties and politicians during the last elections in late fall 1992 were often so rude that they repelled voters instead of attracting them. It seems, however, that a wave of public criticism had good results. The standards of behavior in the new and reformed parliament are markedly higher and the new government itself is apparently more professional in approaches and more effective.

Ethics of the Media. The transition from a monistic to a pluralistic society has been abrupt. The newspapers, radio and TV, the most influential media, followed suit, but the majority of reporters, commentators and editors started their professional careers under the old system. For many of them it was easy to exploit a nearly absolute freedom in communications, but to master the expertise necessary for it was a much more demanding task. Understanding the economy and economics, business and management need extensive knowledge and experience. This, again, takes time, and in between it is hard to expect enough support for the subtlest change in the economy, the betterment of business values and ethics. Nevertheless, the media are at least very critical of unethical behavior and give support to the change process.

Foreign Management Behavior. Foreign investors are starting to set up wholly- or partially-owned companies in Slovenia and employing Slovenian managers as well. These managers are then subject to corporate policies, regulations and practices conceived in companies abroad; they accept the new rules, try them out, find them useful and internalize them. Their behavior in business is modified accordingly and observed by their peers in Slovenian enterprises. Examples are set and cautiously followed. This is not a fast process, but the results of it are being felt already.

Management and Other Professional Associations. Management, after decades, is again recognized as a profession. The Management Association of Slovenia promotes its own rules of professional ethics. Several other associations act in a similar manner. The Association of Financial Managers and Accountants, one of the oldest in Slovenia, instituted its own rules of professional conduct thirty years ago; the Association for Advertising Professionals did the same only several years after. The newly established Association of Management Consulting Organizations established its rules of ethics a year ago, and others are following suit. These are all voluntary associations and their sanctions for unethical behavior are necessarily symbolic, but influence individual behavior as well.

Cultural Influences

Consulting organizations, at least the large and prestigious ones, are becoming increasingly global, operating across many countries and many cultures.

In countries which have to adapt to a more developed civilization, consulting shall be an important agent of change. But consulting across cultural gradients involves additional complexity. Blaise Pascal, the great philosopher, wrote long ago: "Verite en-deçu des Pyrenees, erreur au dela" (There are truths on this side of the Pyrenees, which are falsehoods on the other) (Harris and Moran, 1989).

In Slovenia, in the leaden years and in the liberalization period, isolated consulting projects were performed, mostly with very limited success. There were difficulties on both sides. It was not realistic to expect consultant who have spent all their lives in a normal market economy, with private ownership, capital and profits, to give useful advise to managers to whom manipulation and politics were the only sources of power and influence. And it would have been just as unrealistic to expect these managers to concentrate on appropriate return on investment, when profits were a part of the capitalist ideology and equity belonged to nobody.

Even in much more normal circumstances cultural differences bring along complex ethical considerations. In a marketing consulting project it would be ethical for the consultant to advise the client to use very realistic price-setting if this would be normal in the culture of the client's environment. In an Arabic or Balkan culture, however, this could be very bad advice. Everybody there is engaged in speculative pricing and extensive discounts are usual – under haggling and highly emotional negotiation (Harris and Moran, 1989), all using extremely unethical means.

The same is valid when internal power structures are involved in counselling. To propose honest promotion and incentive schemes and management by objectives would be naive at least in a country where intrigue and deceit and extensive internal politics are the rule. International consultants following very strict ethics, valid in their home country, would behave unethically giving advice to clients in a culture with different ethics[3].

Operating across large cultural gradients can be extremely demanding on material and human resources (Tavcar, 1990) and it would predictably be unsuccessful without extensive adaptation to a different culture, as proved repeatedly in Slovenia.

To follow the concept of adaptation may create additional complexities. An international consultant, advising quite ethically a local client in accordance with local culture (and ethics) may find an unpleasant conflict of interest if the client used this advice against competitors. An international company could, in its home country, accuse the consultant of using unethical procedures in the client's country.

Situational Consulting Ethics – and the Client

Even when operating in the same culture, the consultant has to use different styles (implying different degrees of ethics/unethics) according to specific attributes of clients. There is no universal best consulting style, not even the well-known Schein's "process consultation" (Schein, 1987). The same is valid for the consulting ethic, which has to be selected as well.

Consulting can be interpreted as a special case of leadership; then the concepts as promoted by Hersey and Blanchard in "Situational Leadership" (Hersey and Blanchard, 1989) do apply.

The relationship among the consultant and the client may be differentiated according to clients' readiness to cooperate and accept advice and clients' ability to cooperate and to implement the advice received. In the following matrix these concepts are combined with the consulting categories, as defined by A. Maister (Maister, 1989).

A "low capability-low readiness" client has to be instructed, how to act; a "low capability-high readiness" client has to be taught, instructed, made more capable to adopt the advice; a "high capability-low readiness" client shall be influenced to internalize the advice; a "high capability-high readiness" client should be ethically manipulated to implement the advice (which he would equally be able to arrive at, but did not for a variety of reasons).

This model, again, opens an array of ethical dilemmas. The concepts may be effective, leading to the consultant's goal, but the ethics involved may be either disputatious or even contestable. The boundaries of influence, under the full awareness of the client, and of manipulation, even based on the noblest possible intentions, but with the client, hopefully, unaware of the subdued influence, represent an extremely sensitive area in consultant-client relationship.

A less demanding consulting model ("procedures", even "grey hair") can suc-

FIGURE 1. Client – Consultant Relationship

High

1.	2.
"BACKGROUND CONSULTING" Apparently no counselling *The internalization model* The problem is owned neither by the consultant nor the client	"BRAINS" Creating innovative solutions *The expertise model* The problem stays with the client, who is advised upon solutions
3.	4.
"GRAY HAIR" Expertise and experience transfer *The experience model* The problem is is shared by both the consultant and the client	"PROCEDURES" Performing services *The execution model* The problem stays with the consultant, responsible for a good job

CLIENT CAPABILITY (to the left, middle)

Low

CLIENT
High   READINESS   Low

cessfully be used with a very capable and/or ready client, if the client and the consultant agree upon the contents of consulting. On the other hand, it is useless to try a "brains" approach with a less capable and ready client. A "background" approach would, in this situation, become even more ethically sensitive; the responsibility for the ethics of manipulation are entirely with the consultant.

In the situation leadership model the "procedures" would correspond to the "telling" style, the "grey-hair" to the "selling" style, the "brains" to the "participating" style and the "background" to the "delegating" style. Accordingly, the consultant will be completely concentrated on the content of counselling in the "procedures model" slightly less in the "grey hair", even less in the "brains" and very little in the "background" model. In the same sequence the involvement of the client will increase gradually. In the "procedures" model the consultant will not concentrate on the client's personnel, as the consultant has to do the job. The same will happen, apparently, in the "background" model, at least as far as the client will be aware.

The consultant will, however, concentrate on the client's personnel in the "grey hair" and "brains" models, where success will depend upon the acceptance of the consultant's recommendations.

In the Slovenian case, remarkably different client profiles are being dealt with; the degree of differentiation in a country experiencing turbulent change is found to be extreme. Not choosing the most appropriate model on the client "readiness-capability" scale, as well as not selecting the best model according to the contents of the consulting process, may result in a lower degree of client benefit and would in itself be professionally unethical.

The judgments and decisions imposed on the consultant are, in real life situations, complex and even ambiguous. The resulting stresses and even disagreements (Bennett, 1990) with clients experienced by consultants may be extreme, even to the extent where deviant behavior is anticipated.

The notion of culturally conditioned, differentiated ethics of consulting may be disturbing enough, but in the global village it will be encountered quite regularly. The chances for success of consulting in culturally differing environments will depend considerably upon an enlightened use of the situational ethics concept.

Conclusion

The Slovenia Case

An efficient and timely comeback to Europe is a vital necessity for Slovenia. Without an increase in the industrial output, Slovenia would again be condemned to massive economic emigration as a hundred years ago and during the recessionary 1930s. Europe has a limited interest in Slovenia, which is not, as in the past, a gateway to the Yugoslav market; still perceived political risks as well as the relative inefficiency of Slovenian enterprises impeded capital flows to Slovenia.

A mediating business role among Central and Eastern Europe, across the cultural barriers certainly is a chance for Slovenian manufacturing and trading companies. This expert service role, however, is conditioned on having enough confidence in Slovenia, and how can one expect confidence in a business partner which still behaves the Balkan way?

It took only a few decades for the environmental influences to deteriorate the Slovenian business ethics: slowly, invisibly, but to a substantial degree, which, by now, is a major competitive disadvantage. Several driving forces are assisting the reestablishment of standard European business ethics in Slovenia. But the major factor, subdued in the background, is an age-old allegiance of Slovenian people to the European culture and tradition.

To mediate among Central and Eastern Europe is, in essence, a large scale consulting process. The success of this process will, to a large degree, depend on the professional ethics applied. The notion of situational ethics may be the crucial concept in this process.

Situational Consulting Ethics

The main determinants are:

- the environment: attitudes, dynamics, culture,
- the clients: capability and readiness, resources, short- vs. long-term concepts,
- the projects: the appropriate fit between the content of a project and the consulting model used is a major ethical issue in itself.

Situational ethics are only the means to an end. They are an extremely important success factor when managing an organization in a turbulent environment and when the activities are performed across cultural gaps and barriers. Determining the proper position on the continuum of unacceptable absolute ethics and the equally unacceptable absolute unethic calls for a thorough analysis and understanding of the situation and trends in the environment or environments.

The Slovenian case not only proves that but may also serve as a guide to many companies intending to operate in changing and culturally alien environments.

Summary

The consulting process must create added value and bring benefits to the client in a given situation. Therefore, neither absolute ethics nor absolute unethics, but rather situational ethics are appropriate for the consulting process. Strategic consulting decisions are based on ethics and trends in clients' environment as well as on the subject of counselling, client attributes and clients' long- vs. short-term orientation. Consultants have to apply situational ethics to the benefit of clients and to their own benefit and to avoid extremes, where ethically determined activities may endanger either the client or the consultant. The turbulent environment of Slovenia is being used to illustrate the concepts and strategies proposed. Slovenia could serve as a valid model for situational ethics – and even a convenient mediator, facilitating the entry to culturally alien Eastern European markets.

Notes

1. Compare FEACO, ACME, etc. Codes
2. Compare Stutz 88 (180-191)
3. Compare Weiss 92 (251-254)

References

Albert, Kenneth J. 1983: *How To Solve Business Problems – The Consultant's Approach to Business Problem Solving.* NY: McGraw-Hill.
Bennett, Roger 1990: *Choosing and Using Management Consultants.* London: Kogan Page.
Craig, Gordon A. and George, Alexander L. 1992: *Force and Statecraft.* London.

Greiner, Larry E. and Metzger, Robert O. 1983: *Consulting to Management.* Englewood Cliffs, NJ: Prentice-Hall.

Harris, Philip R. and Moran, Robert T. 1989: *Managing Cultural Differences.* Houston: Gulf Publishing Co.

Hersey, Paul and Blanchard, Ken 1988: *Management of Organizational Behavior.* Englewood Cliffs, NJ: Prentice-Hall Intl.

Hofmann, Michael, Rosenstiel, Lutz von and Zapotocky, Klaus 1991: *Die sozio-kulturellen Rahmenbedingungen Für Unternehmensberater.* Stuttgart: Kohlhammer Verlag.

Kubr, Milan 1980: *Management Consulting.* Beograd-Geneve: JUGOR-ILO.

Kubr, Milan 1991: *How to Select and Use Consultants – A Client's Guide.* Geneve: ILO.

Maister, David H. 1989: *Professional Service Firm Management, (4th ed.).* Boston: Maister Associates, Inc.

Maister, David H. 1990: *Professional Service Firm Management,* 1990 Supplement. Boston: Maister Associates, Inc.

Schein, Edgar H. 1987: *Process Consultation, Lessons for Managers and Consultants.* Reading, Mass: Addison-Wesley.

Stutz, Hans-Rudolf 1988: *Management Consulting, Organisationsstrukturen am Beispiel einer interaktiven Dienstleistung.* Bern: Paul Haupt.

Tavcar, Mitja 1992: *Sodelovanje S Svetovalnimi Organizacijami – V Dejavnostni Vidiki Managementa.* Materials for 2nd MBA-EPF, EPF Maribor.

Tavcar, Mitja 1992: *Koncepti In Struktura Izvajanja Ekspertnih Storitev.* Organizacija in kadri 25, 3-4.

Tavcar, Mitja 1992: *The Role of Quasi-Ownership Structures In Transition to Private Ownership of Slovenian Enterprises.* 4th Organization and Information Systems Conference, Bled.

Tavcar, Mitja 1990: *Transcultural Marketing Portfolio.* 10th Annual International Conference, Strategic Management Society, Stockholm.

Weiss, Alan 1992: *Million Dollar Consulting – The Professional's Guide to Growing a Practice.* NY: McGraw-Hill.

Kodeks Zdruzenja Za Management Consulting Slovenije. 1992: Gospodarska zbornica Slovenije, Zdru`enje za management consulting, Ljubljana.

PART V

Concluding Issues

17

The Dilemmas of Business Ethics Courses

José Mª Ortiz Ibarz
and
Alejo José G. Sison

Abstract

Starting off from a general notion of a dilemma as that situation in which any of the alternative courses of action leads to some unwanted consequences, this chapter seeks to address two current and inter-related issues concerning business ethics courses. Firstly, it shall consider the inclusion of ethics in undergraduate and master programs in economics and business administration; and secondly, the "a-rational" choice forced on the students between the teleological and deontological doctrines with which these courses normally end. The authors defend that both issues could only be dealt with satisfactorily from a sound and valid "virtue ethics", properly integrated into the economic and political realms of human activity. Concrete recommendations as to the reformulation of business ethics courses – with an emphasis on rational commitment, as opposed to "value-neutral" presentations – are explained in its concluding portion.

Is Business Ethics an Oxymoron?

Perhaps no other discipline has encountered so strong a resistance to its being included in university programs leading to degrees in economics and business administration as business ethics.[1] The fact is that it seems to have entered on the wrong foot; since in the majority of cases, its inclusion has come about as a vindictive move in favor of conserving the ecological equilibrium, protecting the physical and mental health and safety of consumers and workers, or against corrupt and unfair practices – "scandals" – specially in the financial sector.[2] Ethics has never been called upon for its intrinsic value or unsubstitutable contribution to the flourishing of a truly human life; but rather, always as a "last resort" or a desperate remedy for some unwanted side-effects or harmful consequences of otherwise tolerated,

H. von Weltzien Hoivik and A. Føllesdal (eds.), Ethics and Consultancy: European Perspectives, 217-228.

if not entirely permitted customs or modi operandi. Ethics has been forcibly summoned to the world of business for "extra-ethical" motives; and this has seriously damaged its very content and method.

Neither has opposition stopped, once already in business and economics curricula for predominantly pragmatic reasons. Business ethics is still regarded by many as a threat, an intruder, or at best, a useless parasite of other more "productive" subjects. Its self-proclaimed enemies have slyly made propaganda of its supposedly paradoxical substance: rivers of ink have flowed trying to make sense of and defend such a "theory." [3] Others have adopted a less radical stance: while acknowledging the presence of ethics courses in business schools, they nevertheless consider it merely as a passing fad, a contingent demand of a capricious market that somehow has to be satisfied, for reasons no different than any other consumer claim. Without denying the premise of its problematic or even contradictory nature, the most solid attempts at its justification so far have simply been based on the inevitable "ethical dimension" of human choices and actions (among which, logically, business affairs are counted). [4] Yet, although they may accept the legitimate existence of business ethics courses as providers of relevant criteria for decision-making and action plans; nonetheless, they do not understand the peculiar role and influence of moral norms on such activities, thus putting these on the same plane as other "technical" (versus operations, accounting, financial, marketing etc.) considerations. The scientific foundations of ethics in its specific application to business therefore remains shoddy, if not thoroughly inconsistent. Even if we were to argue successfully for the substance or existence of business ethics (i.e., it is no oxymoron), we would still lack convincing reasons as to the necessity of its inclusion in academic programs, because its contribution to the good of an enterprise in terms of productivity or profit obviously pales in comparison with the other technical subjects.

Added difficulty comes from the firmly rooted attitudes of the group of students to which business ethics courses are addressed. Generally, it is an audience that prides itself in being resolute "men of action" – superior to those who often get entangled in the web of their own theories, in want of efficiency and of the production of tangible results. This prejudice against whatever form of abstract reasoning is cultivated and "taught" in the other courses through snide remarks on the part of professors who unstintingly press for expediency and "practicality". The unrenounceable final intention of all business ethics courses to positively affect human life is taken to be "maximalist" and utopian: that is, far beyond the reach of a single, standard credit course offered to students who, for the large part, already are mature and have made their fundamental value options. [5]

The aforementioned problems are aggravated in the case of MBA programs. These are designed for university graduates (traditional preference has been for those with engineering degrees) with a couple of years' professional experience and who desire to equip themselves with immediately applicable problem-solving techniques to supposedly "true-to-life" situations in which managers and entrepreneurs find themselves. Being a luxury good, it of course demands a corresponding price;

its subjective value becoming even more prohibitive for the full-time students who quit their jobs and normally rely on loans to finance, meanwhile, their expenses. Additional stress comes from the risk of not finding any suitable compensatory employment later on. The addressees of business ethics courses, therefore, already have clearly established life goals and job profiles, none of which favors receptiveness towards this particular subject matter. Business ethics courses may then not only be unnecessary, but likewise inopportune given the peculiar circumstances of their public.

Recently, however, some winds of change have blown in this respect. Journal articles questioning the relevance of actual MBA curricula (specially those offered by American schools) have raised a great deal of controversy not only among the academics – many of whom have hastened to modify their programs – but also, among the different corporations that have traditionally hired MBA graduates.[6] The optimists could claim that there is no real cause for worry; the decline in the demand of MBA graduates being a mere repercussion of the widespread economic recession corresponding to some already known economic cycle. Yet a more realistic – in the sense of "unprejudiced" – stance would be, perhaps, to acknowledge that MBA graduates have failed to meet their employers' expectations: as a result, many firms have decided to avail themselves, instead, of the services of fresh graduates made to undergo some specific in-house training.

As the above-mentioned commentaries suggest, some possible causes for the lack of adjustment between corporate demands and the services actually rendered by MBA graduates are, on the institutional level, the exaggerated importance given by schools to the quantitative, analytic and technical skills to the detriment of the "soft" skills – those with a highly humanistic or "people-oriented" content; the latter being the kind of knowledge capable of unifying the former into an organic and functional whole, while at the same time, lending meaning to any professional's existence as a human being and person. Secondly, schools seem to have overlooked an otherwise obvious fact: even on the premise that both entrepreneurs and managers are not "born" as such but "made"; nevertheless, an entrepreneur definitely requires a different kind of formal preparation from a manager. Relying on a reasonable intuition, we may say that whereas entrepreneurs have a greater need of quantitative and analytical (hard) skills, managers do so of qualitative and comprehensive (soft) ones. On the personal level, corporations commonly complain that MBA degree-holders are overly ambitious and too much on the fast-track (the yuppie prototype); they display an utter lack of commitment to the firm they are connected with and seem to serve only their individual interests. The truth is that unless a previous commitment of one's life with the proper values is made, prudence – understood as "right reason in action" – simply cannot be taught nor acquired. The most one may ever achieve is to impart a high degree of craftiness, astuteness or cunning, often mistaken for prudence, although it is but its mere simulacrum.

As we have said, MBA programs were originally designed for engineers who, after some professional experience, leave their company's production lines to occupy managerial and executive posts. This further schooling was meant to provide them not with the raw, quantitative and analytical skills – which given their background, could already be taken for granted – but rather, with some "practical knowledge" in economics, business administration, business policy and organizational theory. Nowadays, MBA students represent a more heterogeneous sampling, and hardly any previous common knowledge, quantitative or otherwise, could be presupposed. Consequently, of the two-year programs the entire first year is designed as an effort towards "leveling" or homogenization of skills in areas such as accounting, finance, marketing, organizational behavior, operations, business policy, etc. Another significant change is that whereas initially, the MBA curriculum was elaborated, strictly speaking, to prepare entrepreneurs and managers; neither of these two professions will generally be assumed by today's graduates. The current trend is characterized by a preference towards work in a consultancy firm (at least, as the first employment) or in the financial sector (investment banking, stock, currency, options and futures markets, etc.). In short, instead of putting entrepreneurial and management know-how into practice and thus creating wealth, apparently MBA graduates as a whole simply aspire for a comfortable niche in some established corporation from which to acquire or accumulate wealth, even perhaps at the cost of "free-riding" on others.

"Teleology Versus Deontology" or Skepticism?

Before analyzing the alternative between teleology and deontology at which philosophical reflection in business ethics courses often comes to a halt, let us examine the content and the preferred research methods or teaching procedures used in them. The reason for this is that the subject matter of any scientific discipline – including ethics of course – is never alien to the form or manner in which it is approached, cultivated and imparted. [7]

The majority if not all of business ethics textbooks (and courses) are structured as follows. [8] The first few chapters are dedicated to an objective and "value-neutral" exposition of various ethical theories, normally grouped into the teleological (utilitarian, consequentialist, proportionalist, etc.) and the deontological (Kant-inspired rights and duties bound) families, accounts of rival doctrines of socio-economic and political justice (liberal capitalism versus socialism), plus a brief sketch of the author's particular understanding of the corporation's moral status and the individual's role within that context. Next comes a more or less ordered list of cases for discussion, dealing with both "micro-issues" (i.e., conflicts of a limited reach, often calling only for individual action) and "macro-issues" (i.e., problems of a wider scope affecting business policy, and thus demanding corporate deliberation, decision and action). [9] The question of an appropriate language is often skirted – a "technical" in the sense of "special" jargon is as a rule avoided – if not dealt with as "a matter of fact", or as a free and arbitrary choice among one based on rights and duties, one on the maximization of happiness, another on "virtues", etc. [10] In short, there is a very strong implicit appeal to a hypothetical ethical common sense as applied, nevertheless, to avowedly complex business activities.

Rather than elaborate a summary and critique of the proposed teleological and deontological models, we'd like to call attention to what lies behind the presentation of such an alternative. We refer mainly to an unconfessed subjectivism, relativism or skepticism on the part of many business ethics professors (and ethics professors tout court) which makes them unable to do their tasks.[11] Their feebleness in demanding any sort of commitment towards any substantive version of justice and the good from their students is, in a large measure, the mere reflection of the lack of commitment which they perhaps in their own lives suffer. Thus their insistence to function in an exclusively "operational level" of ethical knowledge, as proper to "practitioners" or "ethical consultants", and making a conscious evasion of any meaningful discourse on the foundations of ethical theory.[12] If one does not believe in the truth, or does not believe that the truth can be known, then he absolutely has no business teaching, much less an ethics course. The very foundations of ethics lie on the acceptance of the truth that there is a good life for human beings to live, a good character and good habits for human beings to acquire, good actions for human beings to perform despite all their empirical differences; and that the "practical knowledge" of such a good life, character, habit and action is never indifferent to the kind of lives that human beings actually live (nor to the manner in which they exercise their professions, be it in business or elsewhere). This anthropological "feedback" between thought and action is of the essence for ethics.

As regards case studies, the limits of such a methodology do not seem to be clearly perceived by many business ethics professors either. The indication always found at the first page of the text according to which cases are prepared "as a basis for class discussion rather than to illustrate either effective or ineffective handling of an administrative situation" should serve as a sufficient warning; but unfortunately, for a great number, apparently it does not. An intelligent reaction would be to ask, "what then is the point in discussing the case, or even reading it?" Easily, what could otherwise have been a valuable teaching complement, is trivialized and converted into a game to be won by whoever, by force of rhetoric, manages to dominate the discussion. No ethical catharsis can be hoped to be effected; only a further entrenching of one's rationally unexamined prejudices. And what is even worse, in their quest for a pragmatic version of truth, many ethics professors in business schools cannot but breed staunch skeptics among their students.[13]

Defenders of the case method repeatedly insist on its intuitive appeal and practicality. For a moment, we would like to question both points.[14] With respect to the first, we may say that whereas cases illustrating micro-issues (such as truth in advertising, cheating on expense accounts and contracts, sexual harassment, on-the-job safety, etc.) would rate high on appeal and those concerning macro-issues (corporate conscience, responsibility and legitimacy, the debate between capitalist and socialist systems, for example) low; nevertheless, conflicts evolving from macro-issues are definitely more important for people being trained to occupy senior management and executive posts than those which focus on micro-issues. And as to the second point, we would like to express our doubt as to whether practicality is adequately understood in this context: what are narrated usually are camouflaged true to life events that occurred once, in a very concrete time and place, and which would never happen again. Whatever knowledge the student can draw from such a vicarious experience therefore would depend heavily on his grasp of its epistemological limits and status. Yet this condition for learning from the analysis of cases, we think, is not adequately clarified.

Back to the Virtues

The very proposal of a return to virtue-based ethics would provoke a cynical smile among many of our colleagues. It perhaps would remind them of that all-too-familiar Sunday school preaching that they have received; something completely detached or alien to daily life and work, specially if that consists in business.[15] Once again, we think that this is nothing else but the fruit of an erroneous and biased understanding of the reality of the virtues.

A genuine virtue-based ethics, that is, one faithful to the Aristotelian[16] and Thomist[17] traditions, would not simply incorporate the advantages of a teleological or a deontological version of ethics sans their inconveniences, but more importantly, it would likewise be "true" – meaning one designed in accordance with human nature. Like any form of teleological ethics, it shall pay special attention to the results of one's actions and omissions – their specific contribution to a flourishing life or happiness; but unlike teleological ethics, it shall establish the ethical value of an act at the very moment of its realization, without having to wait for its whole sequence of historical repercussions before issuing any judgment on the same. Thus, it is a model of ethical reasoning that recognizes and takes into account the true limits of an agent's responsibility, without, of course, denying the influence that our actions exert on each other through time. In a similar manner to ethics of a deontological inspiration, it would uphold the validity of absolute – in the sense of exceptionless – moral norms or principles; but these would be truly operative ones, and not merely formal or empty injunctions. Besides, such a model of ethical rationality does not turn its back on human tendencies and inclinations, passions and desires on the pretext of fulfilling moral duties as pure and disinterestedly as possible; rather, it posits a correct ordering of human faculties so much so that all of these are politically and not tyrannically subject to reason, and may thus accompany reason, in the realization of ethically good acts.

Let us now consider how virtues are incorporated into human life according to Aristotelian and Thomist doctrines. First of all, human life cannot be conceived as a mere aggregate of acts, without any underlying element of unity except for the temporal one. On the contrary, we know that human life is comprised of actions in an uninterrupted series carried out by the same subject or agent. Foremost among the integrating elements are the habits. Together with action, habits determine human character. Character is the manner in which a human person reacts and behaves according to an end which he himself freely chooses and to which he directs himself. Through an examination of his character, a person perceives his actions as concrete steps towards the attainment of his conception of a good and flourishing life.

The Thomist treatise on habits is found after his treatise on human action and passions. This outline obeys his guiding intuition according to which habits, together with the "bare" human potencies, are the intrinsic principles of voluntary human actions. In effect, habits are found half-way between operative human faculties and their proper acts; habits dispose these potencies towards particular kinds of acts. Habits, therefore, arise when in a given human operative potency or faculty, there exists a high degree of indeterminacy with respect to its acts; and as regards the potency or the faculty itself, there exists a real capacity for its modification. In other words, habits require, as conditions for their appearance, freedom of action and temporality (inasmuch as being subject to time is indicative of the capacity for change in the human person).

These very same conditions of freedom and temporality which make habits possible make them necessary for human beings: devoid of instincts and of innate manners of doing things, people cannot survive; that is, they cannot prolong their existence in time, were they not to determine their freedom through the acquisition of habits. In this sense, habits are real and operative determinations in the nature of a being who is, at the same time, rational, free and existent in time. The growth of habits in an individual subject or person constitutes his biographical perfection. But habits do not only bring along with them an interior perfection; they likewise entail an external or objectifiable improvement. By reason of the former, habits improve one's character; whereas by reason of the latter, habits improve one's actions and the results of those actions (history may be seen as a series of technological developments brought about by the acquisition of ever better techniques, crafts, skills or habits). Habits, therefore, refer to that which results when a free and rational being, subject to change and time, performs an action and that action somehow remains with him, becomes part of his being and his manner of acting.

Ever since Aristotle, the ontological status of a habit has been established as that of an accident (as opposed to a substance); and among the accidents, it corresponds specifically to that of quality. The genus quality is divided into the entitative (e.g. health or infirmity) and the operative (e.g., dispositions, virtues and vices). Such a metaphysical definition of habit indicates that it is something that necessarily inheres in another, in a substance (that is, human nature as found in a specific individual); that it is a stable or even permanent accident, as quality denotes; and that it affects both the "manner of being" (an entitative quality) as the "manner of acting" (an operative quality) of the subject or agent. A habit is a permanent disposition found in an individual substance – as the person – to act in a determined manner; and as such a disposition, it adds to the "bare" or natural operative potency a new inclination or force, a modification that allows it to act in a specific way as if it were second nature.

Habits are perfective of the nature of the subject himself and of the actions proceeding from his nature. Insofar as the habit acquired conforms to the natural end of that subject or agent it is called a virtue; and when it goes against the correct natural inclinations of the subject it is called a vice. The possession of a good habit or virtue thus perfects the subject or agent in a double manner: objectively, in what refers to his actions or operations; and subjectively, in what refers to his sense of fulfillment and satisfaction, since actions springing from a virtue or good habit always bring along with them a certain pleasure, ease, immediacy and spontaneity. Thus goes the incorporation of virtues and their effects on particular human lives. Next we shall explain how virtues likewise affect and perfect the necessary and constitutive social dimension of human lives in the spheres of economic and political activities.

Present day communitarians[18] have called our attention to an undeniable, but heretofore little-publicized feature of Aristotelian and Thomistic ethics: its necessary linkage with economics and politics forming the triad of "practical philosophy". Until then, the common understanding of these disciplines has been such that ethics referred exclusively to the ordering of private lives; politics, to the governing of the social dimension of individual actions; and economics, to the acquisition and administration of wealth, considered mainly in terms of material goods and benefits. There seems to have been a revival of the idea that in the same way that human beings do not constitute themselves fully as persons without developing their relationships with each other; neither would they be able to reach their final goal or end (a verbal agreement exists on this being happiness or eudaimonia) outside of adequately designed and structured economic and political institutions (as the family, school, the workplace, a religious group, etc. and civil society at large). Ethics therefore could not remain indifferent either to economic or to political activities; nor could it simply function as a limit or a brake applied to activities which, economically or politically speaking, would be permissible or correct. Rather, on this view, ethics is considered as a spring or source of good economic and political theory and action. This of course does not mean that ethics should provide efficient economic models nor set the laws by which government and social life should abide (that would be an intrusion to the legitimate autonomy of these sciences); but neither should economics and politics be cultivated as "sciences" independently of ethics.[19] One cannot first develop an economic theory or a political doctrine and then, later on, summon ethics to rectify it. Going back to our initial concern, we cannot impose an orthodox capitalist model of the economy and a mainstream liberal vision of politics to business students and then, further on, expect them to turn a sympathetic ear to our ethical pleading, remonstrances and imperatives, for example. [20] This simply would not work.

Just how are ethics, economics and politics integrated in the classical scheme? First of all, these three "branches" of practical philosophy are hierarchically ordered such that both ethics and economics are subject to that "kingly craft" of politics. Why is this so? Primarily because politics has as its main objective the attainment of eudaimonia or happiness, which, according to the premises of classical philosophy, could only be achieved in the intertwining of human lives – never in solitude – in a justly ordered city or state. Needless to say that such a state requires certain minor socio-cultural, educational, legal, religious, athletic and business institutions, all of which contribute to the development of necessary aspects of a fully human existence. Ethics, for its part, is entrusted with the cultivation of human excellence or virtue (arete). Virtue arises from a determination of the will to its proper end – the good for man – and culminates in the effective realization of that good through action – thanks to which we call a man good. As we have previously said, virtue is by no means an abstract, ethereal reality; but something concrete and operative – a good habit -which human beings have to face in their ordinary lives through the performance of their activities. Through virtue, human beings are said to truly possess their lives at any given point in time: it is a synthesis of the past (actions already performed, experiences once had, still remain in the substrate of the human psyche and bodily faculties) and the future (a pre-determination of human acts yet to be realized as regards their ends and manner of execution; a capacity to make or do more and better activities) in the present moment (the possession of virtue is, in itself, always an act). The need for economics merely obeys the fact that men are material creatures, and therefore demand a minimum of comfort and well-being (that is, the satisfaction of basic desires and necessities) in order to be really happy. On one hand, it would be extremely difficult if not totally impossible for a human person to lead a flourishing life – or to practice virtue, for that matter – in a state of destitution. Yet, on the other hand, the very desire, possession, administration and use or enjoyment of material goods should issue from and be guided by ethically correct principles. Living an ethically good life, practicing virtue, therefore, is man's best bet so that in spite of economically adverse circumstances, he may nevertheless be "entitled" to happiness, once these contingencies have passed. The contrary, however, does not hold: economic success does not at all ensure one happiness nor personal moral worth.

In conclusion, we hereby propose the recovery of economics – and of business or enterprise, as one of its essential components – as a prudential science or craft, as opposed to the technical or positivist attitude and manner in which it is presently cultivated.[21] And as we have earlier said, the prudential cultivation of economics – the re-establishment of its linkages with ethics and politics – is only possible on the basis of a previous personal commitment to the truly good life for man; one consisting in virtue, and neither in wealth, nor in pleasure, nor in honor or power, primarily (though of course, it leaves room for these, in the measure that they are subject to virtue). This commitment is the conditio sine qua non for the proper teaching and learning of business ethics, both on the part of the professors as well as of the students. Anything outside or beneath this would be, for the well-meaning, a source of continued frustration; and for the ill, an instrument for deceit and self-perpetuation; and for all, unfortunately, but a miserable waste of time.

Notes

1. For an analysis of the different reasons with which ethics has been granted entry into business programs, see Alejo José G. Sison, "Hacia una motivación ética en la empresa" *(Servicio de Documentación Empresa y Humanismo,* 20 Oct. 92, 29-34). The author distinguishes among: a) motives that obey an "internal pressure" within the firm (i.e., ethics as a justification of the actions of executives and employees when their individual interests enter into conflict with those of the collective); b) motives that obey an "external pressure" originating from social demands and c) the correct ethical motive, or "ethics for ethics sake."

2. This is true especially of the recent phase of business ethics history (from 1970 until the present) as characterized by Francis P. McHugh *(Keyguide to Information Sources in Business Ethics,* New York: Nichols Publishing, 1988, 8-14).

3. For a summary and a convincing refutation of the principal arguments against the very possibility, necessity and usefulness of business ethics courses, see Ronald F. Duska, "What's the point of a Business Ethics Course?" *(Business Ethics Quarterly,* I-4, Oct. 91, 335-354).

4. Cfr. Arthur L. Caplan & Daniel Callahan (eds.), *Ethics in Hard Times,* New York: Plenum Press, 1981; Amitai Etzioni, *The Moral Dimension,* New York: The Free Press, 1988; Robert Jackall, *Moral Mazes,* Oxford: Oxford University Press, 1988.

5. Cfr. George L. Pamental, "The Course in Business Ethics: Why don't philosophers give business students what they need", *BEQ,* Oct. 91, I-4, 388.

6. We basically have in mind the heated debate sparked by "The Complex Case of Management Education" (Jane C. Linder and H. Jeff Smith, *Harvard Business Review, Sept.-Oct.* 1992, 16-33) and the follow-up commentaries contained in "MBA: Is the Traditional Model Doomed?" (Louis E. Lataif, et. al., *HBR,* Nov.-Dec., 1992, 128-140) plus the article "Is Management still a Science?" (David Freedman, *HBR,* Nov.-Dec., 1992, 26-38).

7. The peculiarity of ethical method as applied to business contrasted with that of other sciences – natural or pure – and that of the different arts has been the recent object of study by José Mª Ortiz ("Ser el mejor: hacer que otros también lo sean", *Cuadernos Empresa y Humanismo,* 36, 1992, 5-9).

8. Our survey extends to the eight most recommended textbooks (throughout their several editions) in American universities according to the study conducted by the Center for Business Ethics, Bentley College, Waltham, Massachusetts (1 April 1982). For a complete bibliographical information, see Francis P. McHugh, *Keyguide to Information Sources in Business Ethics,* New York: Nichols Publishing, 1988, 31-32; 63-68.

9. We are largely indebted to Robert C. Solomon ("Corporate Roles, Personal Virtues: An Aristotelian Approach to Business Ethics", *BEQ,* July 1992, II-3, 319-320) for these distinctions.

10. Thomas Donaldson's stand on this issue as expressed in "The Language of International Corporate Ethics" *(BEQ,* July 1992, II-3, 271-281) is paradigmatic.

11. It is worthwhile to examine the prefaces of business ethics textbooks wherein one finds not only a formulation of course objectives, but also a profession of their respective authors' ethical creeds (if any). Regarding the former, the majority speak of heightening sensitivity and perceptiveness to ethical issues in business, and secondly, of developing analytical and decision-making skills (i.e. proficiency in the use of ethical terms and concepts) regarding the technical aspects (sic) of these ethical issues. No indication whatsoever is made as to the final set of criteria with which an action may be definitively judged as ethically

sound or unsound (i.e. a true guide to deliberation): in its place, a variety of competing doctrines is simply offered.

12. On a different level, this is precisely that "fatal deceit" of objectivity and neutrality which Alasdair MacIntyre denounces in his *Three Rival Versions of Moral Enquiry* (Indiana: Notre Dame Press, 1990).

13. We have found echoes sympathetic to this opinion from Jean Liedtka ("Wounded but Wiser: Reflections on Teaching Ethics to MBA Students", *Journal of Management Education*, Nov. 1992, 16-4, 405-416); Richard Lipke ("A Critique of Business Ethics", BEQ, Oct. 1991, I-4, 367-384) and Ronald F. Duska ("What's the point of a Business Ethics Course?", *BEQ*, Oct. 1992, I-4, 335-354).

14. George L. Pamental ("The Course in Business Ethics: Why don't philosophers give business students what they need", *BEQ*, Oct. 1991, I-4, 385-393) uncovers the flimsy reasoning behind these suppositions as well.

15. Cfr. John Ladd, "Morality and the Ideal of Rationality in Formal Organizations", Monist, 1970, 54-4, 488-516; Laura Nash, *Good Intentions Aside,* Boston, Mass.: Harvard Business School Press, 1990.

16. The core of Aristotle's ethical theory is, of course, to be found in his Nicomachean Ethics; but its interpretation – as we shall later on propose – should rest on an equally attentive reading of his Politics, Rhetoric and Poetics, at the very least. Together, these writings form the principal sources of his "practical philosophy".

17. The most relevant texts explicative of Aquinas' ethical and political teachings are to be found in the Summa Theologiae I-II and in his Commentaries to the Nicomachean Ethics and to the Politics.

18. Included in this group are very influential contemporary philosophers such as MacIntyre, Taylor and Sandel. For a characterization of this "school" of thought, see Will Kymlicka, *Contemporary Political Philosophy,* Oxford: Clarendon Press, 1990.

19. Pioneering efforts have been admirably accomplished in this regard, particularly in the field of ethical and economic rationality, by Amartya Sen (*On Ethics and Economics,* Oxford: Blackwell, 1987).

20. Amitai Etzioni ("Reflections on Teaching Business Ethics", *BEQ,* Oct, 1991, I-4, 360-361; *The Moral Dimension,* New York: The Free Press, 1988) voices a similar opinion regarding the Neoclassical economic paradigm, which, according to him, would necessarily issue in a utilitarian or a consequentialist ethical-political theory.

21. An on-going research project of the Permanent Seminar on Enterprise and Humanism (a joint venture between the Colleges of Philosophy and Letters and of Economics and Business Administration, the International Graduate School of Management – all of the University of Navarra – with leading Spanish and multinational business firms) consists precisely in the elaboration of such a theoretical corpus together with a custom-designed teaching module.

References

Aristotle. Nicomachean Ethics. Politics. Rhetoric. Poetics.

Aquinas, Thomas. Summa Theologiae I-II. *Commentaries to the Nicomachean Ethics. Commentaries to the Politics.*

Caplan, Arthur L. and Callahan, Daniel (eds) 1981: *Ethics in Hard Times.* New York: Plenum Press.

Donaldson, Thomas 1992: The language of international corporate ethics. *Business Ethics Quarterly*, July, II-3.

Duska, Ronald F. 1991: What's the point of a business ethics course. *Business Ethics Quarterly*, October, I-4.

Etzioni, Amitai : *The Moral Dimension*. New York: The Free Press.

Freedman, David 1992: Is management still a science? *Harvard Business Review*. November-December.

Jackall, Robert 1988: *Moral Mazes*. Oxford: Oxford University Press.

Kymlicka, Will 1990: *Contemporary Political Philosophy*. Oxford: Clarendon Press.

Ladd, John 1970: Morality and the ideal of rationality in formal organizations. *Monist*, 54-.

Lataif, Louis E. et. al. 1992: MBA: Is the traditional model doomed? *Harvard Business Review*, November-December.

Liedtka, Jean 1992: Wounded but wiser: Reflections on teaching ethics to MBA students. *Journal of Management Education*, November, 16-4.

Linder, Jane C. and Smith, H. Jeff: The complex case of management education. *Harvard Business Review*, September-October.

Lipke, Richard 1991: A critique of business ethics. *Business Ethics Quarterly*, October, I-4.

MacIntyre, Alasdair 1990: *Three Rival Versions of Moral Enquiry*. Indiana: Notre Dame Press.

McHugh, Francis P. 1988: *Keyguide to Information Sources in Business Ethics*. New York: Nichols Publishing.

Nash, Laura 1990: *Good Intentions Aside*. Boston, Mass: Harvard Business School Press.

Ortiz, José Mª. 1992: Ser el mejor: hacer que otros también lo sean. *Cuadernos Empresa y Humanismo*, 36.

Pamental, George L. 1991: The course in business ethics: Why don't philosophers give business students what they need? *Business Ethics Quarterly*, October, I-4.

Sen, Amartya 1987: *On Ethics and Economics*. Oxford: Blackwell.

Sison, Alejo José G. 1992: Hacia una motivación ética en la empresa. *Servicio de Documentación Empresa y Humanismo*, 20, Oct.

Solomon, Robert C. 1992: Corporate roles, personal virtues: An Aristotelian approach to business ethics. *Business Ethics Quarterly*, July, II-3.

18

Business Ethics versus Ethics in Business?

Josep M. Lozano

Abstract

This chapter poses the question: Is there a contradiction between business ethics and ethics in business? and proposes a reconstruction of some features of L. Kohlberg's theory in order to find the answer. The relationship between Kohlberg's conventional and post-conventional levels is viewed within the framework of the conflict between egocentrism and decentering defined by Piaget. After reviewing several studies containing guidelines designed according to this perspective, the chapter proposes that the relationship between the two levels be re-thought by establishing a dialogue between deontological ethics and the ethics of virtue. The conclusion drawn indicates that the difference between business ethics and ethics in business should not be considered a contradiction but a means of clarifying and complementing a process of personal and organizational development.

Introduction

In a thought-provoking article Richard De George emphasized that:

"What is gaining such success and popular attention is not business ethics in the academic sense, but ethics in business. . . . Businesses, on the whole, are not interested in the academic field of business ethics. Many of them are interested, however, in inculcating conventional morality in their employees. . . . Instruction in business ethics as an academic subject aims to produce critical ethical thinkers. But this is not what many who call for business ethics courses want." [1]

I feel that a critical reading of Kohlberg's theories can help solve this problem that De George stated so clearly and which is so relevant to the work of teachers and consultants.

H. von Weltzien Hoivik and A. Føllesdal (eds.), Ethics and Consultancy: European Perspectives, 229-251.
© 1995 *Kluwer Academic Publishers. Printed in the Netherlands.*

The Piaget Connection

As we know, Kohlberg's theory has its roots in the work of Piaget and is marked by the desire to clarify and explain the processes that go into shaping valid knowledge (Coll and Gillerion, 1989). Seen from this angle, the knowledge attained should not be regarded as a sort of "portrait" or "revelation" of the nature of things done by human beings, but as something constructed by human beings in their interaction with the objects and realities that make up the world in which they live.

This direct relationship between knowledge and learning should be understood in constructivist terms: knowledge is the product of a learning process (and is not just passively received); learning is a problem-solving process in which the learner takes an active part, and the learning process is directly shaped by the opinions of the learners (Habermas, 1983). Thus, the subjects become progressively and steadily more involved with their surroundings as the result of a continuous process of self-regulation on the part of the subject.

According to Piaget, there is one cognitive process that is absolutely essential to understanding moral development and that is egocentrism. Here, this is not a moral category but simply means cognitive and emotional concentration on one's own point of view: a concentration that is repeated in an ever more complex fashion at the beginning of each stage of development, which development in turn requires the subject to become increasingly decentered, which is in itself an ever more complex process. Egocentrism is a kind of basic matrix for understanding the world – although it can form part of broader views. It is always present and can always be activated (or returned to) as a cognitive process for understanding the world – even the world of morals.

Piaget further maintains that there is a close link between the cognitive processes which have defused the immediate and egocentric initial point of view, in order to situate it within an increasingly broad framework of relations and notions, eventually adapting this particular viewpoint to an increasingly broad reality. [2]

In one of the 20th century's most important works on psychology and ethics (Le judgement moral chez l'enfant, Piaget, 1932), the author makes a distinction between two groups of phenomena: the application of rules and the awareness of rules. He states that awareness develops in a sequence that moves from heteronomy to autonomy, repeating itself constantly at every level of consciousness and thought and therefore also in moral rules. However, according to Piaget, the big difference between obligation and cooperation, or between unilateral and mutual respect is that the former imposes set beliefs or rules which must be adopted in block while the latter only proposes a method of reciprocal control and verification on the intellectual plane and discussion and justification on the moral plane. Regardless of whether cooperation is a cause or a result of reason or is both at once, reason needs cooperation inasmuch as being rational means accepting that the individual is subordinate to the universal. Mutual respect thus appears to be a necessary condition for autonomy in both the intellectual and the moral sense of the word. [3]

One of Piaget's major contributions was the distinction he made between verbal thought and active thought. Active moral thought is gradually shaped through action involving the issues and decisions that make up the subject's outlook. It is the discourse that accompanies the actions and decisions being taken. There also exists a theoretical or verbal moral thought which is linked to active thought by all manner of degrees, but which is as far removed from it as thought can be distant from immediate action. This verbal thought occurs whenever a child is obliged to judge activities of others which do not interest him or state general principles which concern his own behavior independently of his actual actions.[4] Verbal thought usually lags behind active thought.

Piaget thus considers that morals governing cooperation and autonomy (as opposed to morals imposed by moral realism and heteronomy) involve exchanging an absolute and egocentric set of morals for morals based on a relative concept in which the individual is capable of seeing things through others' eyes and therefore shifts from a code of morals based on duty to a code based on what is in the common good. Reciprocity and cooperation between equals is the key to moral autonomy. In order to move towards autonomy we must be able to establish reciprocal social relationships based on equality and mutual respect.

In his study of the development of moral judgement in children, Piaget found that physical and mental maturity are every bit as important as social factors in shaping a moral conscience. Intellectual and moral development are so closely linked that we can talk about moral cognition, albeit a cognition that is contingent on social relationships. Without social processes, the individual is egocentric and egocentrism only produces anomie. Authority-based social relations can only give rise to a heteronomous moral structure. Only cooperative relations, which permit formal discussion between equals (mutual respect) allow the individual conscience to develop morality as an autonomous quality and accept the laws of reciprocity as their own.[5] There are thus three key factors in moral development: cognitive development, relations between equals and overcoming the coercive aspects of adult authority.

The Kohlberg Model

The Kohlberg model for moral education differs from the traditional model, the model based on the "clarification of values" and the model based on virtue.

From the standpoint of ethics, Kohlberg is part of the deontological tradition, calling on the rational or liberal tradition of moral philosophy and, more specifically, the formalist or deontological tradition that embraces philosophers ranging from Emmanuel Kant to John Rawls. One of the basic postulates of this school is that a proper morality is based on principles, i.e. that judgements are made in terms of universal principles applicable to all mankind.[6]

Kohlberg belongs to this tradition not only because of his theory of ethics, but also because it systematizes the most important feature of this theory: his definition of the stages of moral development in cognitive-structural terms.

Kohlberg takes Piaget's premises still further. While Piaget divided morals into heteronomy and autonomy, Kohlberg's division is more complex and attempts to further clarify each stage of moral development and the processes that make it possible to move from one stage to another. His work is particularly notable because it unveils the perspective and structure of moral judgement. Taking Piaget's work as his point of departure, Kohlberg has described six stages of moral judgement with the aim of making these stages transculturally valid. What these stages involve in terms of content, rate of growth and level vary depending upon how individuals interact with their surroundings.

When Kohlberg proposes that we place an emphasis on moral judgement, he is proposing that we direct our attention to the moral discourse that always accompanies any decision made. He understands moral judgement as a cognitive process by means of which we select the relevant elements of a determined situation, reflect upon them and/or rank them in order of the values which really guide us, and make a decision.

Hence morality is not a statement of values, but the decisions made. This means that we must concentrate on the thought processes involved in the decisions made and on our thoughts about the decision-making process. The decision made by a subject is the context of his moral judgement on that particular situation. The reasoning that leads to his decision defines the structure of his moral judgement.[7] Thus, as far as the decision is concerned, moral judgement does not affect the axiological or value content but the formal structure of reasoning.

Dividing the development of moral judgement into stages[8] means that moral thought appears to behave like all other types of thought. The progression through the different moral levels and stages is characterized by an increasing differentiation and integration. As it develops, moral thought can be said to partially generate its own relevant facts or at least expound on these facts in a balanced and coherent manner so that the moral thought embraces an increasingly broad range of experiences.[9]

The social perspective adopted plays a key role in each stage. Kohlberg considers role-taking to be of primary importance. The ability to adopt another's viewpoint is a cognitive skill that is essential to developing moral judgement. We cannot understand what distinguishes each stage of moral development unless we take into consideration the subject's social perspective at that particular stage.

Kohlberg divides the six stages of moral development into three levels or categories, which he calls pre-conventional, conventional and post-conventional (Kohlberg, 1975; Hersh et al., 1979; Rubio, 1989).

Level I: Preconventional. Stage 1: Punishment and Obedience

At this stage what is correct or incorrect is always viewed in terms of literally obeying the rules of authority in order to avoid punishment and damage to either people or property. This is morality understood as "follow the rules and you can't go wrong". The reasons for doing or not doing something are always related to the rules and the power of the authorities. Obedience is valued in and for itself, and adherence to established rules is valued only because failure to abide by these rules would result in punishment. The prospect (or unlikelihood) of punishment alters one's judgement about what should or should not be done. It can be safely said that individuals who are at this stage confuse their own viewpoints with those of authority.

Level I: Preconventional. Stage 2: The Instrumental Relativist Orientation

At this stage what is correct (or good) is understood as satisfying one's own needs or the needs of others through concrete exchanges. Everyone has interests and needs and aims to satisfy them while still accepting that others also have needs to be satisfied. Individuals who are at this stage of development see things in individualistic terms, separating their own interests and viewpoints from those of others and those of authority. Because they acknowledge that everyone has interests and needs to satisfy and that in specific cases these may clash with the interests and needs of others, what is good is always what is good for the particular individual. People at this stage of development handle conflicting interests by voluntarily exchanging goods or services in order to achieve their own ends.

Level II: Conventional. Stage 3: Mutual and Interpersonal Expectations, Relations and Agreement

At this stage what is correct or incorrect is defined in terms of establishing good personal relationships with others. Being good is being "a nice person". If you act the way other people expect you to act, you are acting correctly. This is what Kohlberg refers to as the good girl/good boy approach: doing what is expected of one in one's various roles. From this point of view "being good" is a value per se, but in the sense of having good intentions, feelings or motives which are expressed as consideration for others. Individuals at this stage of development view society as a matter of relationships with other individuals. When they confront problems they are aware that there are shared feelings, agreements and expectations that go beyond their immediate interests as individuals and have a certain priority over these interests. They relate different viewpoints to a specific Golden Rule. Although they are capable of putting themselves in the positions of others, they have no general overview or perception of the social system as a whole.

Level II: Conventional. Stage 4: The Law and Order Orientation

This stage involves a broader horizon of moral reference. What is correct is now defined in terms of society: one must meet one's obligations and commitments to the society in which one lives. People at this stage of moral development think in terms of maintaining social order, helping make their social group work and guaranteeing its welfare. They therefore apply their moral criteria to fulfilling the obligations (in the broadest sense of the word) they accepted upon becoming members of a certain social group. Hence, laws must be obeyed, except in those extreme cases where they conflict with other social rights and obligations. What is good or correct is therefore whatever preserves society or a particular organization as a whole. Individuals are now aware of the social and organizational consequences of their actions: "What would happen if everyone acted like me?" People at this stage are able to distinguish between the viewpoint of society or the organization and the viewpoint of interpersonal relations or motives. They are capable of adopting the viewpoint of the system that defines the roles and rules and therefore view individual relationships in terms of their place within the system. The socio-centrism of the previous stage has become broader and is expressed and experienced in organizational, social, cultural or national terms. The viewpoint of one's own social group does not admit the viewpoint of any other.

Level III: Post-Conventional (or Principled). Stage 5: The Social-Contract Legalistic Orientation

At this stage moral decisions involve considering the rights, values and principles which are or could be acceptable to all those individuals who make up a society in which they want to live in accordance with rules which are fair and beneficial to all. Priority is now given to maintaining the rights, values and basic resolutions of a society even when they conflict with the values and criteria of the specific group to which the individual belongs. People who have reached this stage are aware that there exists a variety of values and opinions and that many of them – including one's own – are peculiar to one's particular group rather than absolute, universal or normal. Nevertheless there are some values and criteria which are not relative. This is true of life and liberty, which must be maintained and protected regardless of majority opinions and/or criteria. Beyond these fundamental (often constitutional) rights, what is correct is a matter of personal opinion and values. Situations and conflicts are experienced and analyzed in terms of respect for and protection of one's own rights and those of others. Hence, laws must be judged in terms of their usefulness: what is right is what is best for the greatest number of people. The outlook of people at this stage has changed: they give priority to society and acknowledge that certain values and rights take precedence over all commitments and contracts.

Level III: Post-Conventional (or Principled). Stage 6: Universal Ethical Principles

This stage involves acting in accordance with universal ethical principles which apply to all humankind. At this stage everything is judged in the light of these principles and laws are only valid if they are established in accordance with these principles. Should laws violate these principles it is the principles which must be upheld. They are principles of universal justice: equal human rights and respect for the dignity of human beings as individuals. They are abstract, ethical principles

(among them, the Golden Rule, the Categorical Imperative)   rather than specific
moral rules such as the Ten Commandments. This is not merely a question of recognized values, but one of principles on which individual decisions are based. Reasons
for a particular action are thus rooted in the fact that as a rational being the individual has acknowledged the validity of these principles and has committed himself to
abide by them. This validity is not subjective: it stems from formal standards of
equal rights and universality. And the motives behind the action are "conscious"ones: the key is one's own moral approval or rejection of these principles.
The social perspective adopted is intrinsically moral, i.e. people at this stage of
development act in accordance with the fundamental moral principles from which
all norms and values derive. Their viewpoint is that of rational individuals who recognize that morals and acts should be based on the premise that one respects others
and that morals are intrinsically important and not just a means to an end.[10] This is
an extremely formal stance that involves being guided by obligations that are
regarded as imperatives for any rational being acting as a moral agent.

Individuals progress from one stage to another as the result of interacting with
their surroundings. In certain situations this interaction provokes a cognitive crisis
at the stage in which one normally operates and opens the door to the next stage.
Kohlberg has arrived at the conclusion that it is more likely that moral change takes
place when discussions succeed in triggering cognitive conflict among the participants. One does not simply change one's stance, but instead begins restructuring
one's way of reasoning about moral issues.[11]

Viewed from this angle, teachers and consultants are not specialists in moral
content, but people who stimulate interactive reflections on moral content. These
reflections always begin at the subject's current level of moral development. This
means that the same problem cannot be handled in the same way for everyone. The
relationship of the teacher or consultant with the individuals involved is vitally
important because cognitive conflict on certain issues can be painful, involving personal crisis and the need to reorder one's beliefs. It is not easy to question what people think about moral dilemmas and decisions and even less easy to question how
they think about them, and we teachers and consultants must be capable of providing more than just cognitive support in this process.

Some Critical Observations on the Kohlberg Approach

The Kohlberg approach has been criticized on various grounds, many of which
have nothing to do with the crux of the problem discussed here, i.e. the relationship
between the conventional and post-conventional levels of moral development in the
organizational world.

The post-conventional level has been questioned on the grounds that it somehow
rephrases western philosophical categories in terms of moral psychology. It has also
been alleged that the model has a sexist bias which elevates masculine patterns to a
norm. Kohlberg's approach has even triggered discussion as to whether there are

two moral orientations: one which focusses more on rights and justice (a more masculine concern) and a second which focusses more on care and responsibility (a more female concern).

More interesting to us is the "adolescent regression" that is evidenced in the step from the conventional to the post-conventional levels. It has two basic characteristics: one is a mixture of skepticism and relativism and the other is moral egocentricity. According to Kohlberg, this is understandable if we analyze what leaving the conventional level behind means to an adolescent. It means entering a stage where one's moral reasoning is no longer conventional but has not yet become post-conventional. It is relativistic because it does not consider the possibility of universal agreement (or objectivity) on ethical principles. What counts is the affirmation of one's personal options: decision, commitment, etc. There are no reasons for deciding on alternative moral criteria and the subject's viewpoint becomes an absolute. Inasmuch as all moral values are relative, we all have to deliberately act the way we honestly believe one ought to act so long as this does not hurt anyone. Hence, the departure from conventional morals might at first involve regressing to pre-conventional morals.

Nevertheless, I feel that we should more thoroughly explore the consequences of arriving at a philosophical understanding of what is involved in Stage 5. As an example, we could say that Stage 5 permits us to justify institutionalizing the market's operating framework, but that the relations that take place strictly within the market, i.e. within the limits of this framework, can be perfectly well approached from Stage 2. This distinction between thinking about society and thinking about the individuals that make up this society can help us understand not only adolescent regression, but also the reason many people never get beyond the conventional level.

Habermas is one of the authors who has most questioned Kohlberg's approach. Naturally, his criticism is centered on Kohlberg's post-conventional level. In Habermas' opinion, even though Stage 5 supposedly involves rights what it actually does is elevate egocentricity to the category of a principle because it deals with the rights of individuals. Habermas criticizes Kohlberg's monological approach (and, by extension, the theories of Rawls) because he feels that the individual cannot establish universal norms unless they are the result of a dialogue. It is not enough for each individual to examine his own conscience in order to determine whether the rules he establishes can be applied on a general basis. Contrary to Kohlberg's belief, it is not enough for individuals to search for criteria that can be generally applied. The proposed norms must be discussed with someone else and jointly verified in order to determine whether they are valid as norms.

The content of universal norms not only needs to be universally applicable. It also requires a procedure that is based on and guarantees this very universality. We must emphasize that the ideal procedure involves dialogue: norms become valid when all the participants in a practical discourse agree that they are moral norms.

Habermas points out one problem inherent to all formal ethical proposals (his own as well as Kohlberg's), which is fundamental to what we are discussing here.

Formal ethics involve a distinction – or perhaps a division – between justice and the good human life, between self-determination and self-realization. This is the root of the practical problems that can be involved in a merely deontological morality. Habermas aims to maintain the distinction between the application of general norms in a given context and the issue of what these norms are founded on, but he is aware that that would cause a decline in motivation that must be compensated for. Habermas indicates that the post-conventional separation of morality and ethics signifies that the cultural evidence, the certainties of the world we live in, no longer include the fundamental moral convictions.[12] Consequently, in order to reduce the gap between judgements and moral actions, we need an internal system of behavioral control which involves moral judgements based on principles and the possibility of individual self-direction. And this system must operate autonomously. How viable is this idea in practice? Habermas himself notes that it in concrete life situations it is not normal to function in this way. But it is nevertheless an inexorable fact: the postulate of universality must act as a knife that makes a clean cut between what is good and what is just, between statements that are evaluations and others that establish norms. And this can cause a clash between conventional and post-conventional morals.

Seen from this angle, life issues become moral issues, though of secondary importance. But it is precisely these issues which reflect people's vital identities! Ideas about what is the moral life are not abstract ideals; they are ideas that are characteristic of concrete identities and form part of one's culture and personality. Habermas himself acknowledges this, but as mentioned above, he regards it as a lack of motivation (which can be compensated for) caused by the way his theory is focussed and not by any shortcoming in the theory itself: socialized individuals cannot behave in a hypothetical manner towards the life form or life history within which they have shaped their identities.[13] But, despite this acknowledgement, he still feels that deontological ethics have no relation to axiological preferences but are linked to the validity of the rules that govern the norms of action. The question is whether, despite what Habermas says, everything dealing with the "moral life" can be pushed so far into the background when it is a matter of moral thought and life itself. This is not a question of hierarchy, but of practical relevance.

The Conflict Between Conventional and Post-Conventional Morals in Organizational Life

As we all know, the business ethics agenda has shifted from the individual to the corporation (Mahoney, 1990). One of the things which has contributed towards this shift has been the increasing analytical and practical attention given to "organizational culture". This means that organizations can be considered in terms of values, but the fact that they have adopted certain values does not necessarily imply a process of moral reflection. Moreover, more attention is being paid to organizational and decision-making processes in companies.[14] I believe that both these viewpoints are an indivisible part of our awareness that we live in a dynamic, plural society that is in a constant state of change, a society where the ability to innovate and create knowledge is of key importance (Corbí, 1992). But this means that a moral education that focusses essentially on content cannot be appropriate for either a changing society (Coleman, 1987) or for its increasingly complex organizations.

In this context, it appears that Kohlberg's conceptual framework could be a good support for business ethics. I feel that there are at least five good reasons why this is so, among them:

a) it emphasizes the process of shaping values and objectives;
b) it emphasizes moral discourse when this is translated into actions;
c) it emphasizes the decision-making process and enables one to formally explore the conflicting values present in every moral decision;
d) it draws attention to the evolution of individuals and introduces the idea that people's moral development is rooted in their actual life circumstances;
e) it views rationality as indivisible from recognition of others, which makes moral development an open discussion with the participation of everyone involved.

Kohlberg's conceptual framework also allows us to consider one of the major paradoxes of moral education in a more operational light: the fact that the majority of moral discourses – which are usually suggested as models and presented as the only truly moral approaches – take post-conventional approaches while most people are still on the conventional level. I believe that this contradiction explains many of the shortcomings in business ethics training and the frequent feeling that ethical discourse and day-to-day life are two very different things.

In recent years, a number of studies have examined the moral language of executives without necessarily relating the results to Kohlberg's theory. Gellerman (1986) systematically studied cases of senior executives (previously considered as "good" executives) who had made decisions which were deserving of censure and which had had disastrous consequences. His conclusion was that there were four major lines of argument used to justify these decisions and all of them were on what Kohlberg had identified as the pre-conventional level and therefore confirmed the hypothesis that adults who are in the first stages of the process are more likely to behave in an immoral fashion.

Another significant study was carried out on Canadian executives (Bird et al., 1989). The objective was to study how moral discourse served as a link between the people involved and focussed on the use they made of this discourse in their interactions. This confirmed Piaget's theory that verbal thought and active thought do not usually coincide and that there is not necessarily any correlation between the use of moral expressions and the actual focus of behavior.

Last but not least, Nielsen's study (Nielsen, 1988) attempted to examine the limitations of moral reasoning as opposed to moral action and how executives perceived these limitations.

All these studies assume that the people being studied actually have a theory that moral action consists in putting this "theory" into practice. The idea is that one has one's own moral ideas or principles and then puts them (or doesn't put them) into practice. This idea appears to be the opposite of Kohlberg's approach. Kohlberg maintains that you should start with practice or rather, with the structure of the moral discourse which is always at stake whenever one is faced with making a decision that involves a choice between conflicting preferences, and see if from there it is possible to develop a formal moral attitude that affects the very structure of the judgement involved in the actual process of judging and deciding.

As mentioned above, Kohlberg's studies demonstrate that it is quite common for adults not to go beyond Stage 4, if they even get that far. A survey (Wood et al., 1988) of 2,267 executives and 205 management students who had taken courses in business ethics provides some significant information. Not only did the great majority of the responses not go beyond Stage 4, but the responses that could be classified as pre-conventional accounted for an important part of the total. Given the limited number of post-conventional responses, we should think about whether it would be feasible to approach moral training solely from the angle of universal moral principles, inasmuch as indications are that in many cases people are simply incapable of using them as a basis for operational reasoning.

A study limited to second-year business administration students (Weber & Green, 1991) attempted to determine if it was true that students were at Stage 4 or higher even before receiving training in moral principles. They found that almost half the students were in the pre-conventional stage and less than 2 percent had reached a post-conventional stage of reasoning.

As we know, Stage 4 is characterized by the fact that the individual reasons as a member of a group, viewing himself within the framework of the society (or group) to which he belongs and adopting its viewpoints when establishing his ideas. Keeping the society (or group) viable becomes a basic moral tenet. However, it can happen that as an individual member of a company an executive will reason on a Stage 4 level but when his viewpoint is that of the corporation (i.e. when for all practical purposes he identifies his social group as the company or organization) the same executive might well reason on pre-conventional levels and act accordingly.[15] I therefore feel that it is essential to discover if people able to reason on Stage 4 as private individuals risk losing this ability when reasoning as executives.

Not all studies agree on the lines described above, but it can be safely stated that they basically coincide on a number of points which will form the hypotheses for future research (Trevino, 1986). I feel that the most important of these points are the following: a) on job-related issues most executives are in a conventional stage of reasoning (Stages 3 and 4); b) the few executives who have reached a post-conventional stage (Stages 5 and 6) are more consistent in their judgements and actions than executives who are at a lower stage of reasoning; c) Executives reason at a lower stage on issues involving their own professional activities than on hypothetical issues. Last but not least, moral development is significantly higher among executives with a higher educational background than among their less educated counterparts. What is the reason for this?

Among adolescents and young people it is day-to-day interaction with others that provokes the cognitive conflict. Later on, it is less likely that this will be the case and around the age of 25 one's level of maturity tends to stabilize unless a destabilization is triggered by something other than daily interaction. The most important destabilizing factor is education: it has been confirmed that education is a requisite for reaching Stages 5 and 6.[16] If that is actually the case, then perhaps education should deliberately aim to provoke this cognitive destabilization (assuming that this destabilization is the cause of the most stable moral growth).

This is important inasmuch as some researchers appear to suggest that not only is it rare for students in the first years of their management studies to have gone beyond the conventional level of reasoning (or in many cases to even have reached Stage 4), but there are actually studies (Conry & Nelson, 1989; Weber & Green, 1991) which reveal that students attending management schools are at a lower stage of reasoning and that the education they receive in these schools does not produce the amount of moral growth normally associated with university-level studies. If that is true, it sheds a certain amount of light on our problem: the demand for conventional moral education predominates in the business world because that is the level of moral development actually attained.

L. K. Trevino (1986) allows us to consider some aspects of conventional morals in terms of organizational culture, which is understood to be "a common set of assumptions, values and beliefs shared by the organizational members. Organizational culture influences thoughts and feelings, and orients behavior."[17] Because, as we have seen, most adults reason only on a conventional level (Stages 3 and 4), the working and cultural context of their organization plays a decisive part in their moral behavior within the organization and shapes their moral judgement.

It should therefore come as no surprise that a conceptual model of moral development that is specially adapted for organizations has now been designed (Reidenbach & Robin, 1991). This strikes me as a logical consequence of the aforementioned theories. If we view moral problems (in terms of both judgement and implementation) within the framework of organizational culture we could conclude that the moral development of a corporation is determined by the organization's culture and, in reciprocal fashion, helps define that culture. In essence, it is the organization's culture that undergoes moral development.[18] The problem now is to clarify the link between moral development and organizational culture.

The danger is that morals might end up being diluted by the organizational culture or becoming so identified with it that they begin to be viewed as a way of managing the organization's values. It is true that every organization has its own value system. The problem is that not all these values are moral. Furthermore, being aware of values when making decisions does not necessarily imply adopting an ethical stance. Values can be reduced to no more than a pragmatic expression of corporate interests or non-critical acceptance of the values transmitted or assigned to the corporation and its executive staff by their most immediate environment.

This is why I am convinced that the line of reasoning proposed here will enable us to understand why ethical demands are expressed in conventional terms: people have either not yet reached the conventional stage or are used to operating on that level. It also allows us to think that perhaps there is no contradiction between the more conventional approaches to corporate ethics and the more critical ones and that they can be understood as two stages in a process of personal and organizational development. However, in order to clarify this we must revise our views on the ethics of virtue and relate them to the Kohlberg theory.

Towards Moral Development Understood as the Construction of Conventional Morals

The danger of cognitive and deontological approaches (like that of Kohlberg) is that they end up paying more attention to autonomy, freedom, rationality and duty than to the people who must act autonomously, freely, rationally and according to universally valid criteria. Moral development is synonymous with personal development: it is the development of people who are educated through practices and relationships which lead them to internalize not only ways of thinking and making judgements, but also ways of feeling, learning and doing which become part of their characters and personalities.

We must therefore consider the possibility that it is impossible to develop morals simply by developing moral judgement and that developing morals also involves developing virtues and educating feelings, motivations, emotions, desires and imagination, all of which are ingredients of a moral identity. We must establish certain habits because morals also involve shaping a way of being through a way of doing.

All ideas about virtue involve joining a concept of human life to an idea of what is good and what is excellent. It is here that the emphasis that the ethics of virtue places on the individual becomes truly important. The aim is to reveal the moral subject as such. As has been graphically stated (Abbà, 1987), the ethics of duty can be said to be ethics based on some outside source or third party (observers, judges, legislators) while the ethics of virtue are based on the first person (the subject). First-person ethics emphasize that every decision must have a dimension that is "attractive" rather than simply "imperative"; a dimension that seductively – and not just through regulations – reveals all the human ideals that are at stake and can be attained.

Here decisions take the form of practical wisdom, which involves using reason, knowledge, perception, action, attitudes, desires and emotions because all of them shape forms of behavior. Decisions made on the basis of practical wisdom are made within the framework of a concrete concept of life and the world. While this obviously requires knowledge, it must be the kind of knowledge that is capable of discerning things, people and events through a definite understanding of what constitutes a good human life. It is not simply a matter of will that is subject to universal standards: there is no such thing as ethics of virtue without an expressed ideal or meaningful life project. Hence, practical wisdom does not emphasize the foundation of norms. Instead it emphasizes the achievement of good in real life.

Here then the idea of a goal takes on a certain priority, which is impossible to discuss in abstract terms. It must instead be viewed in terms of specific ideals that aim to meet a particular (and in this case, conventional) goal of human nature. Unless a purpose for or ideal of human life (telos) is constructed and proposed, moral discourse will become no more than a kind of techné (deed or action performed solely with an eye to its results) or praxis (deed or action performed solely with an eye to the deed or action itself). While the telos of human life must be understood as a certain kind of life it is not something to be achieved at some time in the future, but while the complete life is under construction.[19] Without a purpose, virtues become fragments of a jigsaw puzzle. But the telos is achieved in a community where one not only shares certain human goods, but also, and especially, certain practices and criteria which make it possible to excel in this achievement.

This means that an important part of all moral identity must be conventional and quite radically so (Johnson, 1981). I would therefore like to advance my considered opinion that it is possible to rethink conventional morals, not from the perspective of heteronomy (which would reduce conventional morals to no more than a step on the road towards autonomy) but from the perspective – which is equally moral! – of belonging to a life-world.

If we do not accept this possibility, we confirm the contradiction between business ethics and ethics in business, which we are aiming to eliminate. While deontological ethics always risk reducing concrete decisions to simple individual cases of universal principles, the ethics of virtue always risk taking a concrete form of life and universalizing it as a recognized achievement of virtue. It is my opinion that we cannot overcome this contradiction without taking into consideration the social context in which it occurs.

Our Socio-Cultural Context

Culturally speaking, modernization processes [20] involve segmenting the diverse groups to which we belong and the subjects of conversation within these groups, which produce a variety of values that are not interlinked. As Habermas explains, among Max Weber's beliefs was the idea that Western rationalism is characterized by the fact that Europe has shaped a number of expert cultures, which rethink the cultural tradition, dividing its constituent parts in a strictly cognitive, aesthetic-expressive and practical-moral sense.[21] These divisions are not simply theoretical but also cultural: they affect life forms that are no longer organized on the basis of a single one of the groups to which we belong.

Our culture involves a pluralism that goes beyond simple ideological pluralism (of ideas or beliefs) and includes different life styles, criteria and standards of behavior and their attendant practices and ideals, all of which are an inseparable part of the different groups (professional, family, community, friends) to which every individual belongs. This type of pluralism can ultimately be internalized as a sort of aggregate of values and life stories associated with the individual's different roles.

As a consequence, there is a need for conventional morals on the one hand and on the other the contemporary plurality of the different groups to which one belongs and their fragmented, simplified frames of reference. This makes us wonder about the philosophical, social and organizational links [22] between deontological ethics and the ethics of virtue.

We need fundamental, universally justified principles that permit us to morally and critically confront the variety of existing codes, traditions and practices without this confrontation being no more than the declaration of a series of parallel self-affirmations or a new version of the social contract. These universal principles must be understood as guidelines for moral understanding and reflection, guidelines that presuppose a moral option. This is what Kohlberg labels the "post-conventional" level. However, we must also assume that neither rules nor habits can be deduced from universal principles. They do not give us clues as to how to behave, how to live or what to feel in specific situations. A moral life is impossible without these habits, rules, and ways of behaving, living and feeling. This is what Kohlberg means by the "conventional" level. Hence, if we take the variety of lifestyles and moral thought into account, we are faced with the need to link principles and conventions, consensus and pluralism, change and stability on every level of existence.

It would appear that survival in a plural society can only be guaranteed by establishing certain rules based on universal rights and principles that must be observed if we are to be able to live together, and the obligation to observe them must take precedence over and transcend the different ways of thinking and of understanding life.

We can thus consider deontological ethics and the ethics of virtue as two different moral options or proposals. The ethics of virtue would publicly symbolize a concrete understanding of human life and serve as an example of the good human life. It is a moral option made up of maxims which are followed through conviction and which aims to be attractive. Deontological ethics, on the other hand, publicly symbolize the need for certain shared and common minimums which make possible existence, coexistence, dialogue and encounters between the different moral proposals. However, public life should not be reduced to the simple observance of these minimums, which have been established not just by common agreement but by the desire to shape a minimum code of ethics (Cortina, 1986). Indeed, when deontological and axiological ethics are viewed as two separate moral options, deontological ethics is usually viewed as a code of regulations that reject or prohibit while the ethics of virtue are seen as focussing on attracting or inviting people to behave ethically. Organizational ethics must strive to embrace both conventional and post-conventional approaches.

I would like to stress the fact that although we are talking about ethics that involve minimum and maximum requirements, the moral ideals of both deontological and axiological ethics are complementary. It is not that one represents a minimum code and the other a maximum, as is sometimes implied. A minimum code of ethics is nourished and legitimized by an ideal of universality, of values that condition the possibility of human life and for that very reason are expressed as irrenunciable minimum requirements. Ethical maxims involve commitment to a life idea which is accepted as a regulation but presented as an open possibility. In this sense, deontological ethics is always a minimum code while the ethics of virtue is a maxim. Hence, deontological ethics is critical of the ethics of virtue, constantly dwelling on those aspects of its own life project that cannot be overlooked, subordinated or viewed as an absolute. Likewise, the ethics of virtue are critical of deontological ethics, constantly recalling that moral concretions have priority over ethical theory and that there is no such thing as morals (or moral judgement) without individual and group contexts and situations. The two types of ethics can therefore be said to involve complementary and irrenunciable moral requirements and both of them have their place in public and organizational life. Deontological ethics express the moral commitment to raise the minimums, guarantee them and require them while the ethics of virtue express the moral conflict involved in proposing and committing oneself to abide by certain maxims. Both are irreducible and necessary and any contemporary approach to ethics would apparently need to strike a balance between them.

We can now close the circle and reinterpret the ethics of virtue from a constructivist point of view. Indeed, if human nature involves establishing conventions and setting goals (Wallace, 1978) that are in line with the possibilities open to human life (possibilities that fulfill the anthropological constants but which are neither part of nor defined by nature itself), then deontological ethics are the moral expression of a life project for society while the ethics of virtue are the moral expression of a project for life in society. To repeat an idea expressed earlier: first-person ethics are contingent on third-person ethics. Though the latter cannot replace the former, the ethics of virtue cannot exist today other than in the framework of deontological ethics.

In a pluralistic society the ethics of virtue, life styles or conventional morals – call them what you will – are not self-sufficient and this means that we must learn to operate on two different levels: on the one hand, according to the specific rules and precepts that are part of the moral code that prevails in a particular society or sub-group and, on the other, according to the fundamental and objective abstract principles which are often the result of philosophical thought and which are used to understand and evaluate specific rules and precepts.[23] I believe that the two levels should interpenetrate rather than confront one another.

One element that could help foster this interpenetration would be to enhance first-person ethics (the ethics of virtue) and third-person ethics (deontological ethics) with a greater inter-subjective recognition which would render each type of ethics non-absolute and help overcome egocentrism. In this sense I believe that the constructivist concept of moral projects (understood as such) would enable us to understand moral proposals as the process of establishing conventions that serve as conventional morals.

It can be inferred from this that greater moral attention will be paid to those situations which all moral discourse aims to focus and shape. Although often overlooked, attention to the social conditions surrounding a proposed normative discourse is part of the ethical requirements. This attention cannot be given after the discourse is proposed, as though it were a simple problem of "application". The ethical understanding of decision-making processes also demands that attention be paid to the network of relationships surrounding all decision-making. The practical wisdom and discernment mentioned earlier are not some kind of subjective mystique, but the ability to open oneself to reality and accept it in all its complexity... and with all its limitations.[24] Morals are not simply techné nor are they simply praxis. Morals are rooted in sheer admiration for what human life ought to be and in the passion to attain this state and make it possible. Hence, morals are the recognition of the human condition by the human being. But unless attention is paid to techné and praxis we always risk paying no more than simple, gratuitous lip-service to an exalted idea of morals and indulging in barren laments bemoaning the fact that people and organizations are not what they ought to be.

It goes without saying that the business world is particularly sensitive to these conflicts and contradictions. This is true of both the organization as a whole and the individuals that constitute it and the reason for this may be that organizations have suffered like few others – and have caused others to suffer – the schizophrenic gap between techné, praxis and discernment. I therefore feel that the key concepts of organizational culture, decision-making processes and organizational development must be restated in terms of ethics. As I said earlier, this is by no means a suggestion that values must simply be managed. I feel that the issue of organizational development and the issue of organizations as learners must include the awareness (personal and organizational) of the moral requirements involved in the mission and objectives of every organization. I further feel that individuals and organizations must establish their own requirements and accept the responsibility for living up to them within the web of relationships in which we operate as individuals or organizations.

Consequently, teachers and consultants cannot limit themselves to teaching skills, techniques and abilities. Nor can they limit themselves to proposing values, visions and social ideologies. Moral development (or what we view as education pure and simple) is impossible without a clear definition of the characteristics of people who have been given a moral education in a pluralist society. And it goes without saying that the very lack of such a definition in itself defines a particular project: what Aristotle might have described as reducing education to the mere acquisition of techné.

Certainly, ethics in business could end up being a mere justification of conventional morals. And business ethics could end up becoming not simply critical but also abstract and removed from reality. However, just as we have seen that in a dynamic vision of ethics, egocentrism and decentering are not antagonists but two dimensions that are present in every process of growth, we can likewise consider that the logic of ethics in business and business ethics are not antagonistic but complementary. The challenge then is to successfully link this complementary quality.

I hope that this proposal will not cause readers to react as Alice did at a particularly difficult point in her travels through Wonderland: "It sounded an excellent plan, no doubt, and very neatly and simply arranged; the only difficulty was that she had not the smallest idea how to set about it."

This research was financed by a grant from the Fundació Jaume Bofill.

Notes

1. DeGeorge, 1991, pp. 43,54,49.

2. Piaget, 1964, pp. 106-107. The italics are mine.

3. Piaget, 1932, pp. 81-90.

4. Piaget, 1932, p. 146. I believe that this distinction is very important in terms of methodology because of the consequences it will have on moral education. Indeed, there is an entire school of reflection and moral education that is quite content to emphasize verbal thought, even though it would appear that we cannot actually speak of moral education until we have reached the stage of active thought.

5. Rubio, 1989, p. 494.

6. Kohlberg, 1975, pp. 95-96.

7. Kohlberg, 1975, p. 92.

8. The general characteristics of any stage (Kohlberg, 1975; Hersh et al, 1979) are: a) a stage is a consistent way of thinking about any aspect of reality; b) every stage is a structured whole; c) every stage forms an invariant sequence; d) the stages are hierarchical integrations, i.e. in every stage the typical characteristics of the preceding stage are reordered and restructured to become part of a greater ability to reason and understand; e) every stage represents a formal qualitative change in relation to specific structural elements involved in all moral judgements; f) individuals are not stages.

9. Kohlberg, 1968, p. 314. The italics are mine.

10. The Kantian matrix of this view is evident. However, space prevents me from discussing in detail the strong resistance and objections to Kohlberg's last two stages, which I mention here only in passing.

11. Hersh et al., 1979, p. 90.

12. Habermas, 1983, p. 213.

13. Habermas, 1983, p. 129.

14. This approach (Epstein, 1987a, 1987b) should be understood more as a change of paradigm or approach that re-elaborates and restructures all the previous contributions. It continues to focus on the moral significance of individual's preferences, options and actions in terms of their responsibility in the company; it continues to focus on the consequences of organizational policies and the outcome of corporative action; it continues to focus on detecting, evaluating, anticipating and responding to all the different kinds of internal and external expectations that appear in relation to the company or organization. What is new in this

approach is its emphasis on the interrelation of all the varied elements that make up the process of constituting an organization and constructing the aims inherent to this process, not as an ideological statement but as a key to understanding the decision-making processes.

15. I feel that this approach could enhance discussion on whether moral responsibility can be assigned only to people or whether it can also be attributed to corporations.

16. Conry & Nelson, 1989, p. 14.

17. Trevino, 1986, p. 611.

18. Reidenback & Robin, 1991, p. 273. The criteria behind this model of corporative development are not mere speculations or a simple application of Kohlberg's studies. The model was developed on the basis of a documented study of a number of organizations and their actions. The classification enables us to rank several common elements in order of their importance and can at least serve as a tool for analysis. It proposes an organizational development process that is understood in moral terms and defines five types of organizations: amoral organizations, legalistic organizations, responsible organizations, emerging ethical organizations and ethical organizations.

19. MacIntyre, 1984, p. 219.

20. See Lozano, 1989 and 1990 and the bibliography cited therein.

21. Habermas, 1983, pp. 132-133.

22. In terms of the specific characteristics of each level.

23. Johnson, 1981, p. 294.

24. These limitations are sometimes no more than the limitations of a moral discourse that is incapable of setting its own limits.

References

Abbà, G. 1989: *Felicità vita buona e virtú. Saggio de filosofia morale*. Roma: LAS.

Abbà, G. 1987: Virtù e dovere: valutazione di un recente dibattito. *Salesianum*, vol. 49, pp. 421-484.

Alston, W.P. 1971: Comments on Kohlberg's 'From Is to Ought'. In Mischel, T. (ed), *Cognitive Development and Epistemology*. New York: Academic Press, pp. 269-284.

Aristotles: Etica Nicomáquea. *Etica Eudemia*. Madrid: Gredos (1985).

Baron, M. 1985: The ethics of duty/Ethics of virtue debate and its relevance to educational theory. *Educational Theory*, vol. 35:2, pp. 135-149.

Bird, F., Westley, F. and Waters, J.A. 1989: The uses of moral talk: Why do managers talk ethics? *Journal of Business Ethics*, vol. 8:1, p. 75-89.

Bowie, N.E. 1991: Business ethics as a discipline: The search for legitimacy. In Freeman, R.E. (ed), *Business Ethics. The State of the Art*, Oxford: Oxford University Press, pp. 17-41.

Coda, V. 1991: Entrepreneurial values and the success of the firm. *Finanza, Marketing e Produzione*, special issue, pp. 9-42.

Coleman, J.A. 1987: Valores y virtudes en las sociedades avanzadas modernas. *Concilium,* núm. 211, pp. 365-380.

Coll, C. and Gillieron, C. 1989: Jean Piaget: el desarrollo de la inteligencia i la construcción del pensamiento racional. In Marchesi, A., Carretero, M., and Palacios, J., *Psicología evolutiva (1). Teorías y métodos,* Madrid: Alianza, pp. 165-194.

Conry, E.J. and Nelson, D.R. 1989: Business law and moral growth. *American Business Law Journal*, vol. 27(1), pp. 1-39.

Cooper, D.E. 1985: Cognitive development and teaching business ethics. *Journal of Business Ethics,* vol. 4, pp. 313-329.

Corbí, M 1992: *Proyectar la sociedad, reconvertir la religión.* Barcelona: Herder.

Cortina, A. 1986: *Etica mínima.* Madrid: Tecnos.

1989: Etica discursiva. In Camps, V. (ed) *Historia de la ética (vol. 3).* Barcelona: Crítica, pp. 533-576.

1990: *Etica sin moral.* Madrid: Tecnos.

De George, R.T. 1991: Will success spoil business ethics?. In Freeman, R.E. (ed), *Business Ethics. The State of the Art.* Oxford: Oxford University Press, pp. 42-56.

De George, R.T. 1987: The status of business ethics: past and future. *Journal of Business Ethics,* vol. 6, pp. 201-211.

1990: *Business Ethics.* New York: Macmillan.

Epstein, E.M. 1987b: The corporate social policy process: Beyond business ethics, corporate social responsibility, and corporate social responsiveness. *California Management Review,* vol. 29:3, pp. 99-114.

Epstein, E.M. 1987a: The corporate social policy process and the process of corporate governance. *American Business Law Journal,* vol. 25:3, pp. 361-383.

Escamez, J. 1987: Relación del conocimiento moral con la acción moral: la educación para una conducta moral. In Jordan, J.A. and Santolaria, F.F. (eds), *La educación moral hoy. Cuestiones y perspectivas,* Barcelona, P.P.U., pp. 207-240.

French, P.A. 1979: The corporation as a moral person. *American Philosophical Quarterly,* vol. 16:3, pp. 207-215.

Gellerman, S. W. 1986: Why 'good' managers make bad ethical choices. *Harvard Business Review,* jul-aug, pp. 85-90.

Gilbert, D.R. 1991: Respect for persons, management theory, and business ethics. In Freeman, R.E. (ed), *Business Ethics. The State of the Art.* Oxford: Oxford University Press, pp. 111-120.

Habermas, J. 1981a: *Theorie des Kommunikativen Handelns. Band 1. Handlungsrationalität und gesellschaftliche Rationalisierung.* Frankfurt: Suhrkamp.

Habermas, J. 1981b: *Theorie des Kommunikativen Handelns. Band 2. Zur Kritik der funktionalistischen Vernunft.* Frankfurt: Suhrkamp.

Habermas, J. 1983: *Moralbewusstein und Kommunikatives Handeln.* Frankfurt: Suhrkamp.

Habermas, J. 1986: *Gerechtigkert und Solidarität. Zur Bestimmung de Moral.* Frankfurt: Suhrkamp.

Hersh, R., Reimer, J. and Paolitto, D. 1979: *Promoting Moral Growth from Piaget to Kohlberg.* New York: Longman.

Johnson, C.D. 1981: La persona moralmente educada en una sociedad pluralista. In Jordan, J.A. and Santolaria, F.F. (eds), *La educación moral hoy. Cuestiones y perspectivas,* Barcelona: P.P.U., 1987, pp. 291-320.

Kant, I. 1786: *Fonamentació de la metafísica dels costums.* Barcelona: Laia, 1984.

Kohlberg, L. 1968: El niño como filósofo moral. In Delval, J. (comp), Lecturas de psicología del niño (2). *El desarrollo cognitivo y afectivo del niño y del adolescente,* Madrid: Alianza, 1983, pp. 303-314.

Kohlberg, L. 1971: From Is to Ought: How to commit the naturalistic fallacy and get away with it in the study of moral development. In Mischel, T. (ed), *Cognitive Development and Epistemology,* New York: Academic Press, pp. 151-235.

Kohlberg, L. 1975: El enfoque cognitivo-evolutivo de la educación moral". In Jordan, J.A.

and Santolaria, F.F. (eds), *La educación moral hoy. Cuestiones y perspectivas*, Barcelona: P.P.U., 1987, pp. 85-114.

Kohlberg, L. and Candee, D. 1984: The relationship of moral judgement to moral action. In Kurtines, W.M., Gewirtz, J.L., *Morality, Moral Behavior and Moral Development*, New York: John Wiley & Sons, pp. 52-73.

Kohlberg, L. and Colby, A. 1984: Invariant sequence and internal consistency in moral judgement stages. In Kurtines, W.M. and Gewirtz, J.L., *Morality, Moral Behavior and Moral Development*, New York: John Wiley & Sons, pp. 41-51.

Kohlberg, L., Higgins, A. and Power, C. 1984: The relationship of moral atmosphere to judgements of responsibility. In Kurtines, W.M. and Gewirtz, J.L., *Morality, Moral Behavior and Moral Development*, New York: John Wiley & Sons, pp. 74-106.

Lozano, J.M. 1989: De la condició urbana com a condició postmoderna. *Revista de Catalunya*, núm. 30, pp. 17-32.

Lozano, J.M. 1990: Els límits de la Modernitat per a una comprensió ètica de la gestió pública. *Papers ESADE*, núm. 49.

MacIntyre, A. 1984: *After Virtue*. Notre Dame: University of Notre Dame Press.

MacIntyre, A. 1979: Corporate modernity and moral judgement: Are they mutually exclusive?. In Goodpaster, K.E. and Sayre, K.M., *Ethics & Problems of the 21st Century*, London: University of Notre Dame Press.

Mahoney, J. 1990: *Teaching Business Ethics in the UK, Europe and the USA. A Comparative Study*. London: The Athlone Press.

McCoy, C.S. 1985: *Management of values*. London: Pitman.

Mischel, T. 1971: Piaget: Cognitive conflict and the motivation of thought. In Mischel, T. (ed), *Cognitive Development and Epistemology*, New York: Academic Press, pp. 311-355.

Nielsen, R.P. 1988: Limitations of ethical reasoning as an action (Praxis) strategy. *Journal of Business Ethics*, vol. 7:10, pp. 725-733.

Paine, L.S. 1991. Ethics as character development: Reflections on the objective of ethics education. In Freeman, R.E. (ed), *Business Ethics. The State of the Art*, Oxford: Oxford University Press, pp. 67-85.

Patrick, A. 1987: Narración y dinámica social de la virtud. *Concilium*, núm. 211, pp. 445-458.

Penn, W.Y. and Collier, B.D. 1985: Current research in moral development as a decision support system. *Journal of Business Ethics*, vol. 4, pp. 131-136.

Peters, R.S. 1971: Moral development: A plea for pluralism. In Mischell, T. (ed), *Cognitive Development and Epistemology*, New York: Academic Press, pp. 237-267.

Peters, R.S. 1973: Forma y contenido de la educación moral. In Jordan, J.A. and Santolaria, F.F. (eds), *La educación moral hoy. Cuestiones y perspectivas*, Barcelona: P.P.U., 1987, pp. 115-134.

Peters, R.S. 1981: *Moral Development and Moral Education*. London: George Allen & Unwin.

Piaget, J. 1932: *El criterio moral en el niño*. Barcelona: Martínez Roca, (1984).

Piaget, J. 1964: *Seis estudios de psicología*. Barcelona: Ariel, (1983).

Porter, J. 1987: Virtudes perennes y virtudes contingentes: sabiduría práctica, fortaleza y templanza. *Concilium*, núm. 211, pp. 433-444.

Rawls, J. 1980: Kantian constructivism in moral theory. *The Journal of Philosophy*, vol. 77, pp. 515-572.

Rawls, J. 1971: *A Theory of Justice*. Cambridge: Harvard University Press.

Reidenbach, R.E. and Robin, D.P. 1991: A conceptual model of corporate moral development. *Journal of Business Ethics,* vol. 10, pp. 273-284.

Rubio, J. 1987: *El hombre y la ética.* Barcelona: Anthropos.

1989): La psicología moral (de Piaget a Kohlberg). In Camps, V. (ed), *Historia de la ética (III),* Barcelona: Crítica, pp. 481-532.

1992: *Etica constructiva y autonomía personal.* Madrid: Tecnos.

Solomon, R.C. 1991: Business ethics, literacy, and the education of the emotions. In Freeman, R.E. (ed), *Business Ethics. The State of the Art,* Oxford: Oxford University Press, pp. 188-211.

Trevino, L.K. 1986: Ethical decision making in organizations: A person-situation interactionist model. *Academy of Management Review,* vol. 11:3, pp. 601-617.

Wallace, J.D. 1978: *Virtues and Vices.* London: Cornell University Press.

Weber, J. 1990: Managers' moral reasoning: Assessing their responses to three moral dilemmas. *Human Relations,* vol. 43(7), pp. 687-702.

Weber, J. and Green, S. 1991: Principled moral reasoning: Is it a viable approach to promote ethical integrity? *Journal of Business Ethics,* vol. 10, pp. 325-333.

Williams, G.J. 1990: More on ethical reasoning in business. *Training & Development Journal,* jan., pp. 47-49.

Wood, J.A., Longenecker, J.G., McKinney, J.A. and Moore, C.W. 1988: Ethical attitudes of students and business professionals: A study of moral reasoning. *Journal of Business Ethics,* vol. 7, pp. 249-257.

Additional Reading

Andrews, K. R. 1973: Can the best corporations be made moral? *Harvard Business Review,* May-June, p. 57-64.

Atherton, J.M. 1988: Virtues in moral education: Objections and replies. *Educational Theory,* vol. 38:3, pp. 199-210.

Baxter, G.D. and Rarick, C.A. 1987: Education for the moral development of managers: Kohlberg's stages of moral development and integrative education. *Journal of Business Ethics,* vol. 6, pp. 243-248.

Boatright, J. R. 1988: Ethics and the role of the manager. *Journal of Business Ethics,* vol. 7:4, p. 303-312.

Bunke, H.C. 1988: Should we teach business ethics? *Business Horizons,* vol. 31:4, pp. 2-8.

Donaldson, J. 1989: *Key issues in Business Ethics.* London: Academic Press.

Dunfee, T.W. and Robertson, D.C. 1988: Integrating ethics into the business school curriculum. *Journal of Business Ethics,* vol. 7:11, pp. 847-859.

Ellul, J. 1983: Recherche pour une Ethique dans une societé technicienne. *AAVV: Etique et Technique,* Bruxelles, Editions de l'Université de Bruxelles, pp. 7-20.

Foot, P. 1981: *Virtues and Vices.* Oxford: Basil Blackwell.

Frankena, W.F. 1970: Prichard and the ethics of virtue. Notes on a footnote. *The Monist,* núm. 54, pp. 1-17.

Getz, K.A. 1990: International codes of conduct: An analysis of ethical reasoning. *Journal of Business Ethics,* vol. 9:7, pp. 567-577.

Gilligan, C. 1977: In a different voice: Women's conceptions of self and morality. *Harvard Educational Review,* vol. 47:4, pp. 481-517.

Goodpaster, K.E. 1983: The concept of corporate responsibility. *Journal of Business Ethics,* vol. 2, pp. 1-22.

Hoffman, W.M. 1986: What is necessary for corporate moral excellence? *Journal of Business Ethics,* vol. 5, pp. 233-242.

Hortal, A 1979: El sujeto ético en la era tecnológica. In DOU, A. (ed), *Aspectos éticos del desarrollo tecnológico,* Bilbao: Mensajero, pp. 185-212.

Laczniack, G.R and Murphy, P.E. 1991: Fostering ethical marketing decisions. *Journal of Business Ehics,* vol. 10, pp. 259-271.

Liebert, R.M. 1984: What develops in moral development?. In Kurtines, W.M. and Gewirtz, J.L., *Morality, Moral Behavior and Moral Development,* New York: John Wiley & Sons, pp. 177-192.

McHugh, F.P. 1988: *Keyguide to Information Sources in Business Ethics.* New York: Nichols Publishing.

Mele, D. 1991: Etica y empresa. *Información Comercial Española,* núm. 691, pp. 122-134.

Moussé, J.1989a: *Fondements d'une éthique professionelle.* Paris: Les éditions d'organisation.

Moussé, J. 1989b: *Pratiques d'une éthique professionelle.* Paris: Les éditions d'organisation.

Nino, C.S. 1989: *El constructivismo ético.* Madrid: Centro de Estudios Constitucionales.

Nunner-Winkler, G. 1984: Two moralities? A critical discussion of an ethics of care and responsibility versus an ethics of rights and justice. In Kurtines, W.M. and Gewirtz, J.L., *Morality, Moral Behavior and Moral Development,* New York: John Wiley & Sons, pp. 348-361.

Pesch, O.H. 1987: Teología de las virtudes y virtudes teológicas. *Concilium,* núm. 211, pp. 459-480.

Prandstraller, G.P. 1990: Gli 'agenti' della società della conoscenza: i gruppi professionalli. *Etica deggli affari,* vol. 3:1, pp. 77-90.

Pruzan, P.; Thyssen, O. 1990: Conflict and consensus: Ethics as a shared value horizon for strategic planning. *Human Systems Management,* vol. 9, pp. 135-151.

Sacconi, L. 1991: *Etica degli Affari.* Milà: Mondadori.

Schein, E.H. 1984: Coming to a new awareness of organizational culture. *Sloan Management Review,* winter, pp. 3-16.

Senge, P.M. 1990: *The Fifth Discipline.* New York: Doubleday.

Sethi, S.P. 1975: Dimensions of corporate social performance: An analytical framework. *California Management Review,* vol. 17(3), pp. 58-64.

Tsalikis, J. and Fritzsche, D.J. 1989: Business ethics: A literature review with a focus on marketing ethics. *Journal of Business Ethics,* vol. 8:9, pp. 695-743.

19

Philosophers as Consultants

Andreas Føllesdal

Introduction

Philosophers often serve as ethics consultants. In this chapter I suggest some guidelines about what we should expect from philosophers who provide this kind of service to committees or other groups. We will look at committees or groups that are in charge of developing or assessing institutions or policies, but have no formal political power. Such committees offer room for public deliberation and reasoning about the issues. The philosopher serves as a non-voting consultant at the request of the committee.

I first address some issues about the legitimacy and characteristic features of philosophers' role as ethics consultants, and suggest that the philosopher's expertise be that of a teacher or coach. Throughout, I assume that this account is public and that the role and services must stand up to scrutiny, in the sense that future committees are prepared to solicit the assistance of the philosopher under such conditions. In the last section I draw out some implications of this view concerning the philosophers' obligation when serving as an ethics consultant. I address several issues raised in the literature concerning the responsibility the philosophers bears, suggesting that they be allowed to present their own moral views, and that they have certain obligations of confidentiality.

The Legitimacy of Philosopher-Consultants

Committees and groups may have tasks and mandates that raise dire issues of complicity in clearly immoral acts. Considerable judgment is necessary and unavoidable if the philosopher does not wish to become an accomplice to wrongdoing. However, we should discount other objections presented against joining the arenas of practical deliberation as ethics consultants. Such criticism may be of two kinds; either that the role as consultant threatens the integrity of philosophers, or that the philosopher has nothing to contribute as a consultant. I suggest that these

H. von Weltzien Hoivik and A. Føllesdal (eds.), Ethics and Consultancy: European Perspectives, 253-260.
© 1995 Kluwer Academic Publishers. Printed in the Netherlands.

criticisms do not render the philosopher's contribution irresponsible or irrelevant. Let us consider these worries.

Some fear that philosophers lend legitimacy to a project as "a hired pen, wielding grand language for its theoretical and sanctifying power in service of the employer" (Wikler, 1982: 12). Surely, one important role of philosophy, harking back to Socrates, is to provide a critical view of the status quo; for instance by offering an ideal or criteria by which to identify and measure the flaws of present circumstances. Committees and groups, on the other hand, are bound. They cannot start anew, creating the best arrangements from scratch. Instead, they are remedial, serving to correct procedures or run institutions. Moreover, committees can easily become agents of compromise and political manipulation. By serving as consultants to committees, philosophers thus are said to risk their integrity both as individuals and as a group.

We might think that the philosophical profession may have something at stake:

> One possible result of the increasing participation of philosophers in the public policy arena may be the emergence of adversary philosophers for hire. ... I am not certain that this is a development that the discipline of philosophy, or the public, should welcome. (Weisbard 1987: 785)

Weisbard raises an important point, we cannot assess the risks without a careful account of both the current public images of philosophers and the public assessment of philosopher-consultants. I submit that clear expectations and responsibilities are fruitful steps in avoiding confusing consultancy with philosophical studies generally and with philosophers offering services as critics. The risk is reduced since the acknowledged role of the philosopher is not to offer legitimacy, but to work with the committee on its own terms.

This whole area requires a discussion of what a philosopher can offer.

The Services of Philosopher-Consultants

Some critics wonder what, if anything, philosophers can offer committees or groups dealing with practical issues. For a philosopher to offer consulting services might thus amount to deception. However, I suggest that these criticisms are misplaced and I will show how through an exploration of a particular conception of the philosopher's role.

I submit that the philosopher's role is one of educator or coach, clarifying and improving the moral reasoning of the committee. They are trained in arguing about ethical dilemmas, and seek to increase coherence and consistency among the various moral concerns voiced by the members of the committee. To help the committee arrive at reasoned agreement on common grounds, philosophers offer distinctions and interpretations of moral judgments, policies and principles, juxtaposing them as defensible premises and conclusions.

The philosopher contributes to the process of achieving what John Rawls has called reflective equilibrium among the moral judgments of the committee members: their principles, ideals, and particular moral judgments. This method seeks to establish a consistent web of moral judgments, often with the practical aim of throwing more light on questions we have not yet passed judgment on, where we are in disagreement with each other, and where such disagreement matters:

> It is in equilibrium because at last our principles and judgments coincide; and it is reflective since we know to what principles our judgment conforms and the premises of their derivation. (Rawls 1971: 20)

Skills for creating order and structure among judgments, as premises and conclusions, are taught in philosophy departments, and such skills amount to expertise of a certain kind. The philosopher is expected to identify weaknesses and flaws in arguments, identify worrisome premises and consequences, offer their own considered, argued judgment as to improvements and favored conclusions, and present further arguments and reasonable positions.

Are such skills properly called 'moral expertise'? It would appear appropriate since the subject matters are moral judgments. However, this label may be misconstrued as claiming that ethicists are particularly 'ethical' individuals whose judgments are especially trustworthy. But I think the quality of philosophers' recommendations rests, not on their authority or trust in their character, but rather on the quality of arguments that they have to offer.

Moreover, this kind of expertise is not exclusionary, in contrast to the relationships between many professional experts and their clients. The aim of the philosopher is to improve the knowledge and skills of the client, not to use expert skills on the client's behalf. The philosopher's role is thus to increase the rationality of the committee, by improving the committee's ability to decide what to believe and its ability to weigh reasons for action.

Critics claim that the philosopher's utopian society is unattainable from here. It is uninhabitable by normal people, and out of reach for a committee with a constrained mandate. Critics may thus object to philosophers because of their ideal perspective, or because philosophers ignore the nitty-gritty institutional aspects of public policy, focussing instead solely on issues of personal morality.

In response, we must grant that institutional design is not part of philosophers' training. However, social, legal and political philosophy is typically carried out with these complexities in mind, while insisting that individual ethics and issues of institutional justice must be treated as separate, though related subjects of reflection. Moreover, philosophers have long been concerned with "non-ideal" topics: how to act under the tragic – though very real -constraints of wars of aggression, and addressing the ethical issues of revolution against tyrannies, of civil disobedience, and of whistle blowing. There are many such important and substantive moral issues attached to non-ideal circumstances, where philosophers' training in moral reasoning is relevant.

Fragments of a Code of Ethics

I now consider some moral responsibilities of philosophers serving as educators to committees or groups.

Limits to the Philosopher's Responsibility

Is the philosopher morally responsible for the reports and recommendations made by the committee? I suggest that the role of teacher reduces – without eliminating – the philosopher's responsibilities for the policy results.

The philosopher does not make decisions or resolve issues on others' behalf. To the contrary, the contribution of philosophers is to bolster the rationality of the committee itself, not to take on the responsibilities of the committee. Responsibility for the results is not transferred, because the committee is always free to accept or reject the suggestions offered by consultants – be they philosophers or other expert counsels.

Independent committee members evaluate the alternatives, and their decisions break the chain of responsibility of the adviser for the causal results of ideas. The philosopher has a responsibility to do a reasonable job coaching the committee, but should not be held responsible beyond this, whether or not the committee adopts views contrary to a philosophically more favored position.

The Philosopher's Suggestions: Not Constrained by Political Feasibility

Some claim that radical proposals should not be made to a committee or group; they are either counterproductive, or undemocratic. The role of the philosopher-consultant is not that of the reformer. The philosopher consultant should only provide philosophical perspectives that are congruent with current policies, and limited to the agenda set before the committee.

I suggest that this view is too restrictive. The role of teacher involves pointing out flaws in reasoning and suggesting and assessing principles and routines. These tasks include identifying important solutions and alternatives that are excluded by current politics or from the mandate of the committee. A philosopher-consultant may thus offer radical criticism – but always appealing to the judgments and views of committee members or of the public at large, with the intention of exploring and improving on such commitments (cf. Kamm, 1990: 358; Willigenburg, 1991: 35-39).

Short-term political acceptability may be a prudent consideration for the committee when it finally decides what to recommend, but there is little need for members – or consultants – to constrain themselves in this fashion during initial stages of the deliberative process. Indeed, philosophers may provide creativity and foresight about the sensitive questions and issues that will come up later if current policies are left to unfold by themselves (Menzel, 1990: 423).

Philosophers Need Not Always Seek Agreement

Disagreement within the committee is sometimes regarded as particularly troubling (Benjamin, 1990: 377). Philosophical reflection often serves to find common ground by identifying points of agreement and pinpointing issues of disagreement so that misunderstandings and empirical issues can be resolved. However, the philosopher may also threaten the apparent agreement among committee members (Weisbard, 1987.)

We should note that even when apparent agreement is due to improper reasoning, it is not clear that the philosopher must correct these flaws. The aim of the philosopher is to increase the committee's ability to reason, but this goal is not always improved by identifying all flaws.

Disagreement among committee members is not always regrettable. Sometimes reflection reveals deep-seated disagreement among committee members or among citizens at large on central issues. To bring this disagreement out in the open is often quite in order. Many such conflicts will emerge eventually, and committee discussions offer a better arena for reflection and resolution than the alternatives. On some issues, failure to reach consensus may even be appropriate. A committee may sometimes properly report that there is no reasoned compromise to be obtained and that the issue should instead be decided e.g. by normal majority political procedures, or with concern for both sides.

The philosopher's role may indeed sometimes be to help committee members to see how compromise between different opinions and views may be the morally appropriate solution, given the need for a unanimous recommendation for political decision. (cf. Benjamin, 1990: 387).

Philosophers May Offer Their Own Views on the Issues

The philosopher helps the reasoning of committee members by informing them about alternate reasons for various positions – including those philosophical positions that differ from the philosopher's own. Should, however, the philosopher-consultant also show his/her own hand and present and argue for their own views? Some would find that view worrisome: as teachers and advisers to students, for instance, we often refrain from stating our own views on the matters.

We must consider that the philosopher-consultant enters a particular role – that of teacher, or coach – which severs the direct link between personal values and the obligations taken on within that role. However, I submit that it is often acceptable for consultants to present their own views. The most pressing cases might be when the committee seems headed for gravely mistaken conclusions. This can include conclusions that seem to disregard the impact on certain persons or which fail to express the proper respect for affected parties. In such circumstances, I suggest that it is appropriate – indeed sometimes required – for the philosopher to at least express this concern and show why the conclusions are objectionable. By participating actively in the deliberations, philosophers can provide further guidance to the committee, improving on the commission's reflections by giving reasons for their view and showing the evolution of this view.

Why is it acceptable for philosophers to present their personal views in these circumstances but not necessarily when teaching students? There is certainly a risk of influencing committee members unduly. But the consultant does not have the kind of power over the committee or group as teacher has over students. There are still, to be sure, risks of influencing the committee in drastic ways. For instance, the consultant will quite often present the commissioners with conceptual normative frameworks that serve to improve the argumentative structure of their judgments, but which simultaneously cause "conceptual shifts," thus leading the members to change their moral judgments.

Philosophers' purpose in presenting their own position must be to convey perspectives and train the committee's abilities to reason on moral matters. The task is to help the committee members structure their own judgments. The purpose should not be to disseminate expert opinions that cannot be challenged by the members. The philosopher should therefore take steps to offer reasons for a particular position or suggestion, not merely provide conclusions. The philosopher's influence should – if at all – be due to the arguments and reasons provided (cf. Kamm, 1990: 351). What should matter for the committee, then, is not that the consultant holds a particular view, but what reasons the consultant has for holding this view. This assumption should guide consultants' presentation of their views.

Grounds and Scope of Confidentiality

Can a philosopher be expected to remain silent about what is seen as serious flaws in work on which he/she has consulted? What are the grounds for and limits to the obligations of confidentiality towards a committee?

One might hold that the philosopher must always remain free and independent to serve as a critic of poor public reasoning. However, the philosopher may have gained access to confidential information and insight into internal disagreements among members. It may be apparent, in light of such information or insight, that the results of the committee are not due to arguments and reasoned deliberation, but instead to the wielding of extraneous power – political, economic or personal. However, the philosopher has gained access to this information on the understanding that confidentiality is maintained. This expectation is legitimate and should be honored, in the sense that the philosopher generally does not reveal such disagreement or the sources of disagreement. Public criticism of the conclusions of such committees also should normally be avoided by members, to diminish the threat and real danger of revealing confidential information. Similarly, it should not be revealed by the philosopher who presented various considerations. It may sometimes be permissible and appropriate, however, to report on which reasons were offered during the deliberations.

A responsibility to assess decisions critically is perhaps inescapable for intellectuals and for philosophers as a group. However, I submit that an individual philosopher may legitimately engage in particular deliberative processes, waiving their general right – and sometimes obligation – as a citizen to criticize those decisions in public. As an "insider" to the committee, the philosopher is given an opportunity to express opinions in advance and a chance to argue the case to the members of the committee. It falls on others to criticize the conclusions offered by the committee.

The committee may sometimes defend itself against criticism by falsely claiming that the philosopher accepted or somehow sanctioned their arguments, premises, or conclusions. As far as such claims also violate the philosopher's interest in maintaining personal integrity, repute, or the reputation of the profession, they must be permitted to stop such accusations. If the committee refuses to withdraw such statements, the philosopher may offer a public disclaimer.

One exception to the general requirement of confidentiality requires mention. There are often few philosophers or other social critics who have sufficient knowledge of particular issues in specific cases. The distribution of moral responsibility for criticism between insiders and outsiders fails to hold in such instances. If nobody can serve as an outside critic, the philosopher should be wary about taking on responsibilities as a consultant for that particular project. Nevertheless, when a task is accepted under such circumstances, the committee and the public can not expect the philosopher-consultant to keep silent if the committee reaches what the philosopher regards as highly objectionable conclusions.

What should philosophers do if they find themselves strongly opposed to the conclusions drawn by the committee on philosophical grounds? They may find their own integrity at stake. Their professional reputation seems to require that they be permitted to publicly identify serious flaws in reasoning, or claim that the committee ignored crucial implications. While a committee member can have a dissenting opinion, this option is not open to the consultant. However, I suggest that since it is publicly known that the philosopher-consultant is required to keep confidences, silence on particular matters can not be regarded as acquiescence to the arguments or the results. Moreover, loyalty among philosophers should not lead outsiders to refrain from scrutiny of the suggestions of committees. To the contrary, it falls on other members of the public, including philosophers who are "outside" the committee, to criticize the arguments and conclusions of the committee in public. The philosopher-consultant and the philosopher-critic thus provide two worthwhile and compatible services, contributing in their different ways to public reasoning.

Conclusion

Undoubtedly, the philosopher can serve a valuable role as outside critic. I have suggested that philosophers can also serve a legitimate role as counsels of morality and reasoning within politics as consultants to committees. The philosopher's expertise is that of a teacher or coach. Such services may be consistent with the practice of philosophy, where other philosophers serve honorably and credibly as social critics.

References

Benjamin, Martin 1990: Philosophical integrity and policy development in bioethics. *The Journal of Medicine and Philosophy,* 15, August, pp. 375-90.

Kamm, Frances 1990: The philosopher as insider and outsider. *The Journal of Medicine and Philosophy,* 15, pp. 347-74.

Menzel, Paul T. 1990: Public philosophy: Distinction without authority. *The Journal of Medicine and Philosophy,* 15, August, pp. 411-24.

Rawls, John 1971: *A Theory of Justice.* Cambridge, Mass.: Harvard University Press.

Weisbard, Alan J. 1987: The role of philosophers in the public policy process: A view from the President's commission. *Ethics,* 97, July, pp. 776-85.

Wikler, Daniel 1982: Ethicists, critics, and expertise. *Hastings Center Report,* June, pp. 12-13.

Willigenburg, Theo van 1991: *Inside the Ethical Expert.* Kampen, The Netherlands: Kok Pharos.

20

The Consultant-Client Relationship: Personal Autonomy and Development Through Dialogue

Knut Johannessen Ims

Abstract

The two guiding principles in this chapter are: i) maximizing the awareness of clients' values and minimizing the influence of consultants' values, and ii) the issue of instrumentality, i.e assuring that we are doing what we wish to do. In order to obtain the first principle, implicit or explicit pitfalls of manipulating the "model-weak" person in the relationship will be emphasized. The "model-weak" part may be either the consultant or the client, but as a main rule I will see the client as the object of possible manipulation. The quality of relationship is the unit of analysis, and the research approaches the subject matter from an interdisciplinary point of view. The research should in particular be of interest to those interested in management, taking into consideration that the essence of management and leadership is to "manage" interpersonal relations.

Introduction

In Western societies, consultants are highly visible. They perform activities and rhetoric at different organizational levels and are either blamed or blessed for their advice. They are expected to give advice to clients. To be effective, the quality of the consultant-client relationship is assumed important. The consultant-client relationship even though dealt with in prior research is, however, not without ambiguities and difficulties. Due to the assumed importance of the advice, a more thorough understanding of the dyadic relationship is needed. This chapter brings a new perspective to this literature. Three assumptions will be basic:

H. von Weltzien Hoivik and A. Føllesdal (eds.), Ethics and Consultancy: European Perspectives, 261-279.
© 1995 *Kluwer Academic Publishers. Printed in the Netherlands.*

1 Knowledge cannot be treated as a material resource. Knowledge consists of mental facts or personal constructs. Knowledge transfer, therefore, cannot be separated from the psychological makeup of the persons involved in the information process.

2 The actor's self is of central importance for the knowledge construction process and a person's self is a relational phenomenon, i.e. the self is constituted and sustained in an interactive, social process with important others. It means that the substantive content of the knowledge exchange process, cannot be understood in a vacuum. Parallel with the primary information process the actors signal secondary information elements that are interpreted as either disrespect – or self-respect enhancing – and, as Rawls (1971) holds, self-respect is "perhaps the most important primary good." So respect and self-respect need to be part of the analysis.

3 The most important part of the process of knowledge creation does not have a problem solving, but a problem finding character. This means that the question to be asked is not given, but is in itself a core issue (Pounds, 1969; Schøn, 1983).

With these three basic assumptions in mind, many issues need to be confronted in order to illuminate aspects of the consultant-client relationship in an ethical perspective. What does it mean to receive advice and at the same time act as an autonomous person? How should the client avoid gliding unconsciously into the consultant's world – thinking, seeing and speaking on the premises of the assumed expert? And for the consultant, what does it mean to signal respect for the others and at the same time advise them? In the following the quality of the relationship between the consultant and client will be investigated. It is not only a question of substantive content, i.e. a question of what is to be exchanged or constructed, but most importantly how the process is going on between the persons involved. To protect and enhance each other's self-respect is one thing, but how should the participants behave in order to pose the right questions, i.e. how to "frame and name" a situation that initially is regarded as a mess?

Literature Review

To consult (latin consulto) means to seek the opinion or advice of another person. By consultant (counsellor) I mean persons who make it their business to give advice. When using the verb "consult," I think of the client as asking for advice, and when using the noun "consultant," I think of the giving of advice. There are consultants within many professions – law, computers (system analysts, programmers), auditing, and accountancy, to mention a few.

In general, consultants have overlapping roles. In practice they often act as social scientists, (collecting, interpreting, and analyzing data), as psychiatrists (clarifying distorted perceptions) and educators (supporting and stimulating learning of new skills), and, to cite Benne (1969), "in the effort to integrate these discrepant but overlapping roles, ethical problems arise."

How is the dyadic relationship between a sender and receiver of advice depicted in the literature? Parts of the literature with explicit ethical focus describe different models, listing them as either paternalistic, contract, agency, friendship or fiduciary (Bayles, 1988; Ellin, 1988). Ellin (1988) distinguishes between five models:

- adversary model – a competitive relationship between the parties, where they bargain at arm´s length and where it is necessary to compromise the conflicting interests
- a cooperative model where there is partnership and often mutual trust,
- an agency model in which the professional (consultant) carries out the wishes of the client: "The client determines the ends to be attained, and the professional acts to achieve these ends, being an instrument of the client's will.
- But if the professional is superior" (p 135), then he/she may use the client for his/her own ends, i.e an exploitation model, or
- the professional may work for the client's end, in which case there is a fiduciary model.

Ellin's surprising point is that in a strict sense trust is only necessary in the last model.

The Self and Related Concepts

Benne (1961) makes an interesting distinction between ethical and technical problems. When the self is at stake, the issue is said to be ethical or, as Benne puts it, "What makes the problem of the consultant ethical is that it involves in its solution the future career as a consultant self," and "it is an ethical conflict since its resolution involves recommitment in the self and some new inter-accommodation of the associations significant to the self and of their normative demands upon members" (p. 600-601). Benne poses the question of fit or misfit between consultants' image of their role as a good consultant and the client's image of what a helpful consultant should (or shouldn't) do, i.e. what is proper help. Furthermore he discusses what kinds of influence are involved when the consultant belongs to various associations, is a citizen, and is a member of more "personal" associations such as families and churches. Therefore role segregation is difficult in practice.

A related issue is the problem of loyalty. According to Tranøy (1974), the professional (consultant) must give due interest to the "new" stakeholders – clients and society. This widening of the horizon is important since in some professions there has traditionally been a one-sided and exclusive loyalty to members of the same profession. A changed focus of loyalty is also argued by Winslow (1988) in his analysis of the nursing profession.

In the management science tradition there has been an ongoing concern for getting the results of operational research (developing computer based models) into the hands (minds) of managers (see for instance Schultz & Slevin, 1979). In this literature there are different views on successful "implementation" that might be held by different groups. A management science researcher (a consultant) may think of successful implementation in terms of technical validity, i.e if the model developed works. The user (client) on the other hand, may see the problem in terms of organizational validity, i.e the extent to which the model is used in making decisions – how the model fits the organization. The top manager may see the problem in terms of the contribution to the organizations's effectiveness. This means that the advice is good if it produces a behavior change that is desired and is in accordance with the value system of those in top management. A classical contribution is made by Churchman & Scheinblatt (1965). They suggested a clarification of four relationships or "positions" between expert/researcher (consultant) and manager (client) called mutual understanding, communicator, persuasion and separate function. The ideal situation, called mutual understanding, exists when the manager (client) understands the researcher (consultant) and vice versa.

This means that the manager reacts to what the researcher tries to do in a way that improves the manager's possibility to reach relevant goals. In the communicator position it is important for the researcher to make the manager understand the researcher better. As a contrast to this position the researcher in the persuasion position attempts to understand enough about the manager's position in order to persuade him/her to accept the researcher's results/models. This is a "selling of ideas" case, and implementation means to sell one's own recommendations to the manager. In the separate-function position the view is to look upon management and research as two essentially separate functions. The researcher's (consultant's) task is to work out a complete plan and then present it to the manager (client), whose task it is to either accept or reject the plan.

More subtle forms of manipulation are described by Boland (1979) and Bråten (1983a and 1986b). Boland (1979) challenges the system analysts' (experts') value neutrality by describing how they create the users' (clients') world through the design of information systems. Thus he focuses upon the system developers' ethical responsibility. Through a variety of important examples, the Norwegian sociologist Stein Bråten (1983a) illustrates how model-power mechanisms work. He describes how a model-strong actor, even with the best intentions, influences a model-weak actor through their symbolic interaction. By distinguishing between symbolic ("mental") resources and material resources, Bråten illustrates in a brilliant analysis how model power mechanisms may reinforce existing influence gaps between persons when they begin to interact. Bråten's analysis of model-power mechanisms and his listing of five ways to transcend ("aufheben") the power of the model-strong, are particularly relevant for the client-consultant relationship. In order to minimize the consultant's role, partly based upon Bråten's frame of reference, Ims (1987) used a version of Kelly Role Rep Test (1955) methodology, permitting the client to select the elements for reflection as well as using the clients' (electricity directors) own language.

Interesting contributions focusing on the dyadic relationship between consultant-client have been made by Rogers (1968), Håland (1986), and Løvlie (1982a, 1982b). These authors maintain that the relationship is more important than the methods. Rogers (1968) distinguishes between what he calls a "manufactured" relationship and a helping relationship. A helping relationship involves growth for the client and "the optimal helping relationship" is created by a helper who is a psychologically mature person. A psychologically mature helper is "congruent". This means a unified or integrated person in the sense that whatever feeling or attitude he/she is experiencing is "matched by his/her awareness of that attitude" (p 298).

Rogers states that a process of personal development is essential to a good helper, otherwise words may convey one message, while at the same time the consultant's possible annoyance will be communicated in subtle ways. This may confuse the client. Rogers also comments on the problem of distance between the consultant and client, which is often typical of the professionalization of most fields. The consultant may therefore keep from experiencing the caring "which would exist if. . . (the consultant) recognized the relationship as one between two persons" (p. 299).

An important aspect of a helping relationship is also to keep it free of judgment and evaluation as it will "permit the other person to reach the point where he recognizes that the focus of evaluation, the centre of responsibility, lies within self" (Rogers, 1968 p 302). Negative as well as positive evaluation may be threatening. Valuative procedures work in such a way that they transform a person into an object. Rogers' final point is in accordance with Martin Buber and focuses on the importance of "confirming the other." Buber says "Confirming means. . . accepting the whole potentiality of the other. . . I can recognize in him, know in him, the person he has been . . . created to become. . . I confirm him in myself, and then in him, a relation to this potentiality that. . . can now be developed, can evolve" (Rogers, 1968 p 302). The main point is to accept the other person (the client) as a process of becoming – not as something fixed, already classified, already shaped by the past. The importance of the self concept as a relational and a dialectic construct is excellently developed and discussed by Løvlie (1982a, 1982b). (The self concept will be developed in the frame of reference that follows.)

Openness, trust and accurate information flow between consultant and client are recommended by Argyris (1969, 1985) and Argyris et al (1985) in their distinction between model I behavior and model II behavior. Part of the problem is taking feelings and emotion to be central to the resolution of organizational problems, while most managers (clients) regard feelings and emotions as "bad" or "immature". According to Argyris and his co-authors (1985), the main rule is to be open and face the problems. Due to the "defensive routines", "the brittleness syndrome" and other subtle defense mechanisms of the clients, this is not obvious. Consultants are in a dilemma whenever their values are unacceptable to the client. If the consultant states this, he/she may become an unwanted person in the organization and if acting in accordance with the client's values, there will be no change. In short, this literature problematizes the client's willingness and ability to learn. A related problem is described by Maslow, who pinpoints the tension between the fear of knowledge and the search for knowledge. This fear of knowledge violates the overly mechanistic assumption of knowledge creation – that we always strive for more knowledge, and that more knowledge is always preferable to less. This is also observed in cultural analyses of organizations (Schein, 1992).

Argyris et al (1985, p. 387) argue that a non-directive approach may involve more manipulation and dependence than the forthright approach due to the difficulties with placing responsibility on the client to come up with ideas about how to proceed.

Concerning values of the consultant or a consultant group, Argyris (p. 434) distinguishes between two types of competence, technical, intellectual competence versus interpersonal competence. Both types or levels of competence are important. However, Argyris hypothesizes that if either or both is low, or if either is significantly higher than the other, difficulties will tend to arise (p. 435).

Reflections On the Review of Literature

My review of literature has been eclectic – broad, but relatively superficial and fragmentary. I have searched within quite different fields and my findings differ and are more indicative than authoritative. Hence my research cannot be called comprehensive within any field. My purpose was not to epitomize any field, but rather to generate problems/statements and probe for possible cross fertilization. I am left with many questions and issues which need to be resolved.

When Ellin (1988) asserts that trust is only necessary in the fiduciary model, we may be led to think that trust is a clear and well-defined concept. Butler (1991), however, found that trust was a multi-dimensional concept and found 60 sub-dimensions.

In parts of the explicit ethical literature that I have cited, the main theme is framed as a problem of choosing the appropriate model. I find this unsatisfactory. It may well be of a certain analytical help, but it is not enough. Any model needs to be adapted to the specific concrete reality. We need a methodology as well. There may also be a cross-fertilization by combining different theoretic schools, i.e. the organizational-oriented theory might be complemented with ethical concepts and reasoning. Important ethical concepts such as dignity, pride, and self are not discussed in mainstream organizational literature. In particular, some of the concepts found in the psychotherapy literature, especially the self concept and the emphasis of relationship, seem to be lacking in the other fields. My contribution is synthesizing the ethical, the organizational, the information- and psychotherapy-oriented literature. Developing the first rudimentary elements of a methodology of consultant-client relationships with a highlight on the self concept is the focus of the next section.

A Conceptual Framework: A Sketch of a Tentative Theory of Client-Consultant Relationship in an Ethical Perspective.

This section will develop a frame of reference for the ethical issues of the dyadic relationship between client and consultant. Due to the preliminary character of the theory, the emphasis on relevant concepts will be stronger than the relationships between the concepts. One central concept will be the self. The self concept is nicely introduced by the following Taoist story from ancient China:

> When Yen Ho was about to take up his duties as tutor to the heir of Ling, Duke of Wei, he went to Ch'u Po Yu for advice. "I have to deal," he said, "with a man of depraved and murderous disposition. . . . How is one to deal with a man of this sort?" "I am glad," said Ch'u Po Yu, "that you asked this question. . . . The first thing you must do is not to improve him, but to improve yourself."

A Challenge to the Dyadic, But Asymmetric Relationship Between Consultant and Client

A consulting relationship assumes the existence of an asymmetric relationship in terms of knowledge between the consultant and the client. The traditional perspective states the problem as a transfer of knowledge from the consultant to the client. However, many problems are involved. One pitfall is the generalizing of expertise, when the "experts" talk about knowledge that they are not in a privileged position to talk about. Another problem is manipulation. Manipulation may be explicit as strategic behavior (Habermas; 1982; Ims, 1987) or implicit through model power mechanisms (see Bråten, 1983a). Therefore, a high level of awareness for both consultant and client concerning their respective values is necessary. In the following I will focus on how different value systems may be elicited and made more explicit in order to reduce the risk of non-intentional influence (manipulation).

The analysis is limited to two parties (two persons). The quality of the relationship will be the unit of analysis. The task of personal development, which may or may not be part of an organizational development project, is the subject matter and it is obvious that the two parties will be involved in a sensitive project.

Consultancy as Intervention

An intervention is any kind of research into an organization, a group of people or a person. To put into writing thoughts, values and assumptions concerning an organization or a person is quite a new way of looking into a reality otherwise taken for granted. When written down and introduced to the people in the organization in the form of a report, this may represent an intervention. It is also important to argue our values, otherwise we fail to take responsibility for the ethical dimension in a relationship (Schein, 1985). Furthermore, it is important that the professional consultant has formulated ethical guidelines to regulate these interventions. These guidelines should be communicated to the clients for their well-being, for instance as a written description to the person who will be researched.

Practical judgment (phronesis) will be seen as a central component of decision making and action. Therefore, advice based exclusively on a technocratic understanding of the situation is seldom satisfactory (Nordenstam, 1983). One needs something additional that is part of the context. The more people believe in themselves (have adequate competence and a well-established self-concept), the more faith they will have in their own judgment. Faith in own judgment may strengthen the client's as well as the consultant's independence and autonomy, which in my opinion are ethical values.

Autonomy and Integrity Defined

Autonomy is not independence from other persons in an absolute sense. On the contrary a person has a continuous need to be seen and valued by other persons for confirming mirroring and "anerkennen". Thus we should acknowledge everyman's relational reality and that we are dependent on other people all through our lives. With autonomy I mean self-determination as the ability to say no to wants and claims put forward in the environment. This presupposes a separated self that is able to represent one's own will (Gullestad, 1992).

Integrity is necessary, but not sufficient; for virtues of integrity allow for most any content. An evil tyrant could display integrity to a high degree, so it is important that an impartial spectator could say that the person's notion of the common good is in correspondence with well accepted principles, e.g. ideas of the original position (Rawls 1971). Virtues of integrity are truthfulness and sincerity, lucidity, commitment and authenticity.

The Self Concept

The concept of self captivates the person when experiencing the inner and outer world. This is a phenomenological view of the person and includes feelings of self, i.e. self-esteem. A person's self-respect and dignity are assumed to be central. In correspondence with Rawls (1971) self-respect consists of two aspects: i) the person's sense of their own value, "his secure conviction that his conception of his good, his plan of life, is worth carrying out," and ii) the confidence in one's ability to fulfill one's intentions. As Rawls holds, without self-respect "nothing may seem worth doing – and we may sink into apathy and cynicism" (Rawls, 1971, p 440). Further I believe that one's self-respect is contagious and effects people with whom one interacts (Nordenstam, 1968). Bennis & Nanus (1985) wrote about the management of own and others' selves: "What we observed was that our ninety leaders induced (stemming from their own self-regard) positive other-regard in their employees. And this turns out to be a pivotal factor in their capacity to lead" (p. 62).

As Løvlie writes, "The self is the totality – and cannot be localized here or there – it is inside my skin, but also in the relationship to persons and objects in the world with whom and which I interact." Just where the self begins and ends is an open question; the arbitrariness of self "delineation", according to Gregory Bateson (1972, p.30). The essence of self is relationship. In accordance with the one-world view, man-in-the world constitutes a unity and it is up to us to choose how we divide this unity. Løvlie writes, "We are relationship" (1982, p.110). We usually think of two persons as separate bodies because they are separate in a physical sense. However, when two persons interact they transcend their physical separation. Bråten's theory of model-power, illustrates negative consequences in terms of autonomy of one type of monological relationship. Through interaction we can also be acknowledged (in Hegel's sense "anerkannt") or we may experience alienation, i.e the feeling of not being acknowledged and not regaining one's self (Løvlie, 1979).

Does the consultant make the client feel inferior and incompetent, or give the client a feeling of pride and self-esteem, stimulating an enthusiastic exploration of the world and self? This question relates to the dialectic view of the self concept. Anyone´s self is defined as a relation to other selves. This involves consultants creating the client through their ongoing patterns of interaction, which is filtered through all their past patterns of interaction – and as he creates the other, he also creates himself.

Through the self concept we can account for the dialectic and reflective nature of humans. The subjective and objective aspects of humans presuppose each other. If I can reflect, I can also be responsible, i.e. I can answer for my experience – or I can choose not to respond to certain parts of my experiences. According to Løvlie (1982b, p. 36), one type of irresponsible communication is to send unclear messages which I therefore can disqualify, i.e. use constructs that are "loose" (Kelly 1955).

The Quality of Relationship

Authenticity is a property of interpersonal relationship. This means that the person must behave genuinely, i.e. in accordance with personal values (Argyris, 1969). According to Pollak (1976), methodologies may be a barrier between two persons. This statement needs to be corroborated. A proper methodology, used in a flexible and sensitive way, may be helpful, depending upon the subject matter to be investigated and in general the context. Therefore I maintain that the most decisive factor in the consultant-client relationship is that the first sequence (part) of the dialogue must be free of any kind of technology. This is the I-You part in which the relationship is characterized by connectedness and presence (Buber, 1964). The second sequence may involve purposive-rational action by which I understand either instrumental action or rational choice, or their conjunction. Instrumental action is based on technical rules using empirical knowledge and imply empirical predictions about observable phenomena (McCarthy, 1978).

Dignity and Freedom to Choose

Following Benne (1969), I will illustrate a methodology that tries to maximize the client's freedom to choose, i.e maximize client autonomy. It is important to be aware of model power mechanisms and the threat of cognitive imperialism. Dialogue and dialectics may be used to enhance awareness of one's own values through value clarification, (to protect and enhance the personal autonomy of the client).

I suggest the following steps concerning how to reach value clarification (Benne, 1969, pp. 590-591):

Desirable steps	Role of consultant
1) Increasing awareness of manipulation	Labelling own values to self and clients; allowing client to "talk back"
2) Building protection or resistance against manipulation	Minimizing own values and maximizing client's values as dominant criteria for the change process
3) Setting enhancement of freedom of choice as a positive goal	Using professional skills and authentic relationship to increase client's range of choices and ability to choose

Consultants (practitioners) should be aware of the fact that they are controlling the client (Benne, 1969, p. 591). The professional consultant's methods and solutions are not based upon objective reality, but on a particular set of values that might fruitfully be discussed. The institutional settings and the methodology in which the consultant operates may favor certain kinds of values. Consultants introduce their own values into the relationship both in the definition of the situation and in the setting of standards. Consequently it is useful for the consultant to "have certain values about what needs to be done in the situation itself," and to communicate these values to the client. By recognizing that they are engaged in a certain degree of control and that this is an ethically ambiguous act, the consultants provide some safeguards against the control. This will make it easier for the client to "talk back" to the consultant and to argue about the appropriateness of the values introduced into the situation.

How to build in procedures that may protect against manipulation? One step is to encourage the client to explore personal values and relate what is learned to their own value system. As a matter of fact, the client should determine the direction of the process. The crucial point is that the client's own values should be at the centre of attention. These values should be used as criteria against which any change can be measured. In order to stimulate this value clarification process the consultant should help the client in the value exploration process, often by eliciting and contrasting his/her own values.

The third step is to enhance the freedom of choice as one of the positive goals of the change effort. This means providing the client with data and information that widens the range of choices and creating new experiences for the client that increases the ability to choose (and thus maximize his/her own values).

New experiences may be made through a dialectics of meaning-making and action. One is a presupposition for the other (Løvlie 1982a and 1982b). A person acts and creates meaning and self. The world will be perceived as meaningful if you understand, predict or master it to a minimal degree.

Empathy Versus Inclusiveness

Inclusiveness "is the complete realization of… the 'partner' not by the fancy but by the actuality of the being" (Buber, 1965, p. 97). Empathy means to glide with one´s feelings into the dynamic structure of an object, a tree, an animal or a human, "it means to 'transpose' oneself over there and in there. Thus it means the exclusion of one's own concreteness, the extinguishing of the actual situation of life. . . ." On the other hand, inclusion is "the extension of one's own concreteness. . .the complete presence of the reality in which one participates." Inclusion presupposes a relation between two persons, an event experienced in common, in which at least one of them participates actively, and one person who at the same time lives through the common event from the standpoint of the other. And Buber concludes, "A relation between persons that is characterized in more or less degree by the element of inclusion may be termed a *dialogical relation*" (my emphasis) (p 97).

Real Dialogue

A real dialogue presupposes a symmetry between the partners that does not permit either one to dominate (Bråten, 1983). Løvlie (1984) distinguishes between persuasion, which presupposes a subject-object relationship, i.e. an I-It relationship, and convincing, which presupposes a subject relationship, i.e an I-You relationship. Consultants should have a communicative attitude towards the client which means that the consultant should be able and willing to reach a common understanding with the other part (Habermas, 1982; McCarthy, 1978).

I will distinguish between power, which means threats of punishment or punishment, and manipulation, by which I mean hidden influence, for instance when the consultant, partly on the premises of the client, arranges the conditions in such a way that the client makes the consultant's (master's) words their own (Løvlie).

In terms of Bråten's model power theory I am particularly aware of how to transcend ("aufheben") the model power of the most powerful part.

Contract

A contract is any arrangement in which the parties talk and negotiate how to proceed during the interaction process between consultant and client. One important aspect of the contract is to create security. The critical issue is not whether the contract is formal or informal, written or verbal, but the way in which the negotiations are experienced. If the intention of the dialogue is to break down interpersonal barriers, this may create a fruitful platform for confidential, dialogical and growth-enhancing conversations (Håland, 1985). In this situation we may well be aware of Bråten's theory of model power. Even with the best of intentions one of the participants may slide into a dominated relationship by "swallowing" the premises of the expert. In this way the consultant and the client create a monological state.

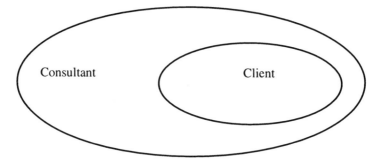

In order to avoid this unconscious "mono-perspective", one may transform the conditions into a dialogical state (Bråten, 1986b). By crossing the border of the meaning horizon or changing the domain, one may establish a symmetric, cognitive conversation in which the complementing and crossing of perspectives are permitted. Crossing of perspectives is a presupposition for awareness and gives an opportunity for a extended creative horizon. In accordance with Bråten (1983; 1986) I postulate that every human being has abilities to enter into a self-reflective dialogue within their own life-world. In order to create a real self-reflective dialogue, both parts (or perspectives) in the dialogue must represent something in common as well as something unique.

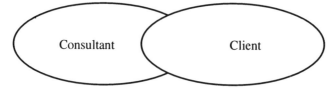

During the contract negotiations, consultants must be aware of their responsibility. They have a professional duty to make the client aware of the consequences of entering into the relationship. This may be a process involving explorative research of the client's personality and culture (which may be analogous to a person's character), leading to organizational change. It is very important for the consultant to talk about the possible consequences in advance in order to give a free choice (informed consent) before the research begins. This also involves the client having the authority to stop the process at any time if it is felt that the organization's integrity is threatened. This right to say no to stop the project should be explicitly agreed. To stop a development project that has gained momentum may be problematic.

Therefore openness, sensitivity, courage and honesty between the participants have to be critical factors in the relationship. It is essential that the development process should be anchored in the individual participant's dignity and his or her inviolable right to stop and drop the project at whatever stage it may have reached. To work through the contract as early as possible, stating these factors, is important.

The Integrity-Flexibility Issue

How flexible should the consultant be when accommodating the client's claims? This is a problematic issue, particularly when accepting a task that may be on the edge of one's professional expertise or builds upon quite different values. When discussing a possible contract, the consultant may experience great pressure to accommodate the wishes of the client. Furthermore, if the consultant is in great need of a contract, the degree of free choice may in fact be limited. Thus, during the contract negotiations, the client may often turn out to be the model-strong actor.

Toward Self-Organized Learning

Up to now single elements have been presented as part of the conceptual model, but what about the processes? With the "two-community theory" as a point of departure, a self-organized learning approach will be encouraged.

The two-community theory of knowledge use (Caplan, 1979; Dunn, 1980) states the problem as a gap between the consultant's and the client's way of looking at the world (often in terms of different ontological and epistemological assumptions). The theory states implicitly that the main problem is a transfer of expert knowledge from the professional to the client. As I see it, personal development is the crucial issue. The purpose is to attain autonomy in the relationship with the expert. A pragmatic issue is involved as well: Will the expert's advice improve anything at all (the effectiveness/ efficiency question)? Due to uncertainties in every structure of the world, the problematic character of causality, and the importance of practical judgement, it will be difficult to rely on any expert's technocratic knowledge (Schøn, 1983). Reflection-in-action is the alternative to the notion of traditional expertise.

The traditional relationship between a consultant, a client, and a resource, i.e. knowledge, may be conceived as involving three elements visualized in the following logical sequence:

Knowledge ⟶ Consultant ⟶ Client

The prototype of this pattern occurs when the consultant interprets the public knowledge of the topic and "injects" this knowledge into the client, who efficiently absorbs the well-organized knowledge. I reject this approach which presupposes a hierarchical relationship. It may work as a stop gap in the short term, but it creates dependence and has little to do with effectively taking control of one's own situation.

Following Thomas & Harri-Augstein (1985), a different perspective on relations that might be called conversational, self-organized learning may be put forward. The term "conversational" points to the fact that no person can know their self unaided: We all need help to exploit our infinite potential – and through conversations and dialogues with others, we can stimulate each other and pool our experiences. By learning, I mean the "construction, reconstruction, and exchange of personally significant, relevant, and viable meaning" (after Thomas and Harri-Augstein, 1985, p. XXIV). "Self-organized" refers to clients' right to define their own learning purpose and that learning may occur naturally and spontaneously from experience through creation of personal meaning. It is important that the meanings are personally significant for some part of the person's life. This perspective enables the client as well as the consultant to participate in a mentally and emotionally active way in order to cultivate and develop their common resources. This perspective involves the consultant helping the client to:

i reflect on self as a person using the client's and the consultant's experience, and

ii explore and experiment on some part of the social or physical environment.

$$\text{CLIENT}_p \longleftrightarrow \text{CONSULTANT}_p$$

The letter p indicates that both consultant and client are concerned with the client as a person and "not merely as a receptacle of knowledge" (Thomas and Harri-Augstein, 1985, p.320).

Dialogue as a Language Creating Process

A communicative dialogue is not governed by egocentric calculations oriented towards one's own success. To the contrary, the interaction is directed at realizing an agreement or a consent as a platform in order to obtain personal goals (Habermas, 1982). As Bråten (1983a) emphasizes, such an interaction may have a dialogical flavor, but is not necessarily a dialogue. It may well be a pseudo dialogue, i.e. a monologue on the premises of the model-strong person. So what is the critical factor?

The crucial point for the consultant is to give the client an opportunity to be expressive. To talk about complicated phenomena that has not yet been put into concepts or categories (at least for one or both of the participants) is seemingly impossible. First the participants must be aware of the dialectic between phenomena and concepts. Concepts are not identical with the phenomena, they are dialectic. Phenomena exist and concepts are constructed in an effort to understand and master the world. We cannot divide the phenomena, but we can divide concepts (Løvlie, 1982a, p. 109). (The notion of the interrelation of everything means that it is up to us – the participants – to choose how we divide this unity. Any division is arbitrary.) In this process the client/participant must have initial help to engage in an ongoing language-creating process.

When the client expresses a word/concept (or even better, a "construct"), consultants should not think of themselves as clairvoyant experts who immediately know what the client means. The biography of the client will probably be different from that of the consultant. Therefore the two parts may well:

1 put different meaning on the same expression
2 put the same meaning on different expressions.

Case 1 is an example of a rich or a loose construct. As a consequence of arbitrariness in the articulation of constructs, one may well have examples of case 1. In case 2 we can speak about pseudo-agreement or -disagreement in the subject matter (Næss, 1961). A pseudo-disagreement can be resolved when the participants during the conversation define the meaning of the expressions.

In order to reach each others' life world, one must define concepts and communicate each others' interpretations. This necessitates learning and openness from both parts through a conversation which must be a mixture of I – You and I – It. Consultants should not regard themselves as the know-all before entering into this process. Their image should rather be that of a student prepared to learn. No doubt this is a demanding and partly a painful process for a well-educated, technically-oriented professional.

Kelly's (1955) concepts of loosening and tightening may be helpful in this phase of the dialogue. "Loosening" is one strategy that makes the conceptualizations so elastic that they cover everything. As a consequence, loosened constructs hinder validity tests of the applicability to reality. "Tightening" or constricting one's construct system makes a conceptualization so tight and limited that most phenomena fall outside of a person's (the client´s) mind (construct system). It will be important to change between loosening up a construct in the beginning and tightening it up later in the dialogue. When grasping the other part's meaning with a concept, one can tighten the concept in order to increase the level of precision. (See also Ims 1987).

I – You, then I – It

What kind of consultant/client relationship is preferable? Following Bråten (1983b) I would suggest that it is essential to distinguish between two different types of interaction. First, we have an external interaction in which the other part is reduced to an "it", an object, a thing in the sphere of "it" (also see Habermas, 1982). The opposite is an I-You dialogue. This is an interaction characterized by here and now experiences, including sincerity and inclusion (Buber, 1964 and Bråten, 1983b). This is a type of inspiring, deep dialogue, and is usually not associated with matter-of-fact (objective) conversations. On such a basis I would postulate that I-You should precede I-it. Therefore, one should first establish a covenant of mutuality and equality between the dialogue partners. Then one may start objective conversations and instrumental thinking and action. This means that achieving each other's life worlds is one premise for planning and designing somebody's future. Thus an external analysis of a person, a group or an organization has partly to be based upon a perspective from within, i.e from the client's world of meaning.

When shall the process be punctuated? When has a mutual understanding in a pragmatic sense been reached? Regardless of the interpreter's capabilities, an attempt to interpret other persons' meanings, based upon words, hints and expressions, is hazardous. At this point the dialectic and debate moment should be brought into play. Interpretations of another person's expressions should not be regarded as a final interpretation, but as a possible interpretation. Thus an interpretation should not be regarded the "one and only" and undiscussable, but as an appropriate point of departure for reflection. My point of view is that any elicitation of important concepts should be debated and be a means in an ongoing dialogue. (Shaw, 1982, in particular p. 65). I will conclude by showing a structured methodology which I have applied and experienced as useful in stimulating an explorative dialogue on the actors' own premises.

The Conceptual Model in Review

In the center of my frame of reference, I have pointed out processes and factors that are important in order to create a dialogical relationship from which both parties should benefit. The essence is that the constructs of both participants should be elicited and be an object for clarification and finally evaluation.

This might occur within a process in which gestures and words were exchanged between the parties. If both parties have an experimental attitude towards words and concepts, but a humble attitude towards the other person, a dialogue may be the way. The dialogue may be viewed as a mutual journey of exploration into the unknown, where goals and information requirements can be formed and developed. Instead of only looking upon "solutions" and information requirements as something that can be uncovered, we should rather regard it as a process of construction, articulation and formulation. Usually one does not find something that is hidden in the expert's head or in the books, but through reflection and talking one creates important aspects of the world. Attitudes in terms of conceit, self-assertion and mastering of technology may be a handicap, whereas openness and ability to communicate are central virtues. As Bennis (1989) strongly argues:

> Free self-expression is the essence of leadership: "Leaders are people who are able to express themselves fully... the key to full self-expression is understanding one's self and the world, and the key to understanding is learning–from one's own life and experiences" (1989 p. 3).

Nobody has described the power of expression clearer than Ralph Waldo Emerson: "man is only half himself, the other half is his expression" (cited in Bennis,

1989 p.2). The central elements of the preferred relationship are depicted in figure 1, as a description of attitudes and behavior which are preferable in order to facilitate a dialogue as a platform for development and autonomy.

FIGURE 1. Central Attitudes and Actions Between the Dialogue Partners

Consultant	open and communicative humble and experimenting (debating and reflecting) listening and exploring loosening and tightening	*Client*

At this point it is important to be aware of the importance of the ladder of inference (Argyris, 1985). We all go through a ladder of inference to make sense out of our world and to act within it. Due to our skilful behavior, our reasoning process is automatic and effortless so we don't pay attention to it. Nevertheless, we build our inferences on different levels of data which may be analogous with rungs on a ladder. The first rung consists of relatively directly observable data, the second rung consists of culturally understood meanings, the third rung of meanings imposed by us, and the fourth rung of the theories we use, i.e. abstract entities difficult to subject to a test.

Due to skilful behavior and a willingness to please and not say what one thinks, one communicates at a generally high level. The more sensitive the evaluations and attributions of others, the stronger the tendency to discuss it only at the most abstract level (rung four). Therefore we typically skip the lowest level of the ladder, thus creating learning avoidance. We avoid testing our theories in use, and thus we reinforce our old behavior instead of changing it.

In order to learn one has to be willing to test one's own theories and assumptions with valid and concrete data. Thus the participants should be aware of the fallacy of discussing meanings, evaluations and attributions, ignoring the building blocks of theory, i.e. the empirical data.

Conclusion

A main issue in this chapter has been to increase the consultants' and clients' awareness of the many traps of manipulation during a physical and symbolic process of interaction. Even with the best of intentions of both consultant and client, there is a danger of gliding into an expert's world view and solutions. Being aware of model power has been central. Establishing the self concept as a platform to understanding a person and giving them due respect and dignity have been essential. Two methodologies have been presented along with a three-step model of value clarification, indicating the importance of eliciting the consultant's and the client's values during the interaction process. This process might preferably take place within a broader context of dialogue in the spirit of the labels of figure 1.

I have attempted to view the information exchange process as a dialogue in which the persons involved are partners in a mutual growth enhancing process, thus criticizing the traditional one-sided instrumental approach to knowledge transfer. Our present understanding of how professionals should interact with dignity and respect for the other in such a dialogue – and at the same time act in an autonomous manner – is at best rudimentary and hopefully it should be a topic for further theoretical and empirical research.

References

Argyris, C. 1985: *Strategy, Change and Defensive Routines*. Boston: Pitman.

Argyris, C., R. Putman and D. McLain Smith 1985: *Action Science*. San Francisco: Jossey Bass Publishers.

Argyris, C. 1969: Explorations in Consulting-Client Relationships in: W.G. Bennis, Benne and Chin *The Planning of Change*, 2nd Ed.. London: Holt, Rinehart & Winston .

Bateson, G. 1972: *Steps to an Ecology of Mind*. New York: Ballantine Books.

Bayles, M.D. 1988: The Professional-Client Relationship, in: *Ethical Issues in Professional Life*, Joan C. Callahan (Ed.). New York: Oxford University Press.

Benne, K.D. 1969: Some Ethical Problems in Group and Organizational Consultation, in: W.G. Bennis, Benne and Chin *The Planning of Change*, 2nd Ed. London: Holt, Rinehart & Winston.

Bennis, W. & B. Nanus 1985: *Leaders. The Strategies for Taking Charge*. New York: Harper & Rows Publishers.

Bennis, W.1989: *On Becoming a Leader*. Reading, Mass.: Addison-Wesley Publishing Co.

Boland, R. J. 1979: Control, Causality and Information Systems Requirements. *Accounting, Organization and Society*, Vol. 4 No. 4

Bråten, S. 1973: Model Monopoly and Communication. *Acta Sociologica*, 16, pp 98-107.

Bråten, S. 1983a: *Dialogens vilkår i datasamfunnet*. Oslo: Universitetsforlaget.

Bråten, S. 1983b: Modeller av dialogiske systemer: Tid og selvrefleksjon. In *Bedriftsøkonomi og vitenskapsteori*, B.W. Hennestad & F.E. Wenstøp (Eds.) Oslo: Universitetsforlaget.

Bråten, S. 1986: Paradigms of Autonomy: Dialogical or Monological? In *Social and Legal Autopoiesis*, G. Teubner (Ed.), European University Institute Publ. Series. Berlin/New York: De Gruytes.

Buber, M. 1965: *Between Man and Man*. New York: Macmillan Publishing Company.

Buber, M. 1964: *Jeg og Du*. Danmark: Munksgaard.

Butler Jr., J.K. 1991: Toward understanding and measuring conditions of trust: Evolution of a conditions of trust inventory. *Journal of Management*, Vol. 17, no. 3, 643-663.

Caplan, N 1979: The two-communities theory and knowledge utilization. *American Behavioral Scientist*, 22, 3, pp459-470.

Churchman, C. W & A. H. Schainblatt 1965: The researcher and the manager: A dialectic of implementation. *Management Science*, Vol 11, No. 4, February.

Dunn, W. N. 1980: The two-communities metaphor and models of knowledge use. An explorative case survey. *Knowledge: Creation, Diffusion, Utilization*, Vol 1 No. 4, June, pp 515-536.

Ellin, J.S. 1988: Special professional morality and the duty of veracity. In *Ethical Issues in Professional Life*, Joan C. Callahan (Ed.). New York: Oxford University Press.

Gullestad, S.E. 1992: *Å si fra. Autonomibegrepet i psykoanalysen*. Oslo: Universitetsforlaget, Det Blå Bibliotek.

Habermas, J. 1982: A Reply to my Critics. In *Habermas, Critical Debates*, J. Thompson & D. Held (Eds.) Cambridge, Mass.: Macmillan Press.

Håland, W. 1986: *Psykoterapi: Relasjon, utviklingsprosess og effekt*. Oslo: Universitetsforlaget.

Ims, K. J. 1987: *Leder i dialog. En studie av informasjonssøk med metoder for personlig utvikling*. Bergen: Universitetsforlaget.

Kelly, G.A. 1955: *The Psychology of Personal Constructs*, Vol. I and II. New York: Norton & Co. Inc.

Løvlie, A.L. 1982a: *The Self: Yours Mine or Ours. A Dialectic View*. Oslo: Universitetsforlaget.

Løvlie, A.L. 1982b: *The Self of the Psychotherapist: Movement and Stagnation in Psychotherapy*. Oslo: Universitetsforlaget.

Løvlie, L. 1979: Dialektikk og pedagogikk. Arbeidsmanuskript. *Oppland Distriktshøgskoles Skrifter* 22.

Løvlie, L. 1984: *Det pedagogiske argument. Moral, autoritet og selvprøving i oppdragelsen*. Oslo: J.W. Cappelens Forlag A.S.

May, W.F. 1988: Contract or Covenant? *In Ethical Issues in Professional Life*, Joan C. Callahan (Ed.). New York: Oxford University Press.

McCarthy, T. 1978: *The Critical Theory of Jürgen Habermas*. Cambraidge: The MIT Press.

Nordenstam, T. 1968: *Sudanese Ethics*. The Scandinavian Institute of African Studies, Uppsala.

Nordenstam, T. 1983: Datautvecklingens filosofi. Två oförenliga traditioner. In *Datautvecklingens Filosofi*, B. Göranzon (Ed.). Stockholm: Carlsson & Jönsson Bokförlag AB.

Pollak, O. 1976: *Human Behavior and the Helping Professions*. New York: Spectrum.

Pounds, W.F. 1969: The process of problem finding. *Industrial Management Review*, Vol. II, no. 1.

Rawls, J. 1971: *A Theory of Justice*. Oxford: Oxford University Press.

Schein, E.H. 1985, 1992: *Organizational Culture and Leadership*. San Francisco: Jossey-Bass.

Schultz, R. L and D. P. Slevin 1979: Introduction: The Implementation Problem. In *The Implementation of Management Science*, R. Doktor, R.L. Schultz and D.P. Slevin (Eds.). Tims Studies in the Management Sciences, Vol 13. Amsterdam: North-Holland Publishing Company.

Schøn, D. A. 1983: *The Reflective Practitioner*. New York: Basic Books Inc.

Shaw, M.L.G. 1982: The Extraction of Personal Meaning from a Repertory Grid. In *Personal Meanings*, E. Sheperd and J-P- Watson (Eds.). Chichester: John Wiley.

Thomas, L.F. and E.S. Harri-Augstein 1985: *Self-organized Learning. Foundations of a Conversational Science for Psychology*. London: Routledge & Kegan Paul plc.

Tranøy, K.E. 1974: Yrkesetikk, personlig moral og offentlig ansvar. Næringsutbygging og samfunnsverdier. *Bedriftsøkonomen* nr. 7.

Winslow, G.R. 1988: From Loyalty to Advocacy: A New Metaphor for Nursing. In *Ethical Issues in Professional Life*, Joan C. Callahan (Ed.). New York: Oxford University Press.

Index

Issues in Business Ethics

1. G. Enderle, B. Almond and A. Argandoña (eds.): *People in Corporations. Ethical Responsibilities and Corporate Effectiveness.* 1990
ISBN 0-7923-0829-8
2. B. Harvey, H. van Luijk and G. Corbetta (eds.): *Market Morality and Company Size.* 1991 ISBN 0-7923-1342-9
3. J. Mahoney and E. Vallance (eds.): *Business Ethics in a New Europe.* 1992
ISBN 0-7923-1931-1
4. P.M. Minus (ed.): *The Ethics of Business in a Global Economy.* 1993
ISBN 0-7923-9334-1
5. T.W. Dunfee and Y. Nagayasu (eds.): *Business Ethics: Japan and the Global Economy.* 1993 ISBN 0-7923-2427-7
6. S. Prakash Sethi: *Multinational Corporations and the Impact of Public Advocacy on Corporate Strategy.* Nestle and the Infant Formula Controversy. 1993 ISBN 0-7923-9378-3
7. H. von Weltzien Hoivik and A. Føllesdal (eds.): *Ethics and Consultancy: European Perspectives.* 1995 ISBN Hb 0-7923-3377-2; Pb 0-7923-3378-0

KLUWER ACADEMIC PUBLISHERS – DORDRECHT / BOSTON / LONDON